WHEN MENTORING MEETS COACHING

MEETS

COACHING

SHIFTING THE STANCE IN EDUCATION

KATE SHARPE &
JEANIE NISHIMURA

Acknowledgements

We are grateful to so many who have contributed to our learning and understanding, and supported us on our journey throughout the writing of this book.

As co-authors and co-creators:

- Our friendship, laughter and fun, deep collaboration, respect and care, unwavering energy, commitment and focus

- As mentor-coaches for each other: our clarity gleaned from accessing and experiencing the wisdom built and shared through years of conversation, reflection, designing, and refining

To our families:

- Tara: our companion on all our writing retreats, providing wisdom, encouragement, lunches, laughter; reminding us to take breaks and to "call it a day"; photographer, capturing our process

- Our families and friends: Carly and Emma, our parents, siblings and friends, believing in us and cheering us on

- Neil: brainstorming the title, helping us refine critical words and ideas, encouraging and supporting us throughout the editing process

- Writing retreats: Sarah and Mark's cabin, the McGregor family cottage, Stillwood Creek, the Sharpe hospitality in Florida, Mary's farm

To our own mentor-coaches and partners in learning:

- Jeanie: Adria Trowhill, Helen House, Cinnie Noble, Laura Atwood, Debbie Nyman

- Kate: Adria Trowhill, Tara Ferguson, Craig Trowhill, the PACT coaches

- Adler Faculty of Professional Coaching: faculty, colleagues, and students

- Our coaching clients and colleagues

To the continuing evolution of the Mentor-Coaching Institute:

- Dr. Joanne Robinson and her vision for what has become possible within this work; the team at OPC/ELC since 2007

- The willingness and commitment of the many participants in the mentor-coaching and coaching courses we have facilitated

- Coach-facilitators for our Mentor-Coaching Program/Institute, as learning partners with us in sharing the mentor-coaching frame and stance within education

- Specific district school boards from across Ontario who have embraced the mentor-coaching stance within their teaching/ leading strategies

To our publisher, Pearson Canada:

- Joanne Close and Chris Allen, who believed in us and our book from the beginning and supported us throughout the process

- Our exceptionally perceptive and skilled editors, Joanne Close and Keltie Thomas

- Larissa Ulisko for our inspired cover and logo

- David Berg for designing the original graphics of our models

- Our "From the Field" contributors for their thoughtfulness and wisdom

We would like to thank the following reviewers for their excellent feedback and suggestions:

- Heather Auden, Manager, Membership Administration, Girl Guides of Canada-Guides du Canada

- Michelle Berggren, B.Ed., C.A.P. Facilitator, High Prairie School Division No. 48, AB

- Barbara Bower, M.A., Professional Learning Facilitator, the Bishop Strachan School, ON

- Alison Chan, Coordinator, Unit Guider Support, Girl Guides of Canada-Guides du Canada

- Lisa Cole, Program Facilitator, Science and Technology (K–12), Durham District School Board, ON

- Linda Crawford, Director, Operations, Girl Guides of Canada-Guides du Canada

- Janice C. Currie, B.Sc.M., Chief Operating Officer, Success College, Maritime Business College, da Vinci College, NS & NB

- Brenda Gabriel, Literacy/Retention Consultant, Lac La Ronge Indian Band, SK

- Joni Heard, B.Sc.N., B.A., B.Ed., Educational Consultant, Ontario Principals' Council-International School Leadership

- Dr. Andrew (Sandy) Hilton, Director, Professional Education, CPA Canada

- Brian Jones, M.Ed., Education Officer/Mentor-Coach Facilitator, Principal on secondment to the Ontario Ministry of Education

- Shelly Niemi, B.A., M.Ed., Administrator, Aboriginal Education, School District No. 57, BC

- Jessie Richards, Curriculum Specialist, triOS College, Business Technology Healthcare, ON

- Carol Rolheiser, Ph.D., Professor, Curriculum, Teaching and Learning, University of Toronto and Director, Centre for Teaching Support & Innovation, University of Toronto, ON

- Jackie Stadnyk, Program Administrator K–8, Renfrew County District School Board, ON

- Reanne Usselman, B.Ed. PGD, M.Ed., Coordinator of Learning, North East School Division No. 200, SK

Table of Contents

PART ONE Building Capacity

PART TWO Mentor-Coaching: Growth, Impact, and Sustainability

Foreword

by Dr. Joanne Robinson

The expression "It's lonely at the top" is heard in many corporations and organizations globally. Generally, we concede that accepting leadership responsibilities means leaving the comfort zone of working in teams with colleagues to strike out on our own to lead an organization. The education sector in Ontario now has a strategy to combat this phenomenon.

Mentoring and coaching are traditionally viewed as effective approaches for minimizing the isolation that is often associated with leadership and positions of responsibility. In education, we use the term *leader* to describe a range of positions. In the K–12 space, this can range from supervisory officers and directors of education through curriculum leaders, principals, vice principals, and teachers. In the higher-education space, this can range from deans through administrators, tenured faculty, contract faculty, and teaching assistants.

What if a formal mentoring program, aimed at these leaders, were to be enhanced by professional coaching skills for the mentors?

In 2007, Kate Sharpe and Jeanie Nishimura created and began facilitating a program to support mentors of new administrators entitled Mentor-Coach Training for Educators. In 2010, a comprehensive study of the benefits and challenges of blending formal mentoring with professional coaching revealed a hugely successful "recipe" for impacting the culture in school districts. The rewards and benefits far outweighed the challenges. The twinning of mentoring and coaching roles that is outlined in this book has made a profound impact on Ontario's leadership capacity building.

The benefits have proven equally positive for the mentors, the mentees, and district committees. When asked about the benefits of the program, *mentors* most frequently referred to

- the coaching skills developed through the program,
- the opportunity to reflect on their own practice,

- the recognition they received, and
- the networking opportunities provided through the program.

The benefits for *mentees* emerged as

- the opportunity for self-reflection,
- the networking provided by the program, and
- role modelling.

District personnel evaluating the program identified the benefits as the necessity to

- set goals,
- monitor progress, and
- evaluate the collective efficacy of all program participants to make it meaningful and valuable to the system.

Mentees and mentors reported one consistent challenge: finding the time to benefit fully from the program (Robinson, 2010, p. 81).

The evidence supported the claim that the pairing of mentoring and coaching can be a powerful strategy for building capacity, reducing feelings of isolation, and promoting sustainability across a system. Networks and purposeful collaborations strengthen all of us.

Since the original piloting and launching of the Mentor-Coach Training for Educators program in 2007, there has been a growing interest in school districts across Ontario to extend the reach of the training to include teachers and non-teaching staff. This speaks to the growing culture surrounding distributed leadership in education and to the relevance of the coaching and capacity-building frame for teachers and students. Higher education is also currently using both mentoring and coaching as effective strategies to support enhanced leadership and teaching practice.

So, as we step back and consider this book's relevance from a broad system perspective and education's central purpose—increasing student achievement and engagement—it is thrilling to see it make a contribution to the two most critical pieces affecting this process: school leadership and classroom instruction (Leithwood, Louis, Anderson, & Wahlstrom, 2004).

Introduction

This book has grown out of our commitment to bring coaching skills and principles to all those involved—directly and indirectly—in education at all levels from Kindergarten to Grade 12 to college and university. Through our extensive experiences in the field, we have witnessed how the stance and skills that coaching brings to education create the conditions for people to be in professional learning conversations differently, be they in offices, classrooms, or hallways. When we create space for people to increase their autonomy, competence, and relatedness (Kaufman, 2013), we see increased engagement and motivation.

It is our belief that the mentor-coaching framework is deeply relevant beyond educational settings. Any mentor, regardless of context, will be able to use the skills and principles outlined in this book to support them in their relationships and conversations to build capacity.

We believe that building capacity sits at the core of education. Building our own capacities, in supporting others as they build their capacities, is vital if we are to maximize our individual and collective potential and engage in the discourses surrounding the systems in which we work. This is what we mean when we discuss building capacity from the inside out.

Central to this book is the belief that all educators are leaders and mentor-coaches engaged in building capacity in themselves and others. We hope that all educators will find this book to be a rich, relevant resource.

We are excited to be collaborating on this book. Having worked closely to develop and facilitate impactful mentor-coaching training for all levels of education, we have been learning and growing in our understanding of the vital role that coaching skills have to play for all leaders, particularly in education, regardless of their context.

In McKinsey & Company's report, "How the World's Most Improved School Systems Keep Getting Better," Mourshed, Chijioke, and Barber share an analysis of twenty top-performing school systems from around the world, and identify "how each has achieved significant, sustained, and widespread gains in student outcomes" (2010, p. 2). The report details the characteristics of system reform, moving along the performance continuum from poor through fair, good, and great to excellent. In the discussion surrounding a system's progression from great to excellent, which is the current reality here in Ontario, the authors describe the shift in balance that is required: from a central focus on accountability interventions to the building of collective capacity. The report suggests that this be done through professional development and training that facilitates increased collaboration, and shared intentionality and responsibility laterally across the organization (that is, not the typical top-down approach).

> Harnessing and enhancing the expertise of those within the system to support both innovation and continuous learning is a critical principle of capacity building in teaching in higher education. As a leader, I build capacity by modelling effective mentor-coaching skills and practices while supporting colleagues as they develop their own skills. As individuals refine their knowledge and application of mentor-coaching strategies, the system benefits from richer and more effective collaborative interaction.
>
> —*Carol Rolheiser, Director, Centre for Teaching Support & Innovation and Professor, Department of Curriculum, Teaching and Learning, University of Toronto*

A model to support this kind of professional learning for leaders and educators—one that accesses both individual and collective engagement—is the essence of mentor-coaching. Embedded in the model are the skills, principles, and structure needed to create an environment where participants can be a part of a mentor-coaching relationship that allows and supports the conversations, intentionality, and action required for continuous improvement and rigour.

Given the centrality of inquiry and the asking of impactful questions in the mentor-coaching process, we feel that it is only fitting to identify the five main inquiries that have directed the design of our Mentor-Coach Training for Educators Program, now called the Mentor-Coaching Institute, and, in turn, the writing of this book:

Inquiries to Support Individual and Collective Capacity Building

1. What do we need to support the professional growth of our leadership and teaching?
2. Who do we want to partner with as we structure our individual learning and growth opportunities?
3. How do we bring ourselves to relationships and conversations that foster learning and growth?
4. What skills do we need to cultivate our ability to hold the space for expanding each other's awareness within meaningful conversations?
5. How can we continue to expand and deepen our collective capacity and commitment to increased levels of student achievement and success?

As educators, our training and experience as certified professional coaches and facilitators has enhanced our skills and our commitment to sharing the coaching mindset and process in service of deep professional growth and change from the inside out. Our educational backgrounds in curriculum development, professional learning and development (from Kindergarten to Grade 12 to higher education), health and physical education (Kate), and drama in education (Jeanie) have grounded us in adult education, experiential learning, the centrality of capacity building in education and leadership, and the importance of the integration of the new learning over time in order for significant growth and change to happen.

In my continuing work with teachers and students in schools, I have realized that integrating my coaching skills into my pedagogy and stance as an educator has further mobilized me as a teacher.

With capacity building as my "bottom line," and the original reason I completed the coach training, I am, as a teacher/facilitator, more agile and better able (read: more skills and competencies) to facilitate the work and conversations. Conceptually, I create a larger and more energized space for student-centred and -directed learning and growth. As I work with teachers, leaders, and parents, my goal is to help them connect more fully to the idea of building capacity in students— supporting them as they access their strengths, voice, and wisdom.

From Kate

Initially, I was drawn to coaching because I saw it as an exciting methodology to support people in becoming ever more purposeful. As a drama teacher, I have always seen the art form as a rich place for students (youth and adults) to build capacity: exploring who they are becoming at the same time that they discover more about others and the human condition. For me, the power of inquiry and the rich variety of drama forms allow for heightened engagement and deep learning. What the coaching frame has added is further rigour around who I am "being." By this I mean paying ever more attention to how I am showing up as a coach-like teacher and facilitator and how I hold the space for participants to step in and step up.

From Jeanie

There is much wisdom on what leaders are to pay attention to—the essential qualities of character and intent that are needed, the critical nature of cultivating relationship, the need for effective communication, and so on. In our experience, what is lacking in the literature and in the training is the depth in mindset and skill development that is required to move from theory to practice. How do you truly support others in building their own capacity? How do you cultivate relationships? How do you become an effective communicator?

Through our professional mentor-coaching training and experience, we explore the critical nature and rigour of the skills of listening deeply, asking impactful questions, acknowledging and building on gifts and strengths, and holding the focus on what matters. This book explores in depth the critical mindset, frame, and skills that build capacity in leaders to bring themselves to conversations differently and allow those conversations to foster growth and development, in themselves and in others. Having facilitated our workshops with hundreds of leaders—an ever-increasing number of whom are teachers—there is consistent recognition of how challenging it is to be fully present and listen deeply.

There has also been a visceral response to the challenge of shifting from the mindset of "fixing and solving" to the mindset of "building capacity," by listening deeply to what matters and, through inquiry, accessing the resources and wisdom within.

Many leaders have initially expressed the belief that they are leaders because they are good at problem solving, giving advice, and sharing wisdom. Challenging them to shift the focus to the other person, supporting by inquiring rather than telling, has called them to dig deep in terms of the skills they bring to conversations and who they are being in each interaction. For many, the impact has been a recognition of their critical role as leaders in supporting others as they build their own capacities, as well as a more distributed leadership (and lighter shoulders).

As the nature of education morphs and the shapes of curricula shift in this digital age, our role as coach-like leaders in and out of the classroom requires expanded capacities and competencies. Katzenmeyer and Moller (2001) capture this in their statement that teachers "lead within and beyond the classroom, identify with and contribute to a community of teacher learners and leaders, and influence others toward improved educational practice" (p. 5).

For those leaders who are classroom- or lecture-based, the pull of old habits can be hard to relinquish. We challenge them to support their students' growth by inquiring rather than telling and working from an appreciative/growth mindset rather than a deficit/fixing mindset. In each interaction, they must adjust who they are being. The message we hear repeatedly is that the shift helped them to see the student as whole again and let go of the problem-focused "fixing" mentality. They are better equipped to get back to the task at hand—teaching and learning—by fostering capacity building.

Our Mentor-Coaching Program: Designed and Developed

For the last eight years, we have been deeply involved with a provincial initiative that involves situating the coaching mindset and skills within the mentoring framework. The result of our work has been the creation of a robust program that is supporting the professional learning and growth of leaders in education in Ontario.

We knew that creating a mentoring program with the aid and structure of coaching skills, and embedded with the coaching mindset and principles, would bring mentors to the work and conversations with their mentees differently. The training would enhance the skills of the educators to be in the learning relationship and conversations with more attention and intention.

We also knew that the professional learning workshops had to grow out of the very real challenges facing the mentors and mentees—and that intentional practice, feedback, application, and integration beyond the training was critical in fostering learning and building capacity over time.

With these experiences and goals in mind, we set out to design a program that would integrate the coaching frame, principles, and skills into the ancient practice and tradition of mentoring. We wanted to support mentors in navigating the relationship and the conversations with their mentees and within their wider leadership mandates. We knew the program had to include a robust theoretical framework; in-depth coaching skills training; and abundant opportunities to practise, offer and receive feedback, take risks to expand competency and confidence, and observe and model mentoring and coaching conversations, in real time.

We also knew that the program had to be offered as a series of sessions over time, allowing the mentor cohorts ample time, opportunity, and intentionality between sessions to practise and integrate what they had learned (formally and informally) in the "real" world. From the research (discussed in detail later in the book) and our own experience, we know that implementation, practice, and support over time are critical if mentors are to integrate the mentor-coaching mindset and skills moving forward.

Designing and implementing the program has been very rewarding for us both. The process of writing this book has clarified our thinking and made us even more committed to expanding the possibilities of integrating mentor-coaching at all levels to further enhance educational leadership and teaching practices.

The Purpose of This Book

Our purpose in writing this book is to provide *all* those involved in education, from leaders in the early years to leaders in higher education, with the principles, attitudes, behaviours, and skills they need to support capacity building from the inside out.

The idea for this book grew out of past participants' requests for a resource that captured the theoretical and, to a degree, the practical aspects of the training they had received through our program. At the same time, we saw that there would be those who would prefer to read about mentoring and coaching first, and who may or may not choose to take a course. We wrote this book to serve both audiences: those who read independently and those who will read it as part of our Mentor-Coaching Institute.

We hope that all readers will find that the depth and breadth of the theoretical content (principles, attitudes) is balanced with the practical (behaviours, skills) and that all are supported by tools, opportunities for reflection, and demonstration coaching (online videos).

The Organization of This Book

We have divided the book into two parts to support the progression of the mentor-coaching model and skills in order to serve your needs as a practitioner.

We appreciate that each reader arrives with different levels of experiences and training. Thus, in Part One, we have aimed to provide sufficient background information on the theoretical components before moving into the mindset, stance, and skills for mentor-coaching in Part Two. We have also provided a Mentor-Coaching Toolkit and demonstration video on the *When Mentoring Meets Coaching* website (www.pearsoncanada.ca/wmmc). These offer further depth and support and will allow for future updates and additions.

It is our hope that we have created a book and tools that set you up for success. We recognize that the rigour required in holding the mentor-coaching frame brings with it real and deep behavioural change and that embracing and inhabiting this stance is not easy.

Our Invitation to the Reader

Throughout this book, we have provided reflections, inquiry, dialogue, exercises, and tools designed to help get the words off the page and the frame and stance into your bones. We invite you to adapt the material in this book to suit the needs of your own capacity-building practice, as formal mentor-coach, informal mentor-coach, coach-like leader, and teacher. In our experience in facilitating this training, it has been critical for participants to experience the power of being coach and client and observer and to have many opportunities to try on the skills, take risks, and experiment to build capacity.

We invite you to embrace the mentor-coaching approach for two critical reasons:

- Mentor-coaching is a powerful way of being in relationship and in conversation about what matters deeply.

- Mentor-coaching is an inspired methodology for capacity building and making a difference by nurturing individual and collective learning and growth.

As educational leaders, let us be committed to listening deeply to the unfolding, ongoing conversations of our own and others' desires in the world. It is through such collaboration with colleagues, staff, and students that we can discover and uncover who we are becoming.

PART ONE

Building Capacity

1

An Overview

"We need, too, to allow ourselves to be restless spirits—to be in the process of becoming… It's the restlessness that, while confirming what is understood, leads on to the next mystery."

—HEATHCOTE, 1984, P. 23

PREVIEW OF CHAPTER 1

In this chapter, we will learn about

- mentoring and coaching: powerful allies
- integral components of mentoring and coaching
- what happens when mentoring meets coaching
- the guiding principles of mentor-coaching

Mentoring and Coaching: Powerful Allies

We have all heard the terms *mentor* and *coach*. Simply speaking, mentors are often seen as individuals who pass on, or share, their wisdom, experience, and expertise to another. In the professional space, the mentor and the person they are mentoring—the mentee—likely share a similar career path, industry, or function.

By contrast, coaches are often seen as individuals who elicit strengths, wisdom, and solutions from their **clients**. It is not necessary for coaches and their clients to come from similar backgrounds or to share interests, talents, or pursuits. Their relationship is built on the coach's skill in facilitating the client's ability and desire to achieve change rather than sharing experience or expertise.

However, what may be less familiar to many of us is the term *mentor-coach*. Mentor-coaches combine the two roles of mentor and coach into one.

In our experience, twinning the roles of mentor and coach as powerful allies builds the capacity of individuals to facilitate a robust learning partnership that enhances personal development and professional teaching and leadership over time.

Currently, mentors are being asked to partner with mentees in a learning relationship that shifts the traditional focus of the relationship from one of sharing on the part of the mentor to one of focusing on the wants and needs of the mentee through inquiry, reflection, and accountability. As coaches, we know the power and effectiveness of the coaching **mindset** and skills—and that mentors can develop them.

In pairing the roles of mentor and coach, a powerful learning relationship can result:

> "Coaching is unlocking people's potential to maximize their performance. It is helping them to learn rather than teaching them."
> —Whitmore, 2009, p. 10

Client—
a generic term coaches often use to refer to a person who receives coaching

Mindset—
the fundamental attitudes and assumptions we hold

Mentor-Coaching Is...

A collaborative learning relationship and reflective process that is established together by a mentor-coach and a mentee. This co-created partnership, of ongoing support and challenge, evolves over time through structured conversations to facilitate engagement, **capacity building**, desired growth, and change.

Capacity building—
or building capacity: to grow individual (and collective) capabilities and competence from the inside out

Integral Components of Mentoring and Coaching

To see how mentoring and coaching can be combined in the mentor-coach's role, let us look at the characteristics of each.

About Mentoring

Homer's epic poem *The Odyssey* defines the classic mentor role. In the poem, Odysseus, King of Ithaca, asks his close friend and counsellor, Mentor, to watch over his infant son, Telemachus, while Odysseus is on his odyssey, fighting the Trojan War and then making his arduous trip home. Mentor becomes Telemachus's guardian and teacher during his father's long absence, passing on knowledge and wisdom. When Telemachus becomes a young adult, Athena, the goddess of wisdom and war, visits him, assuming the guise of Mentor, and encourages and supports him as he grows into the king he will become.

Figure 1.1 Many scholars believe Homer wrote *The Odyssey* in 800 BCE. Since then, the tale of the poem has been told and retold in many forms, including this lithograph, "Telemachos entertains the Mentor," created by Friedrich Preller, the Elder (1804–1878). Mentor, who holds a staff, and Telemachos are depicted in the centre.

Today, a mentor might work one-on-one or with a group or network of mentees. Essential elements make the ancient tradition of mentoring an effective strategy for developing knowledge, expertise, skills, and experience in people that is used throughout numerous organizations and industries. Two of these elements are

- ongoing support offered to employees new to their role by accessing experienced colleagues with in-depth knowledge, understanding, and wisdom; and

- trust and safety developed within a mentoring relationship necessary to talk about what matters, take risks, address challenges, and build competence, confidence, and efficacy.

Mentoring Is...

Two definitions inform our view of mentoring:

Traditional: Mentoring refers to the relationship (formal or informal) between an experienced colleague and a new or inexperienced mentee, where the wisdom and expertise of the mentor is leveraged to support the mentee in accelerating his or her knowledge, learning, and performance.

continued...

Current: Mentoring is a collaborative learning relationship and reflective process, established between an experienced mentor and a new or inexperienced mentee, which evolves over time to support the intentional learning and growth of the mentee. In current educational systems and structures, the mentoring dynamic is critical and implicit within both formal and informal learning partnerships, as well as in teams and communities.

Leaders—
all leaders in education: the classroom leader (teacher), school leader (vice principal, principal), system leader (supervisory officer), district leader (education director), leaders in higher education (college and university faculty and staff)

In education, in particular, mentoring is needed for new school, classroom, college, university, and system **leaders**. Key factors that contribute to this need are

- the critical importance of effective leadership in schools to enhance student learning and achievement (Leithwood, Louis, Anderson, & Wahlstrom, 2004)

- the complexity of current leadership roles at all levels and the inherent expectations, responsibilities, and challenges specific to each level

- the support and encouragement needed for new leaders on their steep learning curve to get beyond the "sink or swim" imperative and focus on learning and growth

- the desire to overcome the culture of isolation, which can exist in educational settings, through fostering a culture of encouragement and support for new leaders, building rich professional networks

- the reality that face-to-face learning and mentoring are the most favoured ways of learning by all generations, including Generation X and the Millennials (Meister & Willyerd, 2010)

Goals of Mentors

Several goals are key to being an effective mentor. These include the ability to

- nurture a relationship that has as its focus fostering capacity building and reflective practice;

- facilitate conversations to stay focused on what the mentee wants, uncovering new awareness and clarity of learning and action for the mentee;

- enhance personal **presence** and skills to maximize the mentee's learning and growth; and

- shift from being one who offers expertise, advice, and experience easily and quickly to one who invites the mentee to dig deep and access their own gifts and wisdom, in service of building their confidence and competence.

Presence— our internal state or readiness as mentor-coach

Within mentoring, as within education, our focus is ultimately about supporting others in learning and growing as they build their capacities. While we claim this, often we continue to fill the vessel instead of inviting the vessel to fill itself.

> "Ecologists tell us that a tree planted in a clearing of an old forest will grow more successfully than one planted in an open field. The reason, it seems, is that the roots of the forest trees are able to follow the intricate pathways created by former trees and thus embed themselves more deeply. Indeed, over time, the roots of many trees may actually graft themselves to one another, creating an interdependent mat of life hidden beneath the earth's surface."
> —Parks Daloz, 2012, p. xiii

Reflection: Connecting to Mentoring

In a discussion or journal, consider and respond to the questions below.

1. Recall an experience that you had as a mentee (formal or informal) that supported your learning and growth as a leader. In considering this experience, what skills are critical for a mentor?

2. What is compelling to you about being a mentor?

3. What gifts and strengths do you bring to the role, relationship, and process of mentoring?

4. As a mentor, which mentoring skills do you want to enhance?

About Coaching

Coaching—
offering a set of skills and principles designed to support structured conversations to facilitate engagement, capacity building, and change through a co-created process and relationship of ongoing support and challenge

Successful coaches, like successful teachers, have an ability to meet clients or students where they are and structure learning conversations and experiences that access responsibility, action, and commitment. In both cases, the tools are the same: dialogue, inquiry, reflection, and assessment.

As effective coaches, we also hold our clients accountable by sharing in their progress and securing their learning. We create opportunities to acknowledge effort, improvement, and achievements. Once we have established coordinates, new targets are set, manageable steps are identified, and support is provided or accessed for the next leg of the shared learning journey.

SPOTLIGHT

International Coach Federation on Coaching

The International Coach Federation (ICF) is the leading global professional coaching organization for setting standards and core competencies for coaches. The following is how the ICF views coaching:

"ICF defines coaching as partnering with clients in a thought-provoking and creative process that inspires them to maximize their personal and professional potential, which is particularly important in today's uncertain and complex environment. Coaches honor the client as the expert in his or her life and work and believe every client is creative, resourceful and whole. Standing on this foundation, the coach's responsibility is to:

- [d]iscover, clarify, and align with what the client wants to achieve
- [e]ncourage client self-discovery

continued...

- [e]licit client-generated solutions and strategies
- [h]old the client responsible and accountable

This process helps clients dramatically improve their outlook on work and life, while improving their leadership skills and unlocking their potential" (ICF, n.d.-b).

As coaches, our primary goal is to elicit the strengths, wisdom, and solutions from the client, helping her or him to access internal and external resources. Over time, coaching fosters growth and resiliency within the framework of a learning relationship.

Foundational Elements of the Coaching Process and Relationship

The following five elements are foundational to the coach and client process and relationship:

1. The intention of the process: growth and change over time
2. The coaching conversation: attention, intention, and action
3. The relationship: authentic, connected, and action-focused
4. The coach: present, listening, and inquiring
5. The client: growth stance

Let us look at each element.

1. Intention of the Process: Growth and Change over Time

The focus of coaching is intentional individual and team growth and change over time.

- Coaching is about the client being deeply engaged in a process that is designed to expand awareness and enhance the capacity to notice and choose actions in service of ongoing learning and growth.

- The coaching process is designed to be clear, clean, and focused, powerfully aligning the client and his or her intentions and goals.

- There is an ongoing commitment to deep reflection and impactful choices leading to effective action and accountability.
- The coach is committed to an ethos of confidentiality and mutual respect.
- The coaching process maximizes the client's engagement through inquiry, dialogue, and reflection that serves to increase her or his attention and intention going forward.

Engagement = Attention + Intention

2. The Coaching Conversation: Attention, Intention, and Action

The coaching conversation is structured to invite the client to engage in deep reflection to expand awareness and choices regarding capacity building and desired change over time.

- The client chooses the agenda and the path of the conversation, thus keeping the focus centred on her or his growth and development.
- The agreement is that it is the client's work throughout the conversation. The coach asks questions that foster exploration and new discoveries, perspectives, and possibilities for action.
- The structure of the coaching conversation is about building capacity, exploring where the client is now, where he or she wants to be, and then coaching to support the journey forward.
- Each conversation is a dedicated time for being "on purpose" and intentional regarding awareness, choice, trust, action, and accountability.

3. The Relationship: Authentic, Connected, and Action-Focused

The coaching relationship is collaborative and supportive, based on authenticity, mutual trust, and respect. The coach facilitates the process, using coaching skills to support the client's ongoing growth journey.

- The coaching relationship is a relationship that is "on purpose" and about building capacity in the client over time.

- As it is the client's work, the coach and client collaborate and co-create, keeping the light on the client and on the identified focus of the work they are stepping into.

- Coaching provides the structure, rigour, and commitment that adaptive change and new leadership or teaching behaviours require.

4. The Coach: Present, Listening, and Inquiring

The presence of the coach is critical to the coaching process, the relationship, and the ongoing growth and development of the client. In each coaching conversation, the coach sets the intention of being fully present and open throughout, responding in the moment and accessing intuition in service of the client.

- The coach is skilled in listening deeply and asking the client impactful questions in support of her or his expanding awareness and capacities.

- The coach holds the mindset that growth is about strengths and capacity building, not weaknesses and deficit.

- The work is about shifting—stepping into new and emerging behaviours or perspectives and creating new neuropathways.

- The coach is willing to champion and challenge the client as they strive to create the changes they want.

- The coach sees and speaks to the client's movement and growth, which helps them to notice their own progress.

- The coach remembers that it is the client's work (and thus refrains from fixing, solving, or making assumptions) and only interprets and shares her or his own experience when it is in service of the client.

5. The Client: Growth Stance

The client chooses to be engaged in an ongoing coaching relationship through conversations that focus on her or his own growth and development.

- The client believes that they are resourceful, creative, and expert in their own life and that they hold the wisdom and answers within.

Stance—
orientation toward oneself and others that includes the notions of posture, bearing, and attitude.

Derivation:
From Middle English, denoting a standing place
From Italian: *stanza*

- The client is committed to investing in their own growth and development over time.

- The client recognizes that it is their agenda/work and that their expanding awareness, choices, and actions are enhanced through inquiry and reflection.

Goals of Coaches

As coaches and coach-like leaders, we must be competent in the skills that allow us to

- build collaborative relationships;

- facilitate reflection, learning, action, and results; and

- communicate powerfully.

FROM THE FIELD

Dr. Jean Zu
Professor and Chair, Department of Mechanical & Industrial Engineering, University of Toronto

As I continued my coaching journey of growth, I realized that I wanted the coaching skills to be more consciously part of my leadership style, in fostering other people's growth and supporting their capacity to excel in their work. One of the staff in my department is a great employee with much potential and a very positive attitude. As she was inexperienced in her new management role, several mistakes were made which caused some concerns. I proceeded to coach her by applying the coaching skills I learned from my own coaching. Amazing results happened to her performance, to the delight of both of us.

I am now in my second term as Department Chair, after serving five years in the first term. The three years of leadership coaching has made such a difference in my leadership style.

One of my first opportunities to use peer coaching happened when I offered to coach two colleagues as they implemented tools and strategies they had learned in Additional Qualifications courses in Drama offered through the Ontario Institute for Studies in Education, University of Toronto (OISE/UT). At the time, I was an instructor of these courses at OISE/UT. In turn, my colleagues supported my continuing learning and growth.

We worked together for over five years, in our informal relationships and process, with much time spent in professional dialogue before and after classroom implementation and experimentation regarding, as examples, learning intentions and outcomes, structures for the drama, and strategies to enhance engagement and deepen the learning experience. We also created opportunities for classroom team teaching, observation, debriefing, feedback, and reflection.

I wrote about our process in a research paper (Nishimura, 1989, unpublished) focusing on "the change process itself and on the collegial support that sustained our growth and change." Within focused interviews, my colleagues talked in depth about the impact of having a coach to support them as they integrated multi-layered curriculum and drama strategies that enhanced their practice and thus the learning and growth of their students.

Laura: "I was a little resistant to the methodology, having seen how overwhelming it could be... I'd had some really successful pieces... but the work that it required was daunting... It fell by the wayside... As I began to create my own structures, being able to bounce my ideas off you and having you listen, suggest adaptations...that opportunity was very important... You would say things like 'What do you want the kids to learn?' Eventually that's what helped me to focus and to decide what was my own way."

It was my first experience of the power of coaching over time in supporting in-depth professional learning with teachers. At the time, I did not know that my path would lead to becoming a professional coach in ten years. I also did not anticipate that Kate and I would meet and, in partnership, design, facilitate, and write a book in

continued...

service of sharing this powerful capacity-building frame with leaders and teachers in education.

Opportunities for being purposeful in offering the coaching frame as an impactful methodology to support deep learning at all levels of education continued to grow.

From Jeanie

Reflection: Connecting to Coaching

In a discussion or journal, consider and respond to the questions below.

1. What helps you stay connected to the growth and change you want for yourself?

2. As you reflect on your early experiences as a leader, what kinds of conversations provoked or invoked the most effective action?

3. Consider your learning relationships. What are their essential characteristics?

4. As an adult learner, what heightens your engagement?

5. How does partnering support your learning and growth?

6. Where is the opportunity for you to integrate "the coach approach" into your work?

What Happens When Mentoring Meets Coaching

When we combine mentoring and coaching, a powerful learning model emerges that is more effective than either one on its own. Bringing the attention, intention, and focus of a structured coaching conversation to the ancient and storied tradition of mentoring extends the reach and grasp of mentoring. When paired with mentoring, coaching offers

- a specific set of coaching skills and principles to build relationships and conversation—one conversation at a time

- an invitation for the mentor-coach and the mentee to bring themselves to the conversations differently, creating more space and intentionality for capacity building in "real time"

- an opportunity for the mentor-coach to focus on capacity building by asking rather than telling, remembering it is the mentee's work. By being ever more present in the moment and listening deeply, the mentor-coach can focus on supporting the mentee in living into their strengths and continuing to build their own capacity.

- a path for a structured conversation. These structured conversations expand the mentee's awareness, help them to clarify their choices, and set specific intentions and accountabilities as they move forward.

- support over time, as the mentee continues to grow her or his own capacities and strengths

Combining the tradition of *mentoring* and the structured conversations of *coaching* results in *mentor-coaching*—a specific frame and skill set that facilitates a rich process to support mentees' development.

> "The whole is more than the sum of its parts."
> —Aristotle

$$M + C = M\text{-}C$$

The role of mentor-coach is an obviously interdisciplinary approach to supporting change that builds on the confluence of a multitude of bodies of knowledge including (in addition to coaching and mentoring) the following:

- educational reform
- principles of adult learning and education
- leadership development
- human resources and talent development
- appreciative inquiry
- psychology (e.g., positive, cognitive, behavioural)
- mindfulness, mindset, and stance
- organizational development
- change management
- neuroscience

The Guiding Principles of Mentor-Coaching

In combining mentoring and coaching, six guiding principles coalesce and provide an explicit and purposeful stance for the mentor-coach to navigate the learning relationship, conversations, and process with the mentee. These principles serve to frame the dynamic and to hold capacity building as the focus of the work. They position us as mentor-coach, establishing our mindset and how we **hold** the mentee within this capacity-building relationship.

Hold—
a term used in coaching to establish and protect the space in the conversations and dynamic for the mentee to show up fully and do the required work

4 Inviting curiosity, discovery, and reflection

5 Fostering awareness, possibilities, choice, intentionality, and accountability over time

6 Sharing mentor-coach's own experience and expertise in service of the mentee

2 Holding the mentee resourceful, creative, and expert in own life

3 Supporting strengths, vision, core values, and desired change

1 Co-creating the mentor-coaching relationship: collaborating; building on trust and mutual respect; offering ongoing support, challenge, and encouragement

DIG DEEPER

See the guiding principles of mentor-coaching in action in the demonstration video on the *When Mentoring Meets Coaching* website.

Figure 1.2 The Guiding Principles of Mentor-Coaching
The guiding principles of mentor-coaching are the foundation of the mentor-coach's mindset and stance.

Let us look at how each principle underpins the mentor-coaching relationship and process.

1. Co-creating the mentor-coaching relationship: collaborating; building on trust and mutual respect; offering ongoing support, challenge, and encouragement

The mentor-coach and mentee create the relationship together. As mentor-coach, our ability to offer encouragement and challenges that invite the mentee to stretch and grow needs to be delicately balanced with specific support and resources that will keep the mentee in a place of action. The level of collaboration that this dynamic fosters is often savoured long after the work is finished.

2. Holding the mentee resourceful, creative, and expert in own life

This principle reminds us to operate from the belief that the mentee is competent and an expert when it comes to the reality of their context and opportunities. They are creative and they bring a wealth of internal and external resources, experiences, and talents to their learning, roles, and responsibilities. To **hold the space** and the process, the mentor-coach must remember that it is the mentee doing the work and that the mentee has the insights and answers within. Operating from this fundamental assumption of competence is important in a learning relationship that is focused on growth and movement forward.

Hold the space— to protect space for the mentee to build capacity. This requires the mentor-coach to maintain her or his stance as the facilitator of the mentor-coaching process.

3. Supporting strengths, vision, core values, and desired change

Listening and watching for the mentee's strengths, vision, values, and desire for change ensures that the mentor-coach is grounding the conversations in the reality of the mentee's world and dreams.

Staying connected to the mentee's strengths, vision, core values, and desired change provides vital nourishment to support action and forward movement. As mentor-coach, building our own capacity to listen for these elements keeps us connected to the mentee and to the inside-out approach to growth and movement.

DIG DEEPER

For more on the inside-out approach to growth and movement, see Chapter 4.

4. Inviting curiosity, discovery, and reflection

Accessing the mentee's curiosity and inviting reflection supports a growth mindset and generates valuable energy to fuel forward movement. This inquiring and reflective thinking and feeling not only invokes increased awareness but also translates into new possibilities and choices, more effective action and, ultimately, increased abilities and capacities. The opposite also holds true: no change in awareness results in no new learning and negligible growth, and as a result, the mentee's capacities remain unchanged.

5. Fostering awareness, possibilities, choice, intentionality, and accountability over time

Mobilize—
to set in motion and move forward. Mobilizing requires access to the mentee's desire for change and movement from what is to what will be.

This coaching principle provides structure for conversations that build capacity and **mobilize** the mentee. By progressing from an exploration and deepening of the mentee's current level of awareness to generating possibilities and choices for moving forward, the mentee is mobilized and purposefully oriented.

Over time, the conversations and process of mentor-coaching also support the mentee's intention, momentum, and accountability. In building capacity, especially in new behaviours, consistent support is essential in the early stages (when new neurocircuitry is being established) to overcome the pull of old or familiar patterns, ideas, roles, or behaviours. While research (Speck & Knipe, 2001) has shown that adult learners are particularly resistant to integrating new learning into current practices, mentor-coaching works to build capacity and mobilize the mentee to work toward their desired change.

6. Sharing mentor-coach's own experience and expertise in service of the mentee

When the mentor-coach feels that her or his experience may be helpful, asking permission to share is critical to ensure that it serves the mentee. This helps to keep the focus on the mentee's learning and growth by positioning the mentor-coach's experience and wisdom as resources for the mentee to access when he or she feels it would be valuable. In turn, this helps the mentor-coach shift away from the traditional role of mentor, in which the mentor's wisdom drives the process.

DIG DEEPER
To explore how the guiding principles of mentor-coaching are the foundation of the mentor-coach's stance, see Chapter 5.

To maximize the value of the mentor-coach's experience and expertise in the process, the mentor-coach needs to be mindful that what she or he shares is

- relevant, laser focused, and succinct;

- in service of the mentee;

- supportive of forward movement and growth; and

- followed with a question that invites the mentee to make their own meaning and connections to their particular circumstances.

Liana Lafranier
Principal, Mentor-Coach Training Program Facilitator, and ACC (Associate Certified Coach)

The most significant difference was inherent in my belief that my mentees were creative, resourceful, and whole in their own right. This belief allowed me to coach them through challenges while supporting their trust in self and recognition of their own magnificence as school leaders.

Dr. Heike Bronson
Vice Principal and Mentor-Coach Training Program Facilitator

As a mentor, I felt I was better able to provide the mentee with a process to help them grow and develop, as opposed to provide them with an abundance of resources, hoping that they would somehow fit to his/her specific needs. It really allowed me to personalize the mentee process by empowering the mentee to build a growing awareness of himself/herself, which provided the direction for the mentorship relationship.

Reflection: Connecting to the Guiding Principles of Mentor-Coaching

In a discussion or journal, consider and respond to the questions below.

1. As an adult learner, what is important about each of these principles for you?

   a) What is the impact of each principle on you? on your willingness to stretch and reach beyond your current capabilities?

   b) Which principle most supports you as you build your own capacity?

   c) Which principle do you value most when in a challenging learning zone?

2. As you consider building capacity in others, which principle feels like a consistent place of strength that you already hold?

    a) What has this principle made possible for you? for others?

3. Which principle feels like a challenge for you?

    a) How will your strengths or gifts support you in building your capacity with this principle?

    b) How will being more purposeful in embracing this principle impact you? others?

4. Which principle, if embraced, will have the most impact on enhancing your capacity to be an effective mentor-coach?

    a) How will embracing this principle support you?

    b) What will it make possible?

Mentor-Coaching: A Learner-Centred Model

Lean into—
to apply one's whole self to an endeavour or challenge

In mentor-coaching, the mentor's role has evolved from being the wise, experienced advisor to being an experienced partner who, as facilitator, supports the mentee in building his or her capacity and becoming ever more purposeful. The mentee is an active partner in the professional learning and development as it is his or her learning needs that are the focus of the conversations with the mentor-coach. As a student or an adult learner, the mentee is invited to **lean into** the support, challenges, and encouragement provided by his or her mentor-coach and the collaborative partnership.

Since the learning path is co-created, the mentor-coach is a true partner with the student in the learning process, inquiring (rather than advising) and supporting the mentee as they take increasing responsibility for building their own capacities. This can be hard to do, when time and external forces can interfere and encourage the mentor-coach to "fix" the mentee and "make" the capacity building happen.

DIG DEEPER
For an in-depth discussion of the mentor-coaching structure and skills, see Chapters 4, 5, 6, and 7.

Holding the space for the mentee and their capacity building requires that the mentor-coach maintain her or his stance as the facilitator of the mentor-coaching process. The structures and skills of the mentor-coaching process keep the focus on the learning and work required of the mentee. When learning is challenging for the mentee, we, as mentor-coach, need to ensure that we do not step in to fix and solve the issue, offering our own experience and solutions rather than holding the space for the mentee to dig inside and find the path or solution for themselves—in other words, building their own capacities.

Opportunities Within Education

There are a number of contexts in which the mentor-coaching frame can be found in educational and learning institutions and departments:

- formal mentor–mentee relationship (e.g., supporting individuals new to their role—administrator, team leader, teacher, professor, system leader, or support staff)

- formal coach–client relationship (e.g., leadership coaching)

- informal mentor–mentee relationship (e.g., supporting a colleague or student)

- being coach-like as a leader, consistently holding the capacity-building, strengths-based inquiring frame

- collaborative inquiry

- professional learning partners, teams, and communities (e.g., teacher and early childhood educator in full-day Kindergarten classrooms; teaching assistants and librarians supporting faculty)

- mentoring and coaching approach within a teaching environment (e.g., teacher with student(s) and student with student)

- resource teachers who foster enhanced teaching practices and student achievement through their work with classroom teachers (e.g., literacy and numeracy coaches)

- teaching assistants working with undergraduate students

A New Pedagogy to Support Deep Learning

When we consider recent directions in educational system reform and the need for innovations in new pedagogies relative to higher-order skills and qualities for deep learning, we recognize that mentor-coaching aligns with these directions. Mentor-coaching is a pedagogical model that can help teachers and students develop these higher-order skills and qualities. Depending on where you live, they may be the 3 Cs, the 5 Cs, or what have been recently identified as the 6 Cs (Fullan, 2013): character education, citizenship, communication, critical thinking and problem solving, collaboration, and creativity and imagination.

As teachers, when we arrive to the "two-way learning partnership" with students, inhabiting the skills and stance as mentor-coach, we are grounded in and effectively walking the talk, living and modelling the 6 Cs. As we explore more closely in the following chapters, the skills and change model we offer are predicated on a dynamic that draws on the student or mentee's higher-order skills and qualities. Without them, our work is suspended.

As a pedagogical model and stance, mentor-coaching aligns with specific teaching practices and roles that best support deep connection, learning relationships, and capacity building with and for students:

1. The teacher as designer of powerful learning experiences

2. The teacher as a source of human, social, and decisional capital in the learning experience

3. The teacher as partner in learning with students, accelerated by technology (Fullan & Langsworthy, 2013)

FROM THE FIELD

Participant
Mentor-Coach Training Program for Educators

In my training as a mentor-coach, I received strategies to support my work as an ISRT (In-School Resource Teacher)... [These included giving myself] permission to slow down and listen. This is essential to building a strong relationship... My next steps are to give specific feedback to support staff and students and to hold myself accountable by scheduling time with them. I am better prepared to meet challenges and build strong teams... When we care, we learn!

2 Mentor-Coaching Builds Capacity

"I am not a teacher, but an awakener."

—ROBERT FROST

PREVIEW OF CHAPTER 2

In this chapter, we will learn about

- building capacity and mobilizing for growth
- mentor-coaching as an impactful approach for professional learning
- mentor-coaching and educational leadership

Building Capacity and Mobilizing for Growth

Building capacity is the fundamental mandate of all educators. It is the art of creating dynamic space, curriculum, conversation, and processes that support students and ourselves, as educational leaders, in stepping into learning and growth with engagement, motivation, and commitment. Building capacity reminds us of the power of education to transform people.

As Stober (2006) notes, "Rogers (1951) proposed that human development is directional (forward) and that within the individual framework of the person, people have a basic striving to reach their full capacity" (p. 20). For educators, the "forward" movement of capacity building is propelled by professional learning and growth.

Building personal or professional capabilities and competencies can also be compared to building a house. The process progresses in a particular direction. This directionality requires an agenda with clear intentions; a design; something to build on; and materials, skills, and strategies with which to build.

Basic "Building Materials"

In mentor-coaching, the capacity-building agenda comes from the mentee—the goals they set and the changes and results they want to achieve—and so do the materials. During the process, the basic building materials emerge through the mentee's expanding awareness and choices:

- believing in self, others, possibilities, and opportunities
- strengths and gifts
- access to internal and external resources
- willingness to be vulnerable and engage in the disruptive process of growth
- commitment
- hunger and restlessness
- creativity

- acceptance

- adaptability and flexibility: supporting oneself, resilience

- independence and interdependence

- taking full responsibility for self

The mentee's pre-existing frame of reference is broadened, deepened, or disrupted through provocations and new connections generated in purposeful conversations with the mentor-coach and subsequent experiences. As new ideas, perspectives, and learning emerge, they also serve as the building materials for growth. Forward movement begins. The mentee is drawn onward by the opportunity to integrate and try on "new" possibilities. New ground is claimed and results are achieved. This style of professional learning—a style that involves a commitment to personal growth and intensive work with others—is supported by a number of researchers, including Katz and Dack (2013), who have written extensively on what constitutes true professional growth.

DIG DEEPER

For an in-depth discussion of the mentee's agenda, see the mentor-coaching model in Chapter 4.

Creating the space for these kinds of purposeful, capacity-building conversations establishes an important precedent. The mentee and mentor-coach develop a taste for the satisfaction and clarity of relevant, focused conversations.

> "Capacity building concerns competencies, resources and motivation. Individuals and groups are high in capacity if they possess and continue to develop these three components in concert."
> —*Fullan, 2011, p. 9*

Accessing and supporting the *growth* of individual and collective competencies, resources, and motivation is the top priority of leaders, mentors, and teachers. However, the layered and sometimes elusive nature of change can make sustainable growth difficult to realize.

Reflection: Building Your Own Capacities

In a discussion or journal, consider and respond to the questions below.

1. What kinds of conversations serve to provoke and invoke new ideas and new perspectives for you as a leader? as a teacher? as a person?

2. Where do you find the "disruptive" experiences and learnings that support your own capacity building?

3. What helps you integrate and stabilize enhanced capacities and movement forward?

A Strengths-Based Approach to Capacity Building

Our greatest opportunities for growth lie within our greatest **strengths**. Thus, identifying and leveraging strengths is central to capacity building within the mentor-coaching model and process. The mentor-coach consistently listens for, acknowledges, and recruits the mentee's gifts and talents.

Discovering our strengths, *creating* opportunities to expand their depth and breadth of application, and *claiming* or "owning" (Seligman, 2002) them and their impact is a powerful way to increase our capacity, performance, and fulfillment.

Each of us has a strengths profile that is uniquely ours, enduring, and constantly developing as we recruit and engage our strengths in life and work. What begins as talents or yearnings grows over time, as the learning and energy that is generated by our strengths re-engages us and expands our capacities.

It is important to note that building our strengths is not about ignoring our weaknesses. Instead, we want to *manage* our weaknesses by adjusting our mindset and holding realistic expectations for ourselves as we redesign our process or recruit support. This purposeful and growth-oriented approach frees us to hone our strengths more sharply and helps us to avoid falling into the deficit mindset that weaknesses foster.

Reconfiguring our work as leaders to maximize our strengths can help us access increased levels of performance, commitment, and passion.

Exercise: Managing Weaknesses

Begin by clarifying whether a weakness pertains to your skills, knowledge, or talents. Take steps to acquire any skills or knowledge that may improve it. After that, if you still feel your performance is subpar, consider the following four strategies for managing a weakness outlined by Buckingham and Clifton (2001).

1. **"Get a little better at it"** (p. 151). This might require some hunkering down, but having a realistic goal in terms of what "a little" means is important. If this strategy becomes "too draining," Buckingham and Clifton recommend trying the following one.

2. **Use one of your strongest strengths to "overwhelm your weakness"** (p. 151). According to Buckingham and Clifton, strengths are "malleable" (p. 44) and can "trump" (p. 155) a weakness. As a result, leveraging a strength to support a weakness builds capacity.

3. **"Find a partner"** (p. 155). Knowing what our weakness is and accessing the support of a partner who has strength in that domain is a skill and critical to maximizing our performance.

4. **"Just stop doing it"** (p. 158). Often, when we recognize that we have exhausted all possible strategies for managing a "particular persistent weakness" (p. 157) we need to consider stopping. According to Buckingham and Clifton, reorganizing our work habits or responsibilities to minimize the weakness can be a powerful strategy for managing it.

Recruiting Strengths as a Practice

Due to its transformative effect, operating from an appreciative or strengths-based mindset is a valuable practice to introduce early in a mentor-coaching relationship. This means consistently inviting the mentee to recruit their strengths into their leadership roles, teaching, work, and so on, particularly when you can hear that they are feeling under-resourced or are operating from a deficit mindset. This subtle shift can have a direct impact on the mentee's engagement, perceived level of competence and, in turn, confidence.

"Practice is a process of personal transformation."
—Hanson, 2011, p. 5

When faced with an opportunity or challenge, purposefully recruiting some of your top strengths can provide energy, focus, and momentum. Thus, as mentee or mentor-coach, it is a useful practice to have a robust list of strengths available as a visual reminder to access and purposefully weave them into conversations, experiences, and planning.

Exercise: Go to Your Strengths

Keeping your top five or six signature strengths consistently in mind can make them accessible in your work and life. Complete the VIA Survey on character strengths (see the Mentor-Coaching Toolkit), to identify them. Then post a list of these character strengths on your computer or desk.

Mentor-Coaching: An Impactful Approach for Professional Learning

Current research around the efficacy of coaching and mentoring within professional learning supports our practice of combining these roles (Jayaram, Moffit, & Scott, 2012). In the research, the assumption is that the mentor brings specific expertise and experience to the coaching process. As the mentor-coach supports the learner over time, she or he shares wisdom, experience, observations, inquiries, feedback, and reflection.

We have not found much depth of discussion in professional learning and development literature regarding the principles, attitudes, behaviours, and skills a mentor-coach needs to employ and integrate as they work with a mentee. We call this the **mentor-coach's stance,** and it is integral to the work that the mentor-coach does with their mentee to support them in building their own capacity and integrating the new learning. For us, this is where the mentor-coaching frame offers so much more to the whole process and relationship surrounding professional learning.

> **Mentor-coach's stance**—
> the principles, attitudes, behaviours, and skills a mentor-coach needs to employ and integrate as he or she works with a mentee

Coaching: A Critical Component of Effective Professional Learning

Increasingly, decisions to invest in human resources and professional learning are data driven and hinge on the professional development or training's proven impact on learning outcomes. In education, the investment needs to transfer directly into improved practice and, thus, improve student performance. Fortunately, a large body of evidence has emerged on the critical role that coaching can play in this domain (Bush, 1984; Showers, 1982; Showers, 1984; Knight, 1998; Knight, 2007; Batt, 2010; Slinger, 2004). Let us look at some of the key findings.

As early as 1980, Joyce and Showers identified the critical components of effective professional development for teachers. More recently (2002), they quantified the efficacy of each of the cumulative aspects, as captured in the table on the following page. Peer coaching is identified as, by far, the most impactful component. The implication of Joyce and Showers's finding is that by providing on-site, collegial support over time, coaching fosters in-depth integration.

Cumulative Aspects of Effective Professional Learning and Development

Components	Knowledge	Skill	Transfer
Study of theory	10%	5%	0%
Demonstrations	30%	20%	0%
Practice	60%	60%	5%
Peer coaching	95%	95%	95%

—Joyce & Showers, 2002, p. 78

> "Successful transfer requires a period of practice of the skill in context until it is tuned to the same level of fluidity as elements of the previously existing repertoire… If we had our way, *all* school faculties would be divided into coaching teams who regularly observe one another's teaching and provide helpful information, feedback, and so forth. In short, we recommend the development of a 'coaching environment' in which all personnel see themselves as one another's coaches."
>
> *—Joyce & Showers, 1982, pp. 5, 6*

Clarity regarding the impact of coaching as the most critical aspect of effective professional learning grew out of the recognition that integrating new teaching practices, in service of enhanced student learning and achievement, is a complex and multi-layered process. It requires significant attention, intention, and support over time.

Integrating Professional Learning, Skills, and Behaviours: Putting Learning into Practice

One of the biggest challenges when designing professional learning is to build in opportunities for learners to practise and integrate new learning in their environment (Joyce & Showers, 2002). Trying on the new is often anxiety-producing and messy. Furthermore, as adult learners not very comfortable with "not knowing," we are often in a hurry to become confident and competent at the expense of meaningfully integrating new learning.

Another challenge identified in the research is that "teachers change their underlying beliefs about how to teach something only *after* they see success with students (Guskey, 2002)… Indeed, when teachers do not see success, they tend to abandon the practice and revert to business as usual" (Gulamhussein, 2013, p. 12). This statement has implications for our traditional forms of professional learning—those large-scale events that are led by experts and have no built-in capacity for implementation and support with peers and experienced others. Conversely, the possibility of best practices and new learnings being integrated is greatly enhanced when leaders or teachers have the support over time of one or more mentor-coaches, co-creating a process and relationship(s) that foster journeying toward mastery.

Indeed, research identifies coaching as one of the most impactful processes in supporting teachers in growing their competence and confidence in the application and integration of new skills and strategies (Joyce & Showers, 1980, 1996, 2002; Cordingley & Bell, 2012; Kretlow & Bartholomew, 2010; Kretlow, Cooke, & Wood, 2012; Gulamhussein, 2013). Coaching provides direct, individualized support to the adult learner as they experiment with applying their new learning in "real-life" application within a trusting relationship, where it feels safe to try on new strategies and behaviours. These applications enable the adult learner to reflect, learn, and grow in service of enhancing best practices.

Two primary models for coaching are referenced in research (Kretlow & Bartholomew, 2010). In both instances, coaching is used primarily as impactful follow-up support for teachers who have experienced significant new learning and are eager to implement it into their practice.

The first primary model for coaching is *supervisory coaching*, where a coach will observe a teacher implementing a technique or approach that they have learned recently:

> "The coach conducts an observation of a teacher implementing a technique he or she has recently learned to use in a prior training… After the lesson, the coach provides descriptive, non-evaluative feedback to the teacher regarding the strengths and opportunities for improvement."
> —Kretlow & Bartholomew, 2010, p. 281

"A change in practice is the result of a reflective journey that involves transforming and reconstructing what teachers know, believe and do."
—Bronson, 2007, p. 29

The second model for coaching is *side-by-side coaching*, where a teacher can observe an experienced colleague work with their students to implement a new practice or procedure before they emulate the coach:

> "During a side-by-side coaching session, the coach directly intervenes during the lesson, provides a model and a rationale for the change, and then provides additional opportunities for the teacher to teach the same format again with immediate feedback from the coach."
> —*Kretlow & Bartholomew, 2010, p. 281*

A third model, *peer coaching*, is also highlighted in related literature (Raney & Robbins, 1989; Joyce & Showers, 1996). Collaborative and reflective dialogue sits at the centre of the process and relationship, in which two or more leaders support each other, over time, in refining their understanding and practice. In peer coaching, greater expertise is not assumed in the coach; rather, it involves colleagues collaborating over time, intentionally expanding their awareness, capacities, and practices.

> "Many believe that the essence of the coaching transaction is to offer advice to teachers following observations. Not so. Rather, teachers learn from one another while planning instruction, developing support materials, watching one another work with students, and thinking together about the impact of their behavior on their students' learning."
> —*Joyce & Showers, 1996, pp. 12–16*

The framework of collaborative inquiry within professional learning communities is evident in peer coaching. Dufour and Marzano (2011) state: "It is the *process* of building shared knowledge and the *collaborative dialogue* about that shared knowledge that builds the capacity of staff to function as high-performing teams" (p. 85).

These coaching models—supervisory, side-by-side, and peer—describe concrete and specific frames for mentor-coaching. By integrating these models into her or his stance, the mentor-coach has a broad palette to draw from as she or he interacts with the mentee in service of deep professional learning and enhanced student achievement.

Linking Effective Professional Learning to Enhancing Student Achievement

The central mandate of education is to support the learning and growth of students. Leithwood, Louis, Anderson, and Wahlstrom (2004) highlight the finding that, after classroom teaching, school leadership is the second most important factor in student achievement. Furthermore, according to Robinson and Timperley (2007), leaders "can have a substantial impact on student outcomes particularly through…promoting and participating in teacher learning and development" (p. 2).

Thus, it is critical that leaders are lifelong professional learners, working individually and collectively to enhance their own practices, so that they may continue to support capacity building in themselves and in their students.

> "[An] important shift in thinking about professional learning is the centrality of students to the process. Improvements in student learning and well-being are not a by-product of professional learning but should be its central purpose. Student engagement, learning and well-being should be the reason for teachers to engage in professional learning, the basis for understanding what needs to change, and the criteria for deciding whether those changes have been effective."
> —Timperley & Earl, 2011, p. 22

Cordingley and Bell (2012) analyzed current professional development research to identify characteristics of professional learning that are most closely tied to having a positive effect on student learning outcomes. They found the following approaches to professional learning to be most effective:

- collaborative—involving staff working together, identifying starting points, sharing evidence about practice, and trying out new approaches

- supported by specialist expertise, usually drawn from beyond the learning setting

- focused on aspirations for students—the moral imperative and shared focus

- sustained over time—professional development sustained over weeks or months had substantially more impact on practice benefiting students than shorter engagements

- exploring evidence from trying new things to connect practice to theory, enabling practitioners to transfer new approaches and practices and the concepts underpinning them to practice in multiple contexts

Mentor-coaching as a methodology and stance includes all of these elements. It allows for the leader and student to engage in an ongoing relationship and process that is fundamentally collaborative, focused on deep learning, experimentation, integration, and capacity building.

Coaching and Mentoring and Impactful Professional Learning: Three Reports

A variety of current research reports exploring the most effective professional learning identify a common factor: coaching and mentoring are two of the most effective methodologies to support enhanced professional learning and integration.

McKinsey Report, 2012

The benefits and cost-effectiveness of coaching as a process for supporting increased learning and performance of teachers is highlighted in "Breaking the Habit of Ineffective Professional Development for Teachers" (Jayaram, Moffit, & Scott, 2012). In the report, the authors suggest that educational systems should "make coaching the centerpiece of PD" (p. 2), given its impact on individual and collective skill building and its return on investment.

> "Open, straightforward, in-person coaching is the most effective way of delivering immediate feedback [support] and advice on specific classroom practices. Because coaching is so customized, it can create faster and deeper insights for teachers about what can work in their classrooms, thus creating inflection points in their practice."
>
> —Jayaram, Moffit, & Scott, 2012, p. 7

Centre for the Use of Research & Evidence in Education (CUREE) Report, 2012

Cordingley and Bell (2012), in "Understanding What Enables High Quality Professional Learning: A Report on the Research Evidence," identify professional learning models that are "more likely to improve student outcomes" as being centred on "collaborative enquiry oriented learning." They suggest that "such practices are found in many combinations under many different labels but at their best they tend to be configured under the labels of coaching and mentoring, collaborative enquiry and, more recently, joint practice development" (p. 8).

Center for Public Education (CPE) Report, 2013

In "Teaching the Teachers: Effective Professional Development in an Era of High Stakes Accountability," Gulamhussein (2013) identifies coaching as the critical methodology for supporting individual and group professional learning.

> "For research-based practices, coaching has proved successful in supporting [the] implementation dip and changing teachers' practice… Schools must also empower teachers to be innovators and researchers themselves through professional learning communities, where fellow teachers can serve as a network of coaches for each other."
> —Gulamhussein, 2013, p. 38

This research speaks to what we knew to be true, given our experiences over the last eight years of sharing our mentor-coaching model. Providing a structure and set of skills that can bring people safely together to stretch and try new learning and attitudes *and* improve results, however, is no small feat.

How One School Mobilized Teachers to Build Capacity and Change the "School Culture"

In November of 2012, I was asked to design a professional development session for 20 Grade 8 teachers who were struggling with a challenging group of female students. This cohort included a clique of clever students who had established a stranglehold on the

continued…

social dynamic that was distracting and difficult for teachers to penetrate. Weaker students were being isolated and the atmosphere in the room no longer felt safe. As a result, teachers felt disrespected by the "clique" and had become preoccupied with their negative influence and shortcomings. In short, they were fed up.

In the briefing with senior administrators, I was told that the teachers were frustrated and that they needed some shared strategies for accessing and engaging the students. It was an interesting task, particularly when viewed through the traditional lens of a "consultant" coming in to "fix" or alleviate the teachers' increasing frustration and "provide" strategies that would help align the team and "get things back on track."

I was offered 90 minutes with the team of teachers, so relevance and efficiency were paramount. Fortunately, the administrator, who was the key contact, was familiar with my approach as educator/coach and my commitment to facilitating desired change from the inside out. The administrator believed in the coach approach to supporting change and this helped to clear the space for a capacity-building session. Arriving as the "expert" with a series of "strategies" and presenting them to the group in an attempt to "solve" the "problem" was not on offer.

As I began to design the session, deciding how to introduce and position the session with the teachers felt integral. It was critical for the teachers to see and feel that the session was designed to help them increase their individual and collective capacities for engaging the challenging students. Having someone come in "from the outside" and effectively tell them how to get back on track, thereby diminishing them and their wisdom, would likely build further resentment. The session needed to build capacity and mobilize the teachers, so that they could do the same for the students. Its dynamic needed to be safe and to invite vulnerability and stepping in and up, right off the top.

I decided to combine an inside-out approach with a concept I had encountered in "The Pivot," an article in Fast Company,

continued...

July/August 2012, about startups in Silicon Valley. In examining organizational success and adaptability, the author Andrew Rice referred to Eric Ries's (2012) idea of "the pivot" and how many successful startups use this strategy when they start out in one direction and aren't successful.

According to Silicon Valley mythology, there is no dishonour in starting off in the wrong direction. Obstacles are seen just as other opportunities for inspiration. They are unpacked, a "pivot" or "change in strategy without a change in vision" (Penenberg & Ries, 2012) is identified, and the course is adjusted in order to realize full engagement (and significant revenue, in the case of start-ups). The idea of a "pivot" felt like a positive one and a great frame to offer the teachers, as they considered changes they wanted to make to better access and engage the students.

By positioning the session as an opportunity to identify a possible "pivot," and opening with an activity that focused on the teachers and the reality of their "current conditions" in the classroom, I set the stage for an inside-out approach to capacity building. I also used a simplified version of the path of a mentor-coaching conversation as a frame for the session. Given that I was facilitating the session as mentor and coach, I used my skills and stance as coach to create a coach approach to capacity building and a dynamic that would help the teachers achieve their goals for the session.

Structure of the Professional Development Session

- **Agenda:** predetermined by the administrators, based on perceived needs

- **Attunement exercise:** core teaching and learning values identified by teachers

- **Awareness exercise:** alone and then in groups, the teachers identified what they believed to be the students' strengths and challenges

- **Group exercise:** in groups of four, teachers identified what they wanted to see "more of" and "less of" in their classroom dynamics (i.e., priorities)

continued...

DIG DEEPER

- For an in-depth look at mentor-coaching conversations, see Chapter 8.

- For information about attunement exercises, see Chapter 6 and the Mentor-Coaching Toolkit.

- **Choices:** individually and collectively, the teachers identified how they wanted to begin to make these things happen in their classrooms

- **Action:** next steps were identified. Also teachers recognized that they wanted to access the students' voices to ensure that all were on the right track.

Outcome of the Session

The teachers returned to their classrooms with a greater level of awareness surrounding the students' strengths and challenges as learners, as well as a focused sense of where the most critical change was required. They also had an expanded awareness of their own personal needs within the classroom dynamic, which they had developed in the teaching values exercise. The teachers' abilities to align with and leverage the strengths of the students to address the challenges that had been impeding the learning process were substantially increased. The teachers' capacities for accessing student engagement also increased, providing a win-win.

By working from the inside out, in the space created by the mentor-coaching approach to capacity building and mobilizing, the teachers had been able to access their "competencies, resources, and motivation" (Fullan, 2011, p. 9).

For me, this experience was exciting because it confirmed that applying this approach to a professional learning opportunity that was focused on "school culture," rather than a pedagogical concept, was able to broaden the teachers' perspective and support them in moving toward their desired results.

By helping the teachers shift their perspective, feel less encumbered and more resourced, a cultural shift could begin. Creating the space for them to step back—from themselves, their practices, and the students—allowed them to break out of their mindset about the cohort, and the impact that it was having on them and their practices.

continued...

Feedback from the School's Team Leader

What did the session provoke or invoke in the teachers, or in their practices with the kids?

"I think the session carved out some time for us to sit back and think about the kids as people—and not behaviour problems. In other words, to think about their strengths and to think about, talk about, and focus on what we like, admire, and appreciate in them and hold that up beside the frustrations we were experiencing."

How did the workshop impact the teachers' awareness and perspective?

"I think talking about their strengths and proclivities shifted the perspective back—brought the 'whole girl and the group' into view rather than pinpointing the specific issues."

What was "the pivot" for the teachers and what did it provide?

"I think the pivot occurred around the way they talked about and 'saw' the kids. There was a desire to work with their strengths more and to engage the girls in problem solving. It led to what we ended up calling a 'reset' for the girls—where the teachers invited the girls to talk about what they wanted for themselves and set intentions about getting there."

Anything else you would like to add?

"I think another thing that was valuable was the honouring of and recognition of the teachers' perspectives. They were really in the driver's seat and they were certainly invited to think how they wanted to handle their challenging situation instead of being told what to do—or, worse yet, just expected to figure it out on their own. Makes me want to do it all over again. Also makes me realize how important it is to do this work in situ—when you've got a group that you are working with and trying to figure out—rather than doing it in isolation and in general ways—talking about teens or Grade 8s hypothetically—but these girls right now, right here."

From Kate

An Effective Adult Learning Model

DIG DEEPER

For more on feedback, see Chapter 9.

Mentor-coaching is well suited to meet the needs of adult learners, as outlined in the distillation of Speck and Knipe (2001) and Malcolm Knowles' (1984) research findings below. We have included the word *mentee* with each point to highlight the shared alignment and relevance.

- Adults (mentees) become dedicated to their own learning and professional development when they believe that the goals are realistic, important, and aligned with their experiences and needs. They need evidence that what they learn applies directly to their daily work and on-the-job challenges.

- Adults (mentees) need to be independent and in charge of their own learning and growth and the process that surrounds it.

- Adults (mentees) value real and relevant experiences that will help them achieve their objectives. Time to explore, apply, and integrate their learning into their work, or context, can support increased responsibility and engagement.

- Adult learners (mentees) need ongoing support to integrate new learning into professional practice. Thus, the learning relationship within coaching helps to realize lasting change.

- Adults (mentees) need consistent and relevant feedback throughout the learning process as they grow their skills and capacities.

- Adult learners (mentees) come to the learning process with a depth of experience, knowledge, training, and capacities as well as a strong desire for autonomy.

With the mentor-coaching skills and principles serving as the foundation of the mentor-coach's stance, the mentor-coaching process deeply honours the needs of the mentee as adult learner.

Mentor-Coaching and Educational Leadership

As noted previously, classroom leadership and school leadership are the two greatest factors that influence student learning and achievement (Leithwood, Louis, Anderson, & Wahlstrom, 2004). Leadership itself happens at many levels in many contexts and capacities. The goal of this book is to invite all of us to hold a wide frame for leadership, since it is distributed throughout the culture of the classroom, school, district, and system, and across higher education. Given this, as noted earlier, when we use the term *leaders*, we are speaking to *and of* all leaders in education—the classroom leader (teacher), school leader (vice principal, principal), system leader (supervisory officer), district leader (education director), and leaders in higher education (college and university faculty and staff).

Leadership is, by its very nature, about **directionality** and **intentionality**. The mentor-coaching relationship and process is always about supporting the mentee leader in moving forward with increased awareness and clarity. Within the mentor-coaching frame, we advocate the leadership stance outlined below.

Leaders lead from the inside out. It is vital for leaders to be grounded in their own awareness and experience and to be clear about the importance of always "doing their own work" as they invite others to do the same.

> "Leaders either shed light or cast a shadow on everything they do. The more conscious the self-awareness, the more light leaders bring. The more limited the self-understanding, the more shadows leaders cast."
> —*Cashman, 1999, p. 39*

Leaders are authentic. Authenticity requires a lifelong commitment to self-discovery and self-observation. Asking ourselves, "Where is my leadership coming from?" helps us to consider whether our actions originate from deep within ourselves, or whether they are coming from a more superficial place. Are they coming from our role, our persona, or our expectations for ourselves as mentor-coach? Or, are they coming from the essence of who we are?

> "Authenticity is a collection of choices that we have to make every day. It's about the choice to show up and be real. The choice to be honest. The choice to let our true selves be seen."
> —*Brown, 2010, p. 49*

Directionality— a particular direction of movement, progression, or development

Intentionality— a deliberate purpose

DIG DEEPER
See Chapter 4 for an in-depth discussion of our model of leading from the inside out.

Leaders are present, open, flexible, and resilient. A leader's ability to connect with opportunities and challenges that continuously emerge around him or her takes a great deal of mental and emotional energy. Having another trusted adult whom you can rely on as a listener and thinking partner is incredibly valuable and has also been proven to be emotionally restorative. As research tells us, two of the key predictors of resilience are a strong sense of purpose and a supportive partnership (Hargreaves & Shirley, 2009).

> "*Openness* implies that we are receptive to whatever comes to our awareness and don't cling to preconceived ideas about how things 'should' be. We let go of expectations and receive things as they are, rather than trying to make them how we want them to be… It gives us the power to recognize restrictive judgments and release our minds from the grip."
> —Siegel, 2010, p. 32

Leaders, as reflective practitioners, are mindful and self-aware and foster these qualities in others. Mindfulness is our capacity to be in the moment, experiencing directly, and aware of our own mental processes. As impartial observers of ourselves as leaders—being in the moment, open-minded, and unattached—we cultivate the capacity to pause, experience, observe, reflect, and choose…indeed, inviting reflection instead of reaction.

> "It's not so much what the leader does, given that they are likely pretty good at the doing, it's what they SEE—seeing clearly requires mindfulness and synchronizing with our experience. The discipline trains us to step out from behind the curtain of the restless mind and touch reality directly."
> —Carroll, 2010, p. 55

Relationships are the bedrock of leadership. Relationships, cultivated and fostered, serve as the foundation of leadership and teaching, generating energy and synergy. It is the mutual trust, respect, and shared commitment that supports the growth and development of the individuals and the collective, as the path forward emerges.

> "I want a world full of great leaders… I want us all to stop thinking only in terms of accomplishments, of task and completion, of beating the competition…of winning praise, and instead, live our lives forging the

deepest relationships we can with ourselves and with one another. I want us to respond to adversity by deepening our engagement in our lives. It isn't complicated. We've got to make connections—at a deep level. Create them. Every day. On purpose. Make more and more of them."
—*Scott, 2009, pp. 297–298*

Leaders stand as part of the circle. As leadership and teaching in the twenty-first century shift from a hierarchical position to a flatter or more-distributed approach, leaders are recognizing the centrality of the relationships to growth and change. Coaching supports this shift by providing an infrastructure for dialogue and engagement.

"To succeed in a networked world requires leaders to think in terms of attraction and co-option rather than command. Leaders need to think of themselves as being in a circle rather than atop a mountain."
—*Nye, 2011, p. 101*

Leaders build capacity one conversation at a time. Leaders and teachers hold a deep belief in the expanding capacity of self and others by being purposefully coach-like in conversation to support others in accessing their own strengths, wisdom, clarity, and intentionality. A leader is someone who sees more in others than they see in themselves.

"It could be argued that all leadership is appreciative leadership. It's the capacity to see the best in the world around us…to see with an appreciative eye the true and the good, the better and the possible."
—*Creelman & Cooperrider, 2001*

Leaders recognize that everyone brings their whole self to work. Leaders and teachers understand that we each bring our whole selves to work each day. It is arbitrary and counterproductive to try to separate our working/student lives from our broader personal and emotional lives. There is such beauty and creativity available when our whole selves are recognized and invited into the relationships and the work.

"The organizations in which we sought to be of help were very different, but their leaders—whether CEOs, unit heads, or team leaders—all shared one thing in common long before they met us: A deep and abiding recognition that their people bring their humanity to work with them every single day; that the absolute division between the work realm and the personal realm is naïve and unhelpful; and that twenty-first century leaders must find a more effective way to engage the emotional lives of their organizations and leadership teams."

—*Kegan & Lahey, 2009, p. xiv*

Leaders foster rich professional dialogue and support structures. Being in deep professional conversations and relationships with colleagues and students over time builds relationships and support structures that foster sustainable growth and connection, individually and collectively.

"[Leaders use] robust dialogue to surface realities [within]…relationships… [using] their rigor and intensity to explore the depths of the situation. They will flush out assumptions, push for goals being realistic and compelling, and invite the best imaginative and critical skills of their people."

—*Hall & Duval, 2003, p. 35*

Leaders hold, inhabit, and mobilize a deep commitment to purpose and vision. Vision and purpose serve as the compass for leaders and teachers, informing mindset, choices, behaviours, relationships, attention, mobilization, and intentionality.

"Great leaders face the uncertainty of today's world with hope: they inspire through clarity of vision, optimism and a profound belief in their—and their people's—ability to turn dreams into reality."

—*Boyatzis & McKee, 2005, p. 3*

FROM THE FIELD

Bill Tucker
Visiting Associate Professor, Faculty of Education, Western University; former Director of Education, Thames Valley DSB

Educational leaders throughout a school system must be able to demonstrate a cadre of skill sets and competencies regardless of role, environment, or situation. Key among these is the ability to build relationships based on mutual respect and trust. My

continued…

leadership experience has been that the authentic mentor/coach connection serves as foundational in that aspect. The professional growth of all staff, regardless of their position in the organization, becomes both intrinsic in nature and sustainable. In our board, we found that the ability of our leaders to provide mentorship/coaching to staff allowed us to move as a system from the "whats" of education to the "whys" and "hows," resulting in much deeper and more meaningful conversations and impacts on student learning.

As an associate professor currently supervising and working with graduate students, the use of powerful mentorship/coaching strategies is twofold in purpose. First, it creates opportunities for my students to reach higher levels of understanding and achievement in the areas of self-awareness and self-learning. Second, a large percentage of the faculty's graduate students already occupy leadership positions within their respective boards of education and the intentionality of the mentorship/coaching approach is to model stratagems that they can use within their own roles and responsibilities.

"Leadership, if it is to be effective, has to have an explicit 'making-a-difference' sense of purpose, use strategies that mobilize many people to tackle tough problems, be held accountable by measured and debatable indicators of success, and be ultimately assessed by the extent to which it awakens people's intrinsic commitment, which is none other than the mobilizing of everyone's sense of moral purpose."
—Fullan, 2001, p. 20

Aligning Mentor-Coaching with Educational Leadership Research

The intent of the role of mentor-coach is anchored and aligned with Leithwood and Riehl's (2003) landmark study and well-documented understandings of successful educational leadership. The researchers cite "three broad categories of practices [that] have been identified as important for leadership success in almost all settings and organizations" (p. 5). These practices include "setting directions, developing people, and developing the organisation" (p. 5).

Important Practices for Leadership Success

Setting Directions	Developing People	Developing the Organization
• identifying and articulating a vision • creating shared meanings • creating high-performance expectations • fostering the acceptance of group goals • monitoring organizational performance • communicating	• offering intellectual stimulation • providing individualized support • providing an appropriate model	• strengthening school culture • modifying organizational structure • building collaborative processes • managing the environment

—Leithwood & Riehl, 2003, pp. 1–12

These three broad categories define and streamline practices that are central to impactful school leadership. In turn, these practices have emerged in a variety of state and provincial leadership frameworks that define capacities and competencies central to the role.

As an example, in the State of New York, the 2008 Interstate School Leaders Licensure Consortium (ISLLC) Standards have been adopted to outline the standards and functions of high-quality school leadership behaviours. Recently, the ISLLC Standards are being used within our mentor-coaching program to support mentee growth and intentionality. In Ontario, as part of the broader province-wide mentoring initiative, districts are required to integrate a mentee learning needs assessment that focuses on the Ontario Leadership Framework (OLF) (Institute for Education Leadership, 2013).

In the research following the implementation of our program, both mentors and mentees revealed that expertise in setting direction was the leadership domain most influenced by participation in the initiative (Robinson, 2011).

FEEDBACK FROM THREE SCHOOL LEADERS

Jane Morton
Principal, Mentor-Coach Training Program Facilitator

I listen better; I come at problems from a place of curiosity; my feedback is more objective and I am less defensive when it comes to receiving my own feedback. I tend to stay further away from the problems of others, instead believing (trusting) that "they" who own the problem also own the solution. *And* it's a lot of fun! Our board mentors strongly believe every administrator in the system needs this training.

Liana Lafranier
Principal, Mentor-Coach Training Program Facilitator, and ACC (Associate Certified Coach)

Approaching school leadership from the point of inquiry has allowed me to more easily suspend judgment and be more flexible in my decision-making, planning, and managing.

Karin Schmidlechner
Principal and Mentor-Coach Training Program Facilitator

Before mentor-coaching, as principal, I didn't always see each person's full potential in my building. However, mentor-coaching has provided me with a model to support self-discovery and potential for everyone. Possibilities are explored, staff are collaborating, leading and stretching their own capacity.

Coaching opportunities present themselves around every corner in my day: walk-throughs, teacher performance appraisals, critical conversations, planning sessions, school improvement plan team meetings, just to name a few. Mentor-coaching allows me to gain insight into how each staff member may contribute to the school team and, in turn, it allows my staff to gain insight into how they are doing and being their best.

Carol Rolheiser
Director, Centre for Teaching Support & Innovation and Professor, Department of Curriculum, Teaching and Learning, University of Toronto

I work with a wide array of leaders, faculty, staff, and students across our university with a focus on enhancing teaching and learning. Often our interactions involve challenging problems, high-stakes activities, and competing priorities. People need to be heard and my goal is to help create a space where that is possible.

My training as a mentor-coach has influenced my awareness of what stance I need to assume in any given interaction in order to support the goals of the person with whom I am interacting. I have adopted this same approach in working with my staff and providing both training and ongoing mentoring-coaching for them in order to enhance our effectiveness as a team. Daily we see the payoffs as we develop our individual and collective skills and capacity.

Reflection: What Does It Take to Build Your Capacity and Mobilize Yourself?

In a discussion or journal, consider and respond to the questions below.

1. As a leader, what does it take to build your own capacities? to get you moving?

2. As a teacher, what supports you in staying open and rigorous with yourself as you continue to expand your own best practices?

3. As a parent, how do you support your children in finding their wings and taking flight?

4. As an athlete, what supports you in growing your competence, comfort, and confidence?

5. As an artist, what supports you in accessing the vulnerability and exhilaration to increase your fluency and creative mastery?

3 Learning in Relationship

"If you want to go quickly, go alone.
If you want to go far, go together."

—AFRICAN PROVERB

PREVIEW OF CHAPTER 3

In this chapter, we will explore

- the importance of being in relationship
- what "learning in relationship" makes possible
- the mentor-coaching relationship
- what sets the mentor-coaching relationship apart
- critical aspects of the mentor-coaching relationship

The Importance of Being in Relationship

As wisdom within neuroscience and psychology continues to grow, researchers are finding "hard evidence" of what many of us, particularly educators and leaders, have sensed already: that being in relationships with others is critical for surviving and thriving.

> "We are social beings that grow and flourish when our relationships are intact; our survival is inextricably linked to the quality of our relationships, and our growth and development occur in the context of relationships. Indeed…growth-fostering relationships are a central human necessity."
> —*Hicks, 2011, p. 6*

Goleman (2006) describes the social brain as orchestrating our thoughts, feelings, and interactions in relationships. It is "the only biological system in our bodies that continually attunes us to, and in turn becomes influenced by, the internal state of people we're with" (p. 10).

What "Learning in Relationship" Makes Possible

"I've known some of these people for years and have never had professional conversations like this."

—*Mentor-coach training participant*

Research (Robinson, 2011) tells us that learning together makes a difference, both at cultural and relational levels. The laughter and rich conversations that come with the stretching and growing together makes learning and digging deep something we value as adult learners. As well, the tradition of mentoring has always capitalized on the opportunities for growth inherent in relationships that support capacity building over time.

Relationships grow in safe and nourishing environments, where we feel a sense of ownership, purpose, and autonomy and have the space and resources to grow. The mentor-coaching relationship offers such an environment, as its main components are learning and relationships. In our work surrounding the mentor-coaching initiative, we have realized that the dynamic between the two—the learning and the relationship—is where the "magic" occurs. The synergy that comes from the partnership between mentor-coach and mentee provides a structure and creates a space for deep learning to occur. We call this "turbo-charged" learning. As in any powerful learning relationship, the learning that is possible within a mentor-coaching relationship reaches well beyond that which could happen on one's own and spreads through the organization's social and human capital: networks of relationships and the skills-and-knowledge base of individuals.

Robinson (2011) captures this dynamic when she states that the mentor-coaching relationship effectively provides a frame to move from a "'sink or swim' treatment of newly appointed leaders to a culture of support and community of learners" (p. 23).

> "In the Ontario study, mentors had the opportunity to meet with mentees, colleagues, learning teams and lead mentors, continually bringing an enhanced level of expertise related to their professional practice through socialization and 'the personal networks [that] play an important role and enhance the development of individual competence' (Mieg, 2006, p. 757). The networking and opportunity to layer and learn interactively from and with colleagues showed positive results. The principal's job can be perceived as isolated and remote, but the opportunities to meet, collaborate and share expertise emerged as a strong conclusive benefit of the [mentor-coaching] program."
> —Robinson, 2010, p. 87

How Is Learning in a Relationship Unique?

In his book *Ungifted*, Scott Barry Kaufman (2013) explains that contextualized learning, learning *with* someone and *within* a particular context or role, leads to a greater sense of competence and autonomy. Kaufman references Deci and Ryan's (2008) theory of self-determination, suggesting that our highest levels of intrinsic motivation are accessed when a learning experience satisfies our top three foundational human psychological needs:

"The underlying principle is that success is most likely to occur when people engage in environments in which they are active participants in the learning process, and are challenged and supported."
—Kaufman, 2013, p. 136

1. Autonomy: the desire to feel in control of one's decisions

2. Competence: the desire to feel capable of mastery and accomplishment

3. Relatedness: the desire to feel a sense of connection to one's peers

Mentor-coaching provides the ideal setting for this type of learning to occur. As the mentee navigates his or her learning path, the mentee has a co-pilot and supportive witness in the mentor-coach. Through purposeful conversations, the mentee's autonomy, decisions, competence, and growing mastery are consistently reflected back and forth between the mentor-coach and mentee. This allows for deepening the cognitive connections being made. This, in turn, helps to cement the learning, build capacity, and assist the mentee in accessing deeper intrinsic motivation.

Kaufman (2013) points out that the goals that grow out of intrinsic motivation feed the need for autonomy and take processing to a deeper level, engaging greater persistence and, ultimately, resulting in a higher level of performance.

How Relationships Influence Learning

> "When I have been able to transform a group—and here I mean all the members of a group, myself included—into a community of learners, then the excitement has been almost beyond belief. To free curiosity; to permit individuals to go charging off in new directions dictated by their own interests; to unleash the sense of inquiry; to open everything to questioning and exploration; to recognize that everything is in process of change—here is an experience I can never forget."
>
> —Rogers, as cited in Kirschenbaum & Henderson, 1989, p. 304

Every classroom teacher knows the impact that the relationships among students can have on learning. It is very simple: the relationships either help or hinder the learning. Similarly, as students, we have all felt the impact of our relationships with our teachers on our learning. Being with a teacher who really "gets us" and appreciates us for all that we are prompts us to dig deeper and try harder.

In "Towards a New End: New Pedagogies for Deep Learning," Fullan and Langworthy (2013) speak directly to the future and the increasing centrality of student-teacher relationships and technology's emerging role within the dynamic:

> "Learning is rooted in relationships, and supportive relationships can unleash the potential of every student. Yet few teacher preparation programs provide teachers with explicit guidance on how to build these relationships,

especially with students whose life experiences may be quite different from the teacher's own. The future of teaching may ultimately center in deeper relationships built between teachers and students, developed through creative, collaborative, socially connected and relevant learning experiences."
—p. 14

The fundamental assumption of the mentor-coaching relationship is that *learning and growth will occur.* The purpose, direction, and intention of the relationship all contribute to this call to transformation. The mentor-coach's mandate is to support and challenge the mentee as she or he works toward the desired changes or results. Within this shared context, they each bring a lot to the relationship. Thus, both the mentor-coach and the mentee foster an ongoing commitment to stepping into the learning and change they want to achieve.

Reflection: Relationships and Learning

In a discussion or journal, consider and respond to the questions below.

1. How have the relationships in your life influenced your learning? As you consider this question, think of a moment when a learning relationship supported your growth:

    a) What was made possible that might not have been possible without the relationship?

    b) How did the relationship influence your learning?

    c) What was accessed in you that otherwise may not have been?

    d) Who were you *being*? Who was the other person *being*?

    e) How did this relationship support you as a learner?

2. How have your relationships supported another's learning? As you consider this question, think of a moment when you supported another's learning, through the relationship that existed:

    a) What was your role?

    b) What did it require of you?

    c) What felt critical in your approach or stance?

    d) What was made possible for you? for the other person?

    e) What has the lasting impact of this experience been for you?

Creating a Culture of Learning and Accountability

Just as relationships are key to learning and growth, relationships can also get in the way and stifle them. If hierarchical forces or cultural norms embedded within an organization, school, department, or team discourage curiosity and drive—or view initiative and shared learning as risky—individuals will hold back or seek out other ways to express their deeper needs and gifts.

Edmondson's (2003) work examines how workers in teams or partnerships can "overcome the interpersonal risks they face every day at work, to help themselves, their teams and their organizations to learn" (p. 235). Edmondson was intrigued by the fact that "people… are reluctant to engage in behaviors (learning behaviours, asking questions, seeking help, experimenting or seeking feedback) that could threaten the image others hold of them" (p. 235). The problem with this, she says, "is that it precludes learning" (p. 236). Since asking questions, asking for help, or asking for feedback can carry a risk of being seen as ignorant, incompetent, or even disruptive, they may be avoided.

To overcome this, Edmondson's (2003) research suggests creating an organizational culture where staff members have the opportunity to set challenging goals and step willingly into the learning and collaboration to facilitate those goals. According to Edmondson, this requires a feeling of "psychological safety" (p. 237). This is a cultural dynamic where a fine balance of "structure without rigidity" and "safety without complacency" (p. 252) is purposefully developed. Edmondson calls this the "learning zone" (p. 11).

As illustrated in Figure 3.1, certain characteristics are essential for Edmondson's (2003) "learning zone" dynamic to take root. Without them, other dynamics take over, resulting in "comfort," "apathy," and "anxiety zones" (p. 11) that are less conducive to risk-taking and learning.

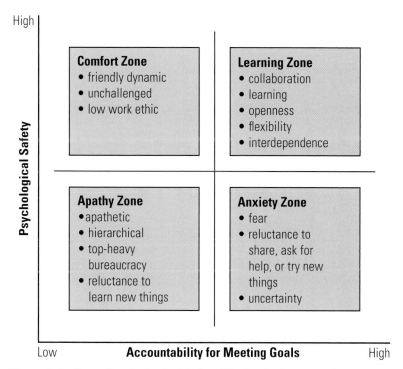

High

Psychological Safety

Comfort Zone
- friendly dynamic
- unchallenged
- low work ethic

Learning Zone
- collaboration
- learning
- openness
- flexibility
- interdependence

Apathy Zone
- apathetic
- hierarchical
- top-heavy bureaucracy
- reluctance to learn new things

Anxiety Zone
- fear
- reluctance to share, ask for help, or try new things
- uncertainty

Low   **Accountability for Meeting Goals**   High

Figure 3.1   Does Psychological Safety Hinder Performance?
Adapted from Edmondson (2008)

The "learning zone" is a culture that encourages mentees, students, and staff members to expand their capacities and step into challenges. It is an environment that fosters trust, openness to new ideas, flexibility in trying new things, and a feeling of interdependence and willingness to turn to colleagues for insights or expertise. From a mentor-coaching perspective, this zone also includes a dynamic where best practices and knowledge are the "common and explicit property of all" (Cooperrider & Whitney, 2005, p. 9) and need to be shared.

As mentor-coach, our mission is to build capacity from the inside out. We operate from an appreciative stance, focusing on who the mentee is rather than on who they are not. We help them to access strengths, expand awareness, mobilize resources, and secure desired results. These are concrete ways to foster a climate that is both psychologically safe and charged for growth.

Keeping the mentee's learning front and centre is the most critical element of our mission as mentor-coach. When learning is no longer occurring, the partnership shifts from a purposeful mentoring and learning relationship to a "buddy" system.

Focusing on the mentee's learning "wants" and **growing edges** is a useful way to begin the mentor-coaching relationship together.

Growing edge— also called a "learning edge"; the threshold between knowing and competence and not knowing and experimentation

Mentor-Coaching in Action

Start by Asking Questions

At the outset of a mentor-coaching relationship, ask the following questions to keep learning central to the process:

- What do you know about yourself as a learner that would be helpful for me to know, as your mentor-coach?
- How do you learn best?
- What fosters curiosity in you?
- What is your experience with feedback as a learner?
- How can we create a space for feedback that will be meaningful for you?
- What advice do you have for me, as your mentor-coach, to ensure that we are working together in a way that suits you?
- What concerns you about entering into this learning relationship?
- What is it you are wanting from me in this learning relationship? What do you want from yourself?

"A learning relationship exists when we learn from, or through, others. Such relationships will vary according to the characteristics of the groups involved, the context within which they operate, and the strength of the relationships."

— Fowler & Mayes, 2000, p. 11

The Mentor-Coaching Relationship

The centrality of the relationship in the mentor-coaching process cannot be overstated. Whether we are working with adults or young students, one-on-one or in groups, the authenticity, reciprocity, and trust that is established through the work creates a dynamic learning relationship and the conditions for the kinds of conversations that make transformation possible.

The mentor-coaching relationship both supports and grows out of the work that the mentor-coach and mentee do together. We point this out because many people initially believe that the "work" cannot start until the mentor-coach "gets to know" the mentee. Our experience has proven otherwise. By focusing on deep learning from the beginning of the process, the relationship grows, fuelled by growing awareness and aligning intentions with what matters to the mentee.

> "The relationship is a place of meaningful contact, growth and change."
>
> —Spoth, Toman, Leichtman, & Allen, 2013, p. 386

FROM THE FIELD

Mentee
Photographic Artist

The honour and support within the mentor-coaching relationship allowed me to fully trust in the process without question. I know I was honoured and felt a deep trust in this relationship, which allowed me to fully embrace the journey. The most fascinating aspect to me was the questions that were asked of me, that made me stop dead in my tracks. Questions that made me realize the power of choice and that everything I needed was within me, I just needed to access it. With gentle guidance, patience, and commitment, my mentor-coach encouraged me to continue to look within. Years later, I can continue to access the tools I need to continue to grow.

What Sets the Mentor-Coaching Relationship Apart?

The five factors that make the mentor-coaching relationship unique are detailed below.

Factor 1: The Relationship Is Co-created

This idea of "co-creating" the mentor-coaching partnership and relationship is central because of what it infers. The mentor-coach and mentee are standing together, co-creating the relationship *and* shaping the process: the nature of the work, focus, roles and responsibilities, expectations, and so on. These elements are identified and agreed on at the outset and serve as the foundation as the mentee designs his or her intentions for moving forward. The mentor-coach offers questions and support in service of the mentee's path forward—one informs the other in a relationship of mutual respect, trust and reciprocity, awareness, choice and action, provoking reflection, and learning.

Factor 2: Mentor-Coaching Includes a Mindset That Builds Capacity and Accelerates Learning

The mindset and stance of the mentor-coach has a significant impact on the relationship and the mentee's learning and growth that sets the relationship apart from other structured learning partnerships. The mindset is designed to build capacity and accelerate learning in the mentee through the following characteristics:

- an appreciative or strengths-based frame

- operating from an assumption of competence

- centrality of learning, growth, and transformation

- expanding mindfulness, awareness, reflection, and intention

- offering and receiving feedback as a gift in service of learning, growth, and stretching beyond comfort zones

- maximizing potential; minimizing interference (Gallwey, 2000)

- inviting multiple perspectives

- responsive versus reactive

"If you tell me, I will listen. If you show me, I will see. But if you let me experience, I will learn."

—Lao Tzu

Factor 3: A Reciprocal Learning Relationship Is Created

We often hear how much mentor-coaches appreciate the reciprocal nature of the learning partnership. For both mentor-coach and mentee, new awareness is provoked (or invoked) through the work they do together.

In our work with seasoned leaders of the Mentor-Coaching Institute, the comments of one mentor-coach in particular underline this idea of reciprocity. She said that she was close to retirement as a principal of a large urban high school. However, as a result of the work she had been doing with her mentee, she was delaying her retirement because their work together was providing an opportunity for her to reconnect with and share what she had learned and loved about her job. The conversations with her mentee had effectively reinvigorated her by reconnecting her with the deeper purpose, mastery, and autonomy she had developed as a leader. Her experience

DIG DEEPER

See Chapters 2 and 5 for a detailed exploration of the capacity building and mobilizing process and the coaching mindset and stance, respectively.

demonstrates how the mentor-coaching relationship can support the resilience and engagement of leaders in any context and create a ripple effect that reaches well beyond the official objectives of a mentoring initiative.

Looking at this from a systems theory perspective, we can see the exponential growth in the complexity of the dynamic in and around the mentor-coaching relationship as the different players and layers come together. We can see that something greater than the sum of its parts starts to emerge. As the effects of the relationship are integrated by mentor-coach and mentee, and ripple out beyond them to the broader culture, something entirely new is created.

Factor 4: Mentor-Coaching Provides a Thinking Partner

With the reality of our busy lives, compounded by the endless flow of information, messages, requests, and distractions in today's digital world, we may often feel that we are not moving fast enough or being productive enough. The "tyranny of the urgent," whether driven by our minds or external sources, can undermine our long-term view and crowd out our objectives, including plans for personal learning and growth.

We know that slowing down, reflecting, and consolidating our learning does not happen by accident. Providing a proactive and appreciative stance, structure, and process to help make this happen is important. The mentor-coaching relationship is a place and space where we can do this. Having a thinking partner in a mentor-coach helps the mentee stay clear and focused on her or his goals and diminishes distractions. Furthermore, as we will explore in Chapter 8, the structure of the mentor-coaching conversation slows things down and pre-empts the reactive and deficit mindset that can creep into our hurried lives.

It is important to note that a mentee may benefit from or require more than one mentor-coach depending on the specificity and diversity of the mentee's learning needs.

Dufferin R. Worden
P. Eng., Lead Mechanical Engineer, SNC-Lavalin Nuclear Inc.

Partway through pursuing a degree in mechanical engineering, I found that I was really struggling with my grades and lack of motivation for my field of study. Still committed to earning a degree that would set me up for the future, and not wanting to just give up, I started working with my mentor-coach to help me re-evaluate my career path and get myself back on track for success. In our many coaching sessions, she would challenge me to "cast a wider net" by having me think more about the bigger picture of where I wanted to be rather than the difficulties I was experiencing in the present.

My mentor-coach encouraged me to brainstorm my thoughts and ideas about what I wanted in a career, providing me with a sounding board to express myself without context. We would work together to translate these thoughts and ideas into tasks and actions for me to follow up on—whether it was researching a company or profession, or seeking out people to job shadow.

The mentor-coach's method of keeping me engaged and focused on the short-term goals would ultimately greatly contribute to my long-term success. Through our mentee-coach partnership, I was able take a step back, gain some perspective, and ultimately recommit myself to earning a degree and pursuing a career in mechanical engineering.

Factor 5: Mentor-Coaching Provides Infrastructure for Organizational Learning

"Teaming is the engine of organizational learning. By now, everyone knows that organizations need to learn—to thrive in a world of continuous change. But *how* organizations learn is not as well understood."
—Edmondson, 2012, p. 14

When we consider the value of mentor-coaching within organizations, and its contribution to the ongoing calls for structures to support increased learning and engagement across all levels, we see that it addresses a deeper need. The mentor-coaching frame, roles, structure, principles, and skills are a concrete approach and transferable infrastructure for supporting organizational learning. This approach for learning in relationship creates clear pathways for sharing intellectual capital, practices, stories, histories, and the individual and collective wisdom of leaders and practitioners throughout organizations. The connections and support networks that develop through the mentor-coaching conversations engage people and increase their sense of belonging, connection, and ownership.

Cautionary Note

The five factors unique to the mentor-coaching relationship are dependent on the openness, honesty, and rigour of the learning conversations and co-creating that take place within the dynamic. If an evaluative component pre-exists in the relationship between the mentor-coach and mentee, or becomes part of what the mentor-coach brings to the relationship and conversations, the dynamic can be critically compromised. Mentor-coaching people who report directly to us is a complicated endeavour, as the hierarchical nature of the relationship can undermine the mentee's trust and willingness to share.

Critical Aspects of the Mentor-Coaching Relationship

What does it take for the mentor-coaching relationship to flourish? The following diagram shows the 12 critical aspects.

As we take a closer look at each of these critical aspects in the following sections, we invite you to view them as portals for fostering rich and dynamic interaction within a formal or informal mentor-coaching relationship. The 12 aspects serve as the basis for developing learning relationships within classrooms as well as among colleagues and teams within educational and corporate organizations at all levels.

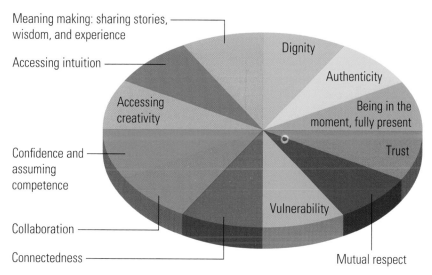

Figure 3.2   Mentor-Coaching Relationship Critical Characteristics Wheel
These 12 aspects are critical to the success of the mentor-coaching relationship.

Dignity

Our desire for dignity is at the core of human interaction. Thus, it is essential that the mentor-coaching relationship is based on deep caring and a profound sense of each other's worthiness and value in the world. This foundation allows the relationship to foster ongoing trust, respect, authenticity, connection, and vulnerabilty—all of which are critical in building a robust and rich relationship for fostering capacity building.

In a relationship, we are easily triggered when we sense that the other person is not responding to us as a worthy or valuable person. Perceived judgments or assumptions being made by the other often feel like violations of our dignity. This activates the limbic brain, and the "fight or flight or freeze" response kicks in. When this happens, we no longer have access to our pre-frontal cortex, the part of our brain responsible for decision-making, planning, self-regulation, and empathy. The pre-frontal cortex essentially shuts down and can take as long as 20 minutes to "come back." Thus, it is critical that the mentor-coach stays out of judgment. The same is true of the mentee. The mentee's own judgments of themselves and feelings of unworthiness may shut them down, influencing their capacity to remember their best selves or to see the path forward. It is the mentor-coach's job to support the mentee in remembering who they are at their best.

Dignity—
"an internal state of peace that comes with the recognition and acceptance of the value and vulnerability of all living things" (Hicks, 2011, p. 1)

"When a mutual sense of worth is recognized and honored in our relationships, we are connected. A mutual sense of worth also provides the safety necessary for both parties to extend themselves, making continued growth and development possible."
—*Hicks, 2011, p. 6*

Authenticity

Authenticity—
to be real, genuine, true to, or congruent with who we are from the inside out; the capacity to show up as ourselves in the world, without pretense

Authenticity is central to knowing who we are within ourselves and our relationships with others. To "know thyself" requires a lifelong commitment to self-discovery, self-observation, and self-reflection. As mentor-coach, being our authentic self in the relationship requires confidence, consistency, courage, and vulnerability. Our capacity to be authentic is essential in establishing an open, trusting, and impactful learning relationship with the mentee. It is also what we are inviting the mentee to access in themselves within the relationship and the work.

As humanistic psychologist, psychotherapist, and educator Carl Rogers (1942) articulated, authenticity is critical in relationships that focus on personal development. According to Rogers, the more the leader or teacher "is himself or herself in the relationship, putting up no professional front or personal façade, the greater is the likelihood that the client will change and grow" (as cited in Kirshenbaum & Henderson, 1989, p. 135).

> "Authenticity is a collection of choices that we have to make every day. It's about the choice to show up and be real. The choice to be honest. The choice to let our true selves be seen… *Choosing authenticity means*
>
> * cultivating the courage to be imperfect, to set boundaries, and to allow ourselves to be vulnerable;
>
> * exercising the compassion that comes from knowing that we are all made of strength and struggle; and
>
> * nurturing the connection and sense of belonging that can only happen when we believe we are enough."
>
> —*Brown, 2010, pp. 49–50*

Internal and external expectations can get in the way of our capacity to show up authentically within a mentor-coaching relationship. Given the nature of the relationship, with the emphasis on the learning and growth of the mentee, both the mentor-coach and the mentee may feel pressure to "make it happen" and find themselves making judgments regarding the depth and breadth of the "progress" being made. Recognizing when either one is feeling the pressure to perform—and discussing it—is important. The pressure to perform is externally driven and therefore requires space for careful consideration. Authentic, internally driven expectations to "live into" are far more compelling and energizing than externally driven expectations to "live up to."

Being in the Moment, Fully Present

Fundamental to any robust and fruitful learning relationship is the capacity to "be in the moment, fully present." When the mentor-coach and the mentee are in conversation, it is essential that each is present to and for the other and the process. The dynamic of the relationship and the work unfold in real time and, thus, require deep presence from each participant, moment to moment.

Trust

Trust is foundational in co-creating learning relationships: trust in self, trust in each other, trust in the relationship, and trust in the process and the desired results. The mentor-coach steps into the relationship with a strong belief in the capacities of the mentee and that the mentor-coaching process will support learning and growth in the mentee over time. Confidence and faith in the gifts and strengths of both the mentor-coach and the mentee is an ongoing and critical aspect within the evolving relationship.

In mentor-coaching, trust starts with mutual respect and the creation of a safe, confidential space for the mentee to show up fully and step into her or his learning and growth within a supportive relationship and process. This trust is built over time, as the mentee consistently experiences being deeply seen and heard and supported through inquiry and reflection, accessing strengths and values, and stepping into opportunities and challenges.

Mutual Respect

As teachers, professional coaches, and facilitators, we are acutely aware of how critical it is to have deep respect for each other and our learning relationships. This is key to co-creating a rich and multi-layered learning environment, fostering engagement, and invoking transformational learning and growth.

Mutual respect is the starting point for a mentor-coaching relationship and its lifeblood that expands over time as the relationship

Being in the moment— the capacity to be deeply connected and fully engaged at the present point in time

"To be the space for whatever happens... always choose now."
—Gallagher, 2009, p. 210

Trust— having faith in someone, believing that they are consistently truthful and authentic

"A person has integrity when there is no gap between intent and behavior...when he or she is whole, seamless, the same—inside and out. I call this 'congruence.' And it is congruence—not compliance—that will ultimately create credibility and trust."
—Covey & Merrill, 2006, p. 62

Mutual respect— an attitude of reciprocal regard for each other, an honouring of who each person is in the world, their strengths, beliefs, feelings, and perspectives and the learning journey evolve. It sets the foundation for the mentee and the mentor-coach to trust themselves and each other, and to take the risks inherent in learning and growth. It allows each to honour the other's unique gifts, strengths, and growing edges.

In the words of one mentee, mutual respect "allows both to consistently come from a place of openness; acceptance; non-judgment; truth telling; …[and] willingness to stretch, step up, and step forward." Mutual respect supports the mentee in feeling seen and heard for who they really are—and invites both the mentee and the mentor-coach to consistently believe in each other as their learning relationship focuses on building capacity.

"Always remember that you are absolutely unique. Just like everyone else."
—*Margaret Mead*

In Japanese, the symbol/word *rei*, shown below, represents the concept of "inviting respect and appreciation" that is expressed by the ritual of bowing to one another. When I participated in a workshop led by Nao Konishi and Takeshi Shimamura at the International Coach Federation Global Conference in 2008, I experienced this ritual firsthand as an impactful way of accessing the mutual respect between two people, acknowledging each other and standing ready to do our best for each other and the relationship.

礼

Our intention as mentor-coach and teacher is to remember, minute by minute, this commitment to mutual respect. When judgments or assumptions regarding the mentee or student show up, it is vital for us to notice them and clear them out of the way. Dorothy Heathcote (1984), one of my mentors over the years, challenged teachers to give every student a "fresh start" each day; this is the wisdom of mutual respect.

From Jeanie

Vulnerability

In listening to Brené Brown speak of the power of being vulnerable at the International Coach Federation Global Conference in October 2012 in London, UK, and later reading her book *Daring Greatly* (2012), we were struck by its relevance within the mentor-coaching relationship and process. We also recognized vulnerability as the core objective of capacity building. As the learner and the facilitator within the learning process, the mentee and the mentor-coach, respectively, are asked to commit to a relationship of deep learning and support over time. This always involves being vulnerable as each leans into growth, experimentation, risk, and stretch.

In embracing vulnerability, Brown (2012) suggests that "rather than sitting on the sidelines and hurling judgment and advice, we must dare to show up and let ourselves be seen. This is vulnerability. This is *daring greatly*" (p. 2). This is exactly what the mentor-coaching relationship invites us to do. It invites the mentee to enter into a partnership that focuses on their learning and growth over time, showing up fully, ready to do the work required to grow their capacity. At the same time, it asks the mentor-coach to support the mentee's growth and development through inquiry rather than giving advice and judgments from the sidelines. Both are asked to stand tall and to be seen deeply by themselves and each other, as they co-create a process that encourages each to "dare greatly."

As mentor-coach and mentee build their relationship with authenticity, trust, mutual respect, and dignity, they build the capacity to be open with each other and create the boundaries needed to feel safe enough to be vulnerable in pursuit of deep learning and growth.

Vulnerability is a fundamental aspect of capacity building. To step up and step out takes courage and commitment over time—exactly what the mentor-coaching relationship fosters.

Connectedness

Belonging is primal. Human connectedness is vital for all of us. Currently, neuroscience research tells us that we are hardwired to connect with others, and that our brains grow when we are in deep relationship with one another. With the discovery of mirror neurons, we now also know how it is that we can experience another's senses and feelings as if they were "real."

Vulnerability— from the Latin word *vulnerare* meaning "to wound"; within relationships, vulnerability involves not knowing, taking risks, and sharing our innermost thoughts, feelings, and dreams

"When we were children, we used to think that when we were grown-up we would no longer be vulnerable. But to grow up is to accept vulnerability... To be alive is to be vulnerable."
—Madeleine L'Engle

Connectedness— the links between people; the ways in which people come together in relationship and community— finding commonalities, shared experiences, energies, passions, and values

"At a neural level, we embed in our brains not just what we physically see, but the mental intention we imagine is going on in someone else's mind… Mirror neurons demonstrate the profoundly social nature of our brains… We use our first five senses to take in the signals from another person. Then the mirror neuron system perceives these 'intentional states' and by way of the insula alters limbic and bodily states to match those we are seeing in the other person. This is attunement and it creates emotional resonance."

—Siegel, 2007, pp. 166–167

Thus, the energy and dynamic of connections within the mentor-coaching relationship have a strong impact on the immediate experience of both the mentee and the mentor-coach, as well as on the space that is created for the mentee's learning and growth.

In a relationship that is all about growing the mentee's capacity, connecting deeply is a gift for both the mentee and the mentor-coach. The connection allows for a relationship and process that supports deep learning and growth in each of them.

Collaboration

Collaboration—
working and creating together, in partnership

Mentor-coaching is a collaborative relationship and process that is fostered through an ongoing commitment to openness, flexibility, deep listening, curiosity, and experimentation. It is useful to think of the mentor-coaching relationship as improvisational, in which the mentor-coach and the mentee are working together without a script, and responding to each other in the moment, in service of the expanding clarity and wisdom of the mentee. As in improvisational jazz, individual responses or riffs are informed by and grow out of what has just happened in the moments before. There is a shared commitment to moving forward and honouring the unique voices as well as the overall themes and intentions.

"Once the realization is accepted that, even between the closest human beings, infinite distances continue to exist, a wonderful living side by side can grow up, if they succeed in loving the distance between them which makes it possible for each to see the other whole and against a wide sky!"

—Rainer Maria Rilke

Confidence and Assuming Competence

The mentor-coaching mindset is based on the belief that both the mentee and the mentor-coach are unique and capable human beings, leaders, and learners. This mindset inspires confidence and supports each of them throughout the relationship by keeping their focus on the gifts and strengths that each possess to support growth and movement forward.

An attitude of assuming competence grows out of this mindset and is augmented by the guiding mentor-coaching principle of "holding the mentee resourceful, creative, and expert in own life." By consistently approaching the mentee in this way, the mentor-coach believes in the skills and capacities of the mentee as she or he navigates through successes and challenges as a learner and a leader.

Kaufman et al. (2009) suggest that "if a coach believes his/her client can change and develop, he/she will behave in a way that facilitates the client's growth and development" (cited in Gregory & Levy, 2013, p. 292). Dweck (2006) also points to the connection between believing and results in learning and capacity building by identifying what she calls "growth" and "fixed" (pp. 6–7) mindsets in relation to intelligence and personal qualities. Through her research, Dweck highlights the enhanced learning and growth of students, teachers, and leaders who consistently believe in the capacity of everyone to grow their abilities through effort, experimentation, and stretching themselves. By being confident and assuming competence, the mentor-coach and the mentee work together to hold a space for learning and growth.

Confidence and assuming competence— consistently believing in the capabilities and agency of self, each other, and the relationship

DIG DEEPER

- See Chapters 1 and 5 for details on the guiding principles of mentor-coaching.

- See Chapter 9 for more on Dweck's work.

"Magic is believing in yourself; if you can do that, you can make anything happen."
—Goethe

Accessing Creativity

By its very nature, creativity is challenging to define. Not only does it mean many different things to many different people but also, within Western culture, a limited view of what creativity encompasses often prevails that confines it to the arts. Thus, creativity in other areas of work and life is not often recognized or valued. Furthermore, in our society, many adults are not used to naming or accessing their creative energies and gifts.

In his book *The Element*, co-written with Lou Aronica, Sir Ken Robinson (2009) challenges us to ask ourselves the question "How am I creative?" rather than the more judgmental "How creative am I?" The underlying assumption in Robinson's question is that all humans are creative as we approach our thoughts, feelings, experiences, and expression through a rich tapestry of gifts, talents, passions, and perspectives. In an effort to make meaning, we generate a variety of ideas as we access our imagination and multiple intelligences (intellectual, emotional, sensory, kinesthetic, social, intuitive, and spiritual). We let ideas incubate, sifting and choosing as a creative process unfolds, usually in a divergent manner.

DIG DEEPER

See the Mentor-Coaching Toolkit for tools and structures to support movement and growth.

As mentor-coach, accessing and cultivating creativity and imagination in ourselves and our mentee supports and enhances the relationship, the process, and the learning journey. Remembering always to hold the mentee (and ourselves) as resourceful, creative, and capable of moving forward is essential throughout. It is also critical for the mentor-coach to be always "in the moment" and open to what is emerging for the mentee within the conversation.

"Creative people are constantly surprised. They don't assume that they understand what is happening around them, and they don't assume anybody else does either."

—*Csikszentmihalyi, 1996, p. 363*

By purposefully inviting the mentee to use a range of creative expressions, tools, and strategies, the mentor-coach also expands the opportunities for the mentee to deepen awareness and discovery. For example, inviting the mentee to pick a card from a deck of word or image cards and then link the word or image to where they are in the conversation, immediately opens up opportunities for further meaning making. The links, metaphors, and connections the mentee makes from such an exercise can expand what they see and where they might start to explore.

Accessing Intuition

Intuition is our ability to access all ways of knowing and to thrive in the known and unknown. We have come to believe that it is an internal sensing, a wisdom that comes from our multiple ways of knowing.

Like creativity, we assume that we all have access to our intuition and that some of us are more aware and more comfortable accessing it than others.

Accessing intuition supports the mentor-coach in being and staying "in the moment" with the mentee and allows both to be open to the possibilities that unfold. By tuning in to our holistic, deep ways of knowing, both the mentor-coach and the mentee expand who they are *being* in the conversation, what is on offer, and how they together hold the space.

> "The greater your intuitive awareness, the more able you are to tap into the greatest potential available within any situation or circumstance."
> —Seale, 2008, p. 6

Intuition—
"a process that gives us the ability to know something directly without analytic reasoning, bridging the gap between the conscious and nonconscious parts of our mind, and also between instinct and reason" (Cholle, 2012, p. 27)

Meaning Making: Sharing Stories, Wisdom, and Experience

Story is one of our primary ways of knowing, meaning making, and connecting.

> "Story is narrative. Words are how we think; narrative is how we link... The practice of story creates a social net that makes us capable of seeing each other's unique contribution and incapable of simply dismissing someone as 'not like me.'
>
> As long as we share our stories, as long as our stories reveal our strengths and vulnerabilities to each other, we reinvigorate our understanding and tolerance."
> —Baldwin, 2005, pp. 10, 18

Meaning making—
scanning for connections by accessing and building on memory, experience, and knowledge; the mind is a meaning-making machine. As human beings in relationship, we make meaning and create connection through story, shared experience, and wisdom.

Accessing our stories within a mentor-coaching relationship and beyond, within the larger organization, supports clarity of vision, values, and the building of collaborative cultures. Within mentor-coaching, sharing stories and experiences is how we build the relationship and the space for growth.

One of the gifts that the mentor-coach brings to the relationship and to each conversation is the capacity to listen deeply to the mentee. By listening intently to the mentee's stories, the mentor-coach supports the mentee in recognizing that the stories themselves are a window into the mentee's strengths and challenges, vision and values, and intentions and dreams. It is also impactful for the mentee, through the support of the mentor-coach, to truly hear his or her own stories.

In addition, opportunities arise for the mentor-coach to share relevant stories in support of the learning and growth of the mentee. Deciding when to share personal stories requires rigour. The mentor-coach needs the capacity to notice whether a story or experience that comes to mind is relevant and then to make a quick judgment about whether sharing it at that time will serve the learning of the mentee.

When it feels right to offer a story or experience, asking permission to share is an approach that the mentor-coach uses to honour the time and space for the mentee to do the work. Sharing the depth and beauty of the story in its essence, rather than taking up too much of the sacred mentor-coaching time with the story also requires discipline. After the mentor-coach shares a story, it is critical to invite the mentee to make her or his own links and relevant meaning from the story. For example, at a particular moment, it may be powerful for the mentor-coach to share the core of their leadership or teaching story, communicating their deep passion and commitment and thus, serving to restore the mentee's access to her or his own commitment and contribution.

DIG DEEPER

See Chapter 7 for more detail around the mentor-coach's approach to sharing stories and experience.

> "Everybody is a story… Sitting around the table telling stories is not just a way of passing time. It is the way wisdom gets passed along. The stuff that helps us to live a life worth remembering… Real stories take time. We stopped telling stories when we started to lose that sort of time, pausing time, reflecting time, wondering time… To know our own story and tell it. To listen to other people's stories. To remember that the real world is made up of just such stories."
> —Remen, 1996, pp. xxvii–xxxi

Reflection: Critical Aspects for the Learning Partnership to Flourish

DIG DEEPER

Use the self-calibration tool in the Mentor-Coaching Toolkit to rate yourself on each critical aspect of the mentor-coaching relationship and to track your progress.

In a discussion or journal, consider and respond to the questions below.

1. What critical aspect is one of your strengths as a mentor-coach? What impact does it have within your mentor-coaching and other relationships?

2. What critical aspect is one of your growing edges as a mentor-coach? What impact does it have within your mentor-coaching relationships? What is possible if you are intentional about enhancing this particular aspect?

Exercise: Intention Setting

1. As mentor-coach, it is important for us to be reflective practitioners, able to observe ourselves and reflect as we set intentions to grow our capacities and skills. Remembering to be concrete and specific as we set intentions enhances clarity and purposefulness. Use the following questions to challenge yourself to set an intention to enhance one or several critical aspects of the mentor-coaching relationship.

   a) Think about a critical aspect you want to be more aware of and more intentional about in learning relationships. What strengths can you draw on to support yourself in experimenting with new possibilities for it?

   b) How will you bring yourself differently to the relationship in order to enhance this critical aspect?

   c) What specific intention do you want to set for yourself? What will that look like "in action" within the relationship? the conversations?

   d) How will you support yourself in stepping into your intention? in holding yourself accountable?

2. Having stepped into your intention, tracking your progress helps you notice and become clear about how you are being and doing. Also, noticing the impact of your intention, through observation and feedback, supports the growth. As you reflect on your progress, consider the following questions:

   a) What is the impact of setting an intention on you? on the mentee?

   b) How does setting an intention impact the relationship?

   c) What is the impact of setting an intention on the learning and growth of the mentee? on your own learning and growth?

To further understand what it takes to work in partnership over time, we examined our own experience of what has been required to build the mentor-coaching project over the past eight years. This led us to identify the following list of critical elements for the mentor-coach and mentee to embrace as they build capacity and sustain momentum:

Qualities

- being present in the experience
- openness
- commitment
- focus
- persistence; perseverance
- willingness not to know, to be vulnerable, to contribute
- curiosity
- courage: stepping up and out; exploring new frontiers
- energy; momentum
- adventurousness
- ability to access humour and zest
- gratitude and humility

Mindset

- abundance, growth, opportunity
- accessing our authentic selves—our gifts, strengths, and passions—and staying connected to them
- deep collaboration
- experimenting, taking risks, challenging ourselves and others, stretching
- reflection
- trust in self, each other, our sponsors, participants, the power of the coaching frame
- accessing our individual and collective creativity
- vision, clarity, and alignment
- evolving confidence and competence
- appreciation of excellence and beauty
- believing in ourselves, the work, and the difference it is making; we build our own capacity as we support others in building theirs
- continuous learning and improvement; rigour
- feedback as a gift: acknowledgement, strengths, and challenges
- observing the impact: ourselves, leaders, teachers, students, and systems growing and flourishing
- recognizing the sacredness of the space co-created for the work and the honour and privilege of learning and growing together
- celebration

From Kate and Jeanie

4 The Mentor-Coaching Model °

"Nothing changes except from the inside out."

—INDIAN PROVERB

PREVIEW OF CHAPTER 4

In this chapter, we will introduce the mentor-coaching model and explore

- working from the inside out
- growing talent toward results
- the role of the collective in supporting learning and growth
- the anatomy of the mentor-coaching model

Working from the Inside Out

For any growth or learning to occur, and new capacities to be built, we always need to begin with ourselves, going inside to "do our own work." This precept forms the foundation of the mentor-coaching model. In our experience, we need to be clear about how we are arriving to the work and what we are bringing, such as abilities, competencies, training, talents, gifts, challenges, growing edges, and so on.

As an athlete on a team, the levels of skill, strength, stamina, and talent that I bring to our coordinated and collaborative efforts determine my value. The more I bring of myself to the game, the more the team will benefit, and the greater the number of opportunities for success we will have. Being able to access and deliver my internal and external resources and to perform at my best are my priorities when I want to maximize my athletic performance and make the greatest possible contribution to my team.

From Kate

In drama education, we are always supporting the participants in working from the inside out. The whole notion of role-playing, which is the core of drama and theatre, revolves around the question of "what if." This allows individuals to take what they know and have experienced and imagine what it would to be like to think and feel as "the other" in a particular context. Authentic role-playing comes from the individual working from the inside out, exploring and creating.

From Jeanie

We believe the same precept of working from the inside out applied by team athletes and in role-playing, as mentioned above, holds true in life and leadership, mentoring and teaching. Growth models from scientific disciplines also inform the design of our mentor-coaching model that starts from within and works outward. In biology, organic growth occurs from the inside out. In a tree, for example, rings of growth begin at the centre of the tree and radiate out. With the addition of each ring, the strength of the tree increases from the inside out. In physics, models of sound structures utilize a strong internal design for support as they extend out from a central core. In chemistry, the model of the atom and its nucleus features negatively and positively charged ions, radiating from the inside out to form matter that grows and extends from the inside outward.

From a leadership and teaching perspective, such growth models from scientific disciplines are extremely compelling and speak directly to what we know to be true from our work and our lives—that the growth, stability, and strength of a leader requires a structurally strong, organic core to anchor and sustain the leader in the work they do beyond themselves. We know that "doing our own work," getting out of our own way, and bringing our full selves to what we do and who we are as leaders and teachers are required for us to fulfill our "moral purpose" (Fullan, 2001, p. 3): to contribute to making something far greater than ourselves. These models also speak to our perspective on leadership in education and provide structure for the design and facilitation of our Mentor-Coaching Institute.

"Teaching, like any truly human activity, emerges from one's inwardness, for better or worse. As I teach, I project the condition of my soul onto my students, my subject, and our way of being together… When I do not know myself, I cannot know who my students are. I will see them through a glass darkly, in the shadows of my unexamined life—and when I cannot see them clearly, I cannot teach them well. When I do not know myself, I cannot know my subject—not at the deepest levels of embodied, personal meaning.
I will know it only abstractly, from a distance, a congeries of concepts as far removed from the world as I am from personal truth."
—Palmer, 1998, pp. 1–2

SPOTLIGHT

Three Key Ingredients for Working from the Inside Out

In Kegan and Lahey's (2009) seminal book *Immunity to Change*, the authors explore the inner workings of change and the cognitive disruptions of capacity building. Their research on the successful integration of the "adaptive challenges" (Heifetz, 1998, p. 26) inherent to all deep and lasting change provides a valuable conceptual frame for the inside-out approach to capacity building and mobilizing.

More specifically, the structures that Kegan and Lahey (2009) outline facilitate a cognitive process for "stepping back" or shifting awareness from a subjective place (looking through) to an objective place (looking at). This creates a larger cognitive space from which to operate and, more importantly, to navigate the process and overcome "immunities to change" (p. x). Facilitating this shift in thinking gives us access to tools, or ways of knowing, that did not previously exist. Our awareness is expanded, which in turn generates new choices and possibilities, more effective action, and ultimately increased abilities and capacities.

Increasing capacity and changing what we see, how we feel, and ultimately what we think and do is more likely to happen, say Kegan and Lahey (2009), if we are connected to "guts, head and heart, and hand" (p. 223)—the three ingredients that working from the inside out requires.

Working from the Gut

- For us to begin and stick with any change or learning process, the desired result, learning, or goal must truly matter. It is not enough for the mentee, for example, to have a goal that they think they "should" or "ought" to reach. For even if it "makes sense," the mentee must experience a genuine desire for change to help them cross the critical thresholds. Reasons can certainly help to motivate, but they do not reach deeply enough into the gut to help sustain growth's disruptive journey.

continued...

Linking Head and Heart

- Kegan and Lahey (2009) point out that in every opportunity for growth or adaptive challenge, "the problem space lies above *and* below our necks" (p. 214). Because resistance or "immunity to change" lies in our thinking/head and feeling/heart, we need to attend to both in order to mobilize ourselves and achieve real, adaptive change.

  Since how we feel about the change that we, or the mentee, are making is critical to the mobilizing process, simply "thinking" or forcing ourselves into action will not support lasting change. Since how we *feel* is intricately tied to how we *know*, we cannot *feel* differently if we do not *know* differently. We need to feel *and* to know that the newness we are experiencing is only temporary, and that the unfamiliarity is proof that change has begun and that we are on our way forward.

The Hand

- No matter how motivated we are, we cannot think our way forward to increased capacities. We need to reach out and take action. Taking the time to support the mentee in identifying and accessing a mindset that will support them in their new "behaviours" and the specific actions they want to take is vital. As mentor-coach, securing the mentee's commitment to action further reinforces accountability.

Avoiding the Outside-In Approach

No doubt working from the inside out may initially feel unfamiliar or uncomfortable in the context of education as it is contrary to the outside-in approach that has historically characterized leadership in many organizations and teaching in many classrooms. The outside-in approach is a more mechanistic, top-down, and hierarchical approach that seeks "results at all costs" and attempts to drive the targets into the organization, often leaving people wondering whether their contribution is valued or even recognized.

Typically, an outside-in approach nurtures a culture of compliance and dependence, where "adherence" is the focus. Leaders and teachers are often positioned within this top-down approach as the "driver" and "expert," and direct reports or students become dependent on the leader or teacher's ability to fix and solve. Another challenge with a top-down, or outside-in, approach is that it often operates from a deficit perspective, where what is missing, weak, or deficient becomes the focus.

> "Central control strategies…are useful to initiate change but as progress is made on a large scale, future improvements increasingly depend on responding productively to differentiated challenges in districts and schools. Sustaining progress ('moving from good to great,' for example) depends on a devolution of authority from the centre."
> —Leithwood, 2013, p. 6

Working from the outside in is a short-term approach with little carry-over to capacity building. Over the long-term, it has critical side effects: attrition, declining retention, increased pressure on succession planning, and decreased engagement. Also, an outside-in approach to leading or teaching often fosters a culture of saying "yes" and doing "no," given that people do not feel safe enough to share their concerns.

Note that an outside-in approach can be helpful for leaders when looking to streamline a decision-making process, disseminate information, or ensure that things get done. However, when viewed through the lens of capacity building, the outside-in approach is limited. In a mentor relationship, where the mentor is positioned as the experienced expert and is using an outside-in approach, solutions and advice arrive from the outside. The mentor's experiences often become the lens through which conversations pass, rather than those of the mentee. In this approach, the focus is on the mentor's experience rather than the mentee's desired learning and capacity building. As a result, the mentee and the mentoring process become dependent on the wisdom and expertise of the mentor, rather than building the mentee's independence, resourcefulness, and sense of self-efficacy.

When an outside-in approach is used in professional development for teachers, the learning typically begins with the arrival of new ideas and practices from the outside rather than growing out of the individual participant's own frame of reference. In fact, the McKinsey Report, "Breaking the Habit of Ineffective Professional Development for Teachers" (Jayaram, Moffit, & Scott, 2012), cautions school systems against working from the outside in and offering programs that "push" externally identified learning onto teachers, rather than "pull" teachers to work from the inside out, and identify their specific learning needs and knowledge gaps. Instead, the report suggests that professional development that works from the inside out and is integrated "with a system for evaluating teachers' strengths and areas for improvement can provide a serious boost to teacher performance and student outcomes" (p. 1).

Growing Talent Toward Results

The mentor-coaching model focuses on the nature of what we are growing toward and the results we are after. As educators and coaches, we are well aware of the critical importance of setting intentions and moving toward the goals and results we desire. Thus, the mentor-coaching model homes in on the realization of the mentee's goals.

Measuring growth and effectiveness is an essential component of growth management and system improvement, so the mentor-coaching model includes a robust results domain. In designing the model, we have strived to find a balance between inviting the growth, expertise, talent, and engagement of the individuals involved and prioritizing measured results and accountability data. This dynamic reflects what we have heard in the field: the need to grow new leaders and teachers who are competent and can manage the weight of the expectations and demands placed on them—new leaders who can nurture themselves from the inside out, while managing what arrives from the outside in. As we considered how to grow talent and capacity toward the desired results, and harness the creative tension with structured coaching conversations facili-tated by coach-like leaders, the mentor-coaching model—working from the inside out—was born.

The Role of the Collective in Supporting Learning and Growth

The other central piece of the mentor-coaching model is the importance of individuals connecting and growing in community, within a collective context. The interactions within the social systems—and the learning and growth that often occur in relationships and conversations—are vital to the sustainability of the process and the resilience of the individuals and the larger system.

In the design of our model, we recognize the importance of creating the space for this dynamic to play out. Thus, the model features a "collective" zone—a layer between the individual and the results the individual is working toward. It is in this interactive, or collective, space that many new possibilities emerge.

In our work as educators and coaches, we are committed to the collective as a vital and impactful space for learning and growth to occur. As teachers of drama and health and physical education, we know that individual students grow within the social dynamic, being provoked and invoked through collaboration, dialogue, and evolving relationships as well as through the collective challenges of the shared experience.

Collaborating with colleagues is critical in enhancing our own professional learning and practice. In fact, our decision to write this book together grew out of our awareness that collaborating in this way would propel our learning and growing and, at the same time, result in a rich resource to support educators in fostering capacity building.

In working with leaders, we constantly see how the collective fosters energy, engagement, and the willingness to take risks—building relationships, skills, and capacities in the process. Further to this, research by Lieberman and Miller (2004) reveals that professional learning within communities of practice takes time because learning is both social and collective, where practitioners learn from and with one another in particular ways:

> "[People] learn through practice (learning as doing); through meaning (learning as intentional); through community (learning as participating and being with others); and through identity (learning as changing who we are)."
>
> —p. 23

The idea of individuals connecting and growing together is the essence of the mentor-coaching relationship and is becoming more and more important as educational reform progresses. The interactive, interconnected, and experiential ways that students and adults are learning together are rapidly emerging as the nexus of the higher-order learning skills and practices (Fullan, 2013). The shifting profile of learning in a digital age requires that we continue to pay special attention to this collective layer and the importance of learning relationships. The relationships, culture, and shared purpose that feed the possibilities within this collective layer create the "magic" that unfolds in a successful classroom as well as in an effective mentor-coaching relationship and process.

FROM THE FIELD

Carol Ann Fisher
Principal, Mentor-Coach Training Program Facilitator

The [mentor-coaching] program grew to include all employee groups: elementary and secondary teachers, learning partners, department heads, curriculum and special education coordinators, Board office staff, facility services staff, developmental early childhood educators, educational assistants. Each sent first their leaders and then potential leaders who desired to mentor new employees and participate in a personal growth opportunity. When we united these participants in their training, we had rich and varied learning and a renewed sense of unity within the district school board... These sessions allowed us all the opportunity to view our leadership and our care for one another in a new and meaningful way. We saw ourselves together as fully involved in the improvement of instruction and service to the students, their families, and the communities in which they live.

The Anatomy of the Mentor-Coaching Model

In the mentor-coaching model, the mentor-coach supports the mentee in exploring first the individual/red zone and then the collective/yellow zone, as they move toward their goals in the results/green zone. Let us examine the dynamics at play in each zone.

The Individual Red Zone

As leader, mentor-coach, or teacher, stepping into growth and desired results begins with us. However, in our haste to increase engagement and build capacity in others, we can easily step over the importance of starting from within.

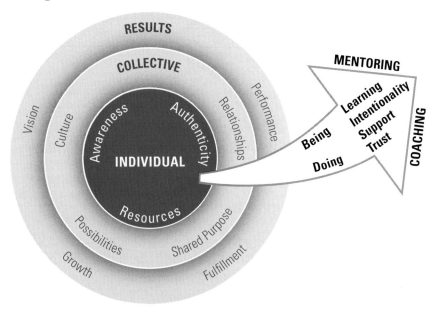

Figure 4.1 The Mentor-Coaching Model: The Individual/Red Zone

Three concentric circles with an arrow running through them, from the inmost circle to the outmost circle, illustrate the mentor-coaching model. The model begins by placing the individual at the centre of the process, the inmost circle coloured red in this diagram, to work from the inside out.

In remembering to begin with ourselves, as the "individual" at the centre of the mentor-coaching model (see Figure 4.1), it is vital to stop and take stock, as indicated by the colour red of the centre circle, and connect to who we are, our role as mentor-coach, and what it is we are wanting.

Initially, our work is to maximize our "personal mastery" (Cashman, 2008, p. 33) by entering into the process authentically—purposefully working from the inside out. We need to heighten our own awareness of who we are and all that we bring to the work: our strengths, expertise, talents, gifts, experiences, fears, values, and purpose. We want to purposefully access the internal and external resources that we will need to support us in our work and our journey. As lifelong learners, we know that our level of self-trust is directly proportionate to how "resourced," or equipped, we feel to take on the task at hand. Or conversely, as we step into any arena, the less equipped we feel, internally (e.g., confidence) or externally (e.g., funding), the less we trust ourselves and our ability to effectively execute the required action. So with our fully resourced and aware self, we embrace the journey, growing and strengthening from the inside out.

This process of beginning from within is the same for the mentee, as the mentor-coaching relationship begins. Through listening deeply and asking questions such as the following, the mentor-coach supports the mentee in connecting with their authentic self and expanding their awareness of what matters to them in their leadership and their learning agenda.

- What do you want?

- How does this matter?

- Where are you now? Where do you want to be?

- What resources do you want to access (internally and externally) to support yourself?

The mentor-coach's role in co-creating these conversations is to see the mentee as resourceful and creative and to ensure that learning, intentionality, support, and trust (LIST) are alive and well, living within the work and the relationship. Furthermore, when we place the student at the centre of the circle, all of this moves into higher relief. If the mentor-coach/teacher does not facilitate or activate LIST, or fails to see the student as resourceful and creative, capacity building grinds to a halt and the opportunity for deep learning is minimal.

"Students were most engaged when what they were learning was meaningful in their lives beyond the classroom… Approaches are effective in stimulating deep engagement when they are implemented in such a way as to enable students' sense of agency and identity, and a learning experience which feels authentic and meaningful whilst progressively handing over responsibility for learning to students."

—*Paul Hamlyn Foundation, 2012, pp. 31–33*

FROM THE FIELD

Steph Cook
Bachelor of Physical and Health Education, University of Toronto

I found working with a mentor-coach, as I transitioned from university and into my professional career, to be a holistic, validating, and empowering process. My mentor-coach first tapped into who I was at my core—what my interests and passions were, what my innate strengths and values were, and what available resources I had at my disposal.

This showed me that it was possible for me to create opportunities from within myself; that I as the mentee had all the available tools already within me. What was essential was both recognizing they were there, and also using them to my advantage.

The relationship I had with my mentor-coach was critical, as I felt that she not only understood who I was at a fundamental level, but that she also believed I had the power within me to realize my goals and visions.

Reflection in the Individual/Red Zone for Mentor-Coach and Mentee

In a discussion or journal, consider and respond to the questions below.

1. What are the characteristics of the relationships that have most supported your learning and growth as a leader? as a teacher?

2. What is the larger purpose for you, as you step into the role of mentor-coach (mentee) and the work it will require as a leader? as a teacher?

3. Where is the learning in this mentor-coaching process for you?

4. What internal resources (such as strengths, qualities, attributes, capabilities, or past experiences) do you want to draw on to support your work and conversations?

5. What external resources do you want to access?

The Collective Yellow Zone

As leader, mentor-coach, or teacher, we next move to the collective/ yellow zone, and proceed cautiously, as suggested by the colour (see Figure 4.2), to begin our collective work as learning partner with the mentee.

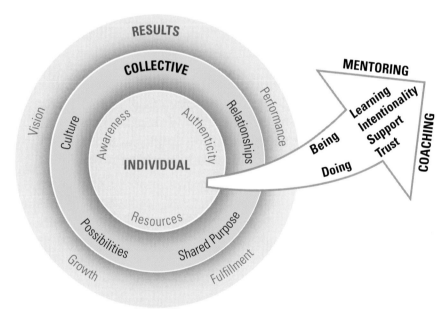

Figure 4.2 The Mentor-Coaching Model: The Collective/Yellow Zone
The middle circle of the mentor-coaching model, shown in yellow in this diagram, is a collective zone between the individual and the results the individual is working toward. Mentee, mentor-coach, and other stakeholders (colleagues, students, parents) grow, learn, and work together in the collective zone toward the desired results.

This is where the mentor-coaching relationship is enhanced, and the process of engagement with the mentee and other stakeholders takes hold. As we step into the collective, we want to align ourselves and the path forward with the mentee and to establish a shared purpose in the work. Aligning ourselves purposefully and co-creating the learning relationship allows a supportive cultural dynamic to take root and new possibilities to emerge.

The idea of alignment, or equal footing, in the collective/yellow zone cannot be overemphasized, given its impact on the interpersonal and learning dynamic that is necessary between the mentee and the mentor-coach. In a more formal mentor-mentee relationship, if a hierarchical tone or "rookie" and "veteran" dynamic drives the rhythm of the interactions, much is lost. The openness and rich dialogue that emerge from honest, direct conversations around growth require a vulnerability that can exist only when shared purposes and authentic relationships have been established.

The path of the mentor-coaching conversations in this collective zone is supported by the coaching principles and skills. The conversations focus on maximizing the connections between the mentor-coach and the mentee and the work at hand. The conversations touch on the areas of learning, intentionality, support, and trust (LIST) for both the mentee and the mentor-coach as they move toward their shared desired results. They consider questions such as the following:

- What relationships are critical to further cultivate your capacity to lead? to teach?

- What kinds of conversations do you want your culture to support?

- How will you continue to increase engagement and commitment?

- What else is possible at the collective level to support the results you are wanting?

Although the importance of the collective layer in building capacity in the classroom is undeniable, it can be easy to step over this layer and its energy, as the pressure around individual scores or results mounts. In providing this model for teachers to help maximize the potential of the collective, we invite educators to consider how the energy surrounding the relationships, culture, and shared purpose that exist in the classroom can be further leveraged to deepen engagement and expand possibilities.

Reflection in the Collective/Yellow Zone for Mentor-Coach and Mentee

In a discussion or journal, consider and respond to the questions below.

1. What do you each want from and for this powerful learning-centred relationship?

2. What do you want to learn together?

3. What are your shared intentions? What are your shared questions?

4. How can these shared intentions and questions support your journey together?

5. How does the culture in your district, school, or classroom align with the spirit of mentor-coaching?

6. What new possibilities are emerging?

The Results   Green Zone

As we "green light" the process and move collectively toward the "results" domain (see Figure 4.3), the mentor-coaching conversations focus on the realization of the desired goal(s) for the mentee. As the mentor-coach managing the process, the signposts at this level remind us that the conversations need to be oriented around specific, desired changes in performance, fulfillment, and growth for the mentee. At this stage, the mentor-coach asks questions such as the following:

- What changes in performance do you want to see?

- What needs to be in place (e.g., core leadership values) to make the process as fulfilling as possible for you?

- What new learning or growth do you want for yourself? for your staff? for your students?

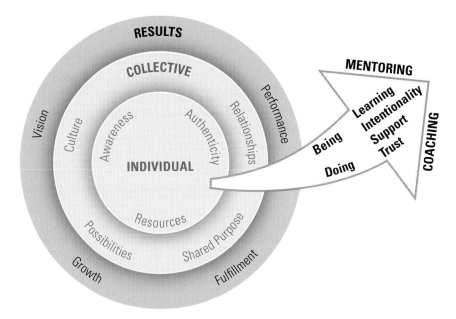

Figure 4.3 The Mentor-Coaching Model: The Results/Green Zone

The outmost circle of the mentor-coaching model, shown in green in this diagram, is a results zone that focuses on the mentee's vision and desired changes in performance, fulfillment, and growth.

It is also important to help the mentee put the structures in place that they will need to hold themselves accountable for the changes or results they want to achieve. Collectively, these indicators contribute to the mentee's overall vision for themselves and the results they seek. Spending some time exploring or touching base on their vision and what they want to achieve keeps the results/green zone compelling.

While supporting the mentee in looking at his or her desired results, the mentor-coach also asks themselves the same questions in terms of their own vision and growth within the relationship.

From the teaching perspective, remembering to stay in the co-pilot seat as mentor-coach, resisting the tug to take the wheel from the students as they navigate toward their desired results, is central to building student capacity from the inside out. Our job, as mentor-coach, is to ensure that support, intentionality, and students' trust in themselves are alive and present in the process.

Reflection in the Results/Green Zone for Mentor-Coach and Mentee

In a discussion or journal, consider and respond to the questions below.

1. What are the shared results you and your mentee are working toward?

2. What will be different when the results are fully realized?

3. How do the results matter individually? collectively?

4. Where does your fulfillment and growth as a mentor-coach fit into your work with your mentee?

5. Who are you becoming as a mentor-coach?

The Arrow Runs Through

The arrow that begins in the centre of the mentor-coaching model and extends through the three concentric circles represents the mentor-coach–mentee relationship and the structured coaching

"When the effective leader is finished with his [her] work, the people say it happened naturally."

—*Lao Tzu*

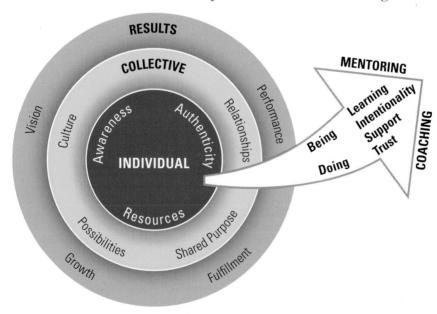

Figure 4.4 The Mentor-Coaching Model: The Arrow Runs Through
The arrow of the mentor-coaching model, which runs through the three concentric circles from the inmost circle to the outmost circle, represents the relationship and direction of the coaching conversations between mentor-coach and mentee that run throughout the work.

conversations facilitated by the mentor-coach. Conceptually, the skills and principles that support the mentor-coach in navigating the conversations sit inside the arrow, as they are the tools that make the journey from the inside out possible. Mentor-coach and mentee travel, in tandem, checking in at the relevant signposts at each level.

The model of the process reminds us, as mentor-coach, that our job is to continually co-create the conditions for learning, intentionality, support, and trust (LIST) in ourselves and in our mentee (see "Mentor-Coaching in Action," below), and to be present as we each move toward our desired results. Who we are *being* and what we are *doing* as mentor-coach needs to work toward this end.

Mentor-Coaching in Action

Remember LIST

Keep the conversations and process vibrant and alive by consistently touching base on the four key elements identified in the arrow of the mentor-coaching model: learning, intentionality, support, and trust in self.

Learning (L)

The mentor-coach helps the mentee keep learning front and centre in the process by helping the mentee to see where it has occurred and secure its impact going forward. It is important to harvest the learning from both successes and challenges. Consider asking

- Where is the learning for you in this?
- What ground have you claimed?
- How does this change your path forward?

Intentionality (I)

Attention and intentionality create engagement and build capacity. The mentor-coach invites the mentee to articulate her or his intentions as the process and conversations continue to unfold. Consider asking

- What do you want to be intentional about?
- What is compelling in this for you?
- What is your desired result?

continued...

Support (S)

The mentor-coach helps the mentee identify concrete support structures to sustain action and focus. Consider asking

- What will help make this happen?
- What support do you need internally? externally?
- What might get in your way?

Trust (T)

The mentee's trust in self is directly proportionate to the resources they have available to support them as they move forward. Consider asking

- How does trust support you?
- Which of the choices feels most aligned with your vision?
- What resources do you want to access to feel more supported?

Mentor-Coach: Remember Who You Are

Being

The mentor-coach helps the mentee notice who they are being in their actions of doing, learning, and growing. Consider asking

- Who do you want to be in the process?
- Who do you need to be in order to do what you want to do?
- What do you want to watch for in yourself?
- What qualities of character are critical for you in this?

Doing

The behaviours and actions of the mentor-coach and mentee should be aligned with their individual and shared desired results. Consider asking

- What do you want to do to support the process?
- What will the "doing" require of you? What do you want to call on in yourself?
- What behaviours do you want to further inhabit?

Alignment Within the Model: Individual, Collective, and Results

The idea of alignment is also central to the mentor-coaching process, as it focuses the energy generated by collective intentionality and connection. Aligning the intentions of all three levels—individual, collective, and results—means that all players step into the process with a shared objective. Just as aligning all four wheels on an automobile to pull in the same direction increases fuel efficiency, minimizes tire wear and tear, and maximizes engine power, aligning the energy, attention, and intentionality of the mentor-coach and the mentee maximizes the power of the relationship and often extends well beyond the formal relationship.

Reflection: Mentor-Coach and Mentee Alignment

In a discussion or journal, consider and respond to the questions below.

1. How has our work together supported your [the mentee's] learning and growth?

2. What conversations have been the most valuable?

3. What feedback do we each want?

4. What feedback feels most relevant right now?

5. What are we learning about ourselves? each other? the relationship?

6. What haven't we considered as we continue to extend the opportunity that this relationship provides?

Reflecting on Our Work from the Inside Out

In our continued work designing and facilitating specialized professional development for educators and organizations, we have come to realize that this rudimentary idea of working from the inside out serves as a valuable portal to what is required of leaders in education and industry today—both in who we are *being* and what we are *doing*. This way of working, which began as the model or conceptual frame for supporting capacity building in others, has now effectively become shorthand for what the world needs from mentor-coaches, teachers, business leaders, and agents of change.

> "As models of leadership shift from organizational hierarchies with leaders at the top to more distributed, shared networks, a lot changes… For those networks to work with real awareness, many people will need to be deeply committed to cultivating their capacity to serve what's seeking to emerge."
> —Senge, Scharmer, Jaworski, & Flowers, 2004, p. 186

Interestingly, in elementary and secondary school settings, we have also shared the inside-out approach for supporting learning and growing with parents. As the boundaries between "in school" and "out of school" learning continue to blur, schools are recognizing that parental alignment is critical—and that parents need to work from the inside out as well to maximize students' learning and growth and avoid working at cross-purposes. Parents have been very receptive to this idea, particularly when it is coupled with a few foundational coaching skills to help bring it to life. This model has also served as a fun counterpoint and welcome alternative to the temptation to engage in "helicopter" or "snowplow" parenting.

Exercise: The Inside-Out Model and Questions

With your mentee, examine the mentor-coaching model (Figure 4.5) and explore each of the signposts (words) in the individual/red, collective/yellow, and results/green zones as well as in the arrow. The questions that follow are some of the key questions for each zone. Throughout the mentor-coaching process, you can use the questions as a reference to choose those that feel the most valuable to consider given the focus or nature of the particular conversation or exploration happening at the time.

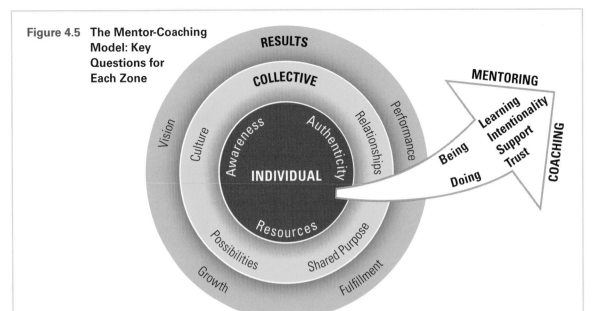

Figure 4.5 The Mentor-Coaching Model: Key Questions for Each Zone

THE INDIVIDUAL/RED ZONE

Awareness
- What results do you want from this learning relationship?
- What strengths/expertise/wisdom do you bring?

Resources
- What internal and external resources do you want to access?
- What will support you in the work?

Authenticity
- Who do you want to be in this?
- Who are you at your best?

THE COLLECTIVE/YELLOW ZONE

Culture
- What kinds of conversations does your system, school, classroom, or relationship support?
- What collective strengths do you want to leverage?

Possibilities
- What new possibilities are emerging?
- How does collaboration support your learning and growth?

Shared Purpose
- What is your shared intention?
- What matters in this for you individually? collectively?

Relationships
- What do you need as you build this relationship?
- What can the relationship make possible?

THE RESULTS/GREEN ZONE

Vision
- Who are you becoming?
- What are the shared results you are working toward?

Growth
- Where is the growth?
- What has shifted?

Fulfillment
- How does seeking fulfillment expand what is possible in your work?
- How do you honour your core values in your work?

Performance
- How can you maximize your potential?
- What interference do you want to eliminate?

PART TWO

Mentor-Coaching: Growth, Impact, and Sustainability

5 Being Coach-like: Presence, Mindset, and Stance

"Our ability to facilitate lasting, sustainable development in others absolutely rests on the presence that we offer to the relationship. Coaching requires that we first do our own inner work; in fact, developing presence is the most important work we can do as a human being. Then, and only then, can we coach in a way that comes close to delivering what coaching often promises."

—SILSBEE, 2008, P. 2

PREVIEW OF CHAPTER 5

In this chapter, we will introduce the aspects of being coach-like:

- presence: our internal state or readiness as mentor-coaches

- mindset: the fundamental attitudes and assumptions we hold as mentor-coaches

- stance: how we position ourselves within the mentor-coaching process and relationship, inhabiting the guiding principles of mentor-coaching

Who We Are Being

The idea of *being* is central to mentor-coaching. As the arrow within the mentor-coaching model indicates, who we *are* as the mentor-coach partners with what we *do* in supporting others in building their capacities from the inside out.

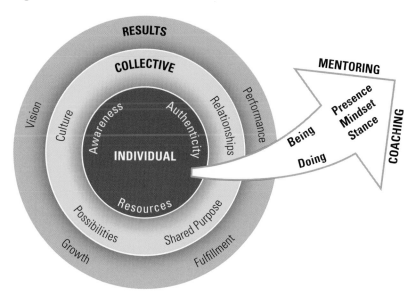

Figure 5.1   Being Coach-like

The arrow of the mentor-coaching model symbolizes the relationship between mentor-coach and mentee—who we are *being* and what we are *doing* in the process and conversations. Cultivating our presence, mindset, and stance enable us to *be* coach-like.

For many of us, considering who we *are* in the moment may be unfamiliar or new territory as Western culture has a predisposition to look at, assess, and judge what people *do,* in terms of actions and behaviours, rather than inviting us to look closely at who we *are* in the midst of what we *do*. However, we believe it is critical for all of us to continuously increase our capacity to notice and reflect on who we are being in the moment and the impact that has on what we want in terms of choices, desired actions, and results. This is what mentor-coaching requires of us, as a mentor-coach, and what we invite the mentee to embrace.

As Figure 5.1 shows, being coach-like has three aspects: presence, mindset, and stance. Let us examine each of these aspects to clarify how we need to *be* in the mentor-coaching relationship in order to support a mentee. As Brené Brown (2010) suggests, we need to "define the gauzy words that are tossed around every day but rarely explained… [G]ood definitions should be accessible and actionable… We need common language to help us create awareness and understanding…" (pp. 2–3).

Presence: Internal State or Readiness

Presence—

the state of being present, in the moment

Derivation:
From the Latin word *praesentia*, meaning "being at hand"

From the verb *praeesse;* from *prae,* meaning "before" + *esse,* meaning "be"

The nature of **presence** is complex and multi-layered. For us, presence refers to who we are *being* in the moment—how we are showing up in the world and in relationships with regard to our energy, bearing, attention, openness, connection, mindfulness, and responsiveness.

> "Energetic presence is our living presence and the message it communicates, whether or not we are conscious of it. This is variously described as the atmosphere we create, the vibes others get from us, or the field or aura surrounding the personal space around the body."
> —Nagata, (n.d.), p. 52

The Presence of the Mentor-Coach

"Only that day dawns to which we are awake."

—*Thoreau in* Walden *(1854)*

DIG DEEPER

See the mentor-coaching presence in action in the demonstration video on the *When Mentoring Meets Coaching* website.

Our presence as mentor-coach is best described as our internal state or readiness. In other words, it is how we bring our awareness and ourselves to each moment within the mentor-coaching process and the relationship.

As mentor-coach, each of us is our own instrument. We offer our presence and mindfulness, coaching principles and skills, tools and strategies, commitment, integrity, clarity, authenticity, and vulnerability. Thus, it is essential that we learn to pay attention to our presence in the moment. As we bring our whole selves to the relationship and the process, presence is the groundwork for change.

"The use of self as an instrument means how the coach 'shows up' in the relationship affects the other's change process... The more the coach is self-aware, the more she can use herself choicefully and with intention in service of the person's learning and growth."

—*Spoth, Toman, Leichtman, & Allen, 2013, p. 393*

The International Coach Federation (ICF) describes "coaching presence" as one of its coaching core competencies, and defines it as the "ability to be fully conscious and create spontaneous relationship with the client, employing a style that is open, flexible and confident" (ICF, n.d.-a).

FROM THE FIELD

Patty Lowry
Copywriter, Top Drawer Creative Inc.

In my experience as mentee, authentic presence is pivotal. It's the binding essence of trust. An emotive, visceral attention that validates you matter, you're being listened to, accepted, and genuinely cared about. It provides an intangible safety net—to unlock the vault, be vulnerable, be real. Without it you are simply a participant. With it you are partners in the process.

The Essential Aspects of the Mentor-Coach's Presence

Listed below are essential aspects of presence.

a) Being in the moment, fully present

b) Mindfulness

c) Centring

d) Stillness

e) Engagement

f) Rapt attention

g) Openness

h) Accessing intuition

We invite you to consider each aspect and its resonance for you as mentor-coach.

a) Being in the Moment, Fully Present

To be a successful mentor-coach, we need to be able to bring ourselves fully to our conversations with the mentee, listening deeply and asking questions that grow out of the mentee's present concerns and desires. Leaders, teachers, and mentor-coaches often find this critical aspect of mentor-coaching challenging to sustain.

Being in the moment involves the capacity to "be with"—open, agile and flexible, and able to respond to whatever is emerging in the moment. It also requires letting go, and not anticipating or predicting. For this, we need to cultivate a heightened awareness within ourselves, a capacity to notice when we are being pulled into assumptions and instead invite ourselves back to the moment, to being present, open, and non-interpretive.

> "Openness implies that we are receptive to whatever comes to our awareness and don't cling to preconceived ideas about how things 'should' be. We let go of expectations and receive things as they are, rather than trying to make them how we want them to be… It gives us the power to recognize restrictive judgments and release our minds from their grip."
> —Siegel, 2010, p. 32

As mentor-coach, it is critical that we are continuously developing our capacity to be present, moment by moment, staying with the mentee—listening deeply and supporting and challenging his or her deepening awareness, possibilities, and intentions.

> "To stay present in everyday life, it helps to be deeply rooted within yourself…to inhabit your body fully. To always have some of your attention in the inner energy field of your body. To feel the body from within, so to speak. Body awareness keeps you present. It anchors you in the Now."
> —Tolle, 1999, p. 94

Reflection: How Do I Ensure That I Am "Here, Prepared to Be Nowhere Else" (Scott, 2002, p. xv)?

In a discussion or journal, consider and respond to the questions below.

1. How do I know when I am indeed fully present? What keeps me there?

2. What strengths do I bring to my capacity to be present in the relationship? the process? the conversation?

3. What habits or rituals help me show up and remain fully present? What keeps me there?

4. What distracts me when I am in conversation? What can I *do* differently in order to *be* more fully present?

5. How can I enhance my capacity to be truly and consistently present?

b) Mindfulness

In Chapter 1, we defined mindfulness as "our capacity to be in the moment, experiencing directly, aware of our own mental processes. As impartial observers of ourselves as leaders, being in the moment, open-minded, and unattached, we cultivate the capacity to pause, experience, observe, reflect, and choose…indeed, inviting reflection instead of reaction."

We are practising mindfulness when we are in the moment with purposeful attention. In a 2014 radio interview, Dr. Ellen Langer, a social psychologist and professor at Harvard specializing in mindfulness, described it as follows:

> "Mindfulness, for me, is the very simple process of actively noticing new things. When you actively notice new things, that puts you in the present, makes you sensitive to context. As you're noticing new things, it's engaging. And it turns out, after a lot of research, that we find that it's literally, not just figuratively, enlivening."
>
> —Langer, 2015

Langer's approach to mindfulness is easy to understand, and is a useful strategy that we can apply to pull us into the present. Like breathing, "actively noticing new things" anchors us in the present moment.

As leaders, teachers, and mentor-coaches, we can all benefit from purposefully enhancing our own capacities to be mindful and integrating mindfulness practices into our lives. Mindfulness is what mentor-coaches, in particular, want to bring consistently to each moment.

As mentor-coaches, mindfulness expands our capacity to be "in" conversations more deeply. Our ability to pause, experience, observe, reflect, and choose how we want to navigate the process and dialogue with the mentee gives us more to work with. We are less apt to get pulled in by the immediacy of the mentee's emotions and better able to maintain our objectivity and hold the larger agenda and purpose of the conversation. We are more mindful of the mentee's energy shifts and subtle changes in body language. We also hear "more," as we are better able to notice (hear, see, and feel) the mentee's deeply embedded beliefs, collapsed distinctions, dreams, hopes, fears, assumptions, and so on.

Exercise: Introductory Mindfulness Meditation

Find a quiet and comfortable place to sit. Close your eyes, or keep them open in a soft gaze, and focus your attention on feeling your breath in your body, inhaling and exhaling. Over several minutes, keep your focus on your breath and the sensations you experience in your body as you continue to breathe. When you notice that you are no longer paying attention to your breathing, call yourself back. It is important not to judge yourself when you find your mind has wandered off and you have forgotten the breathing focus. Continually noticing and inviting yourself back expands your capacity to be in the moment, experiencing being present with yourself.

c) Centring

Centring is an essential aspect of presence, supporting us to go inside and notice where we are in the moment. By cultivating this practice, we can learn to consistently invite ourselves to be present in the moment, letting go of distractions, anxiety, and stress in order to be available to ourselves and to others.

"Centering is an internal process of bringing attention into our bodies, connecting with ourselves, and becoming aware and present. It is a living process of reorganization that shifts us from a state of being triggered or responding automatically into being self-generating, resourceful and creative. When we are centered, we are alert, connected, present, and ready for whatever is next."

—*Silsbee, 2008, p. 155*

As mentor-coach, it is critical to be skilled at centring ourselves as we prepare to enter and participate in coach-like conversations. When we are centred, we are present, available, and open throughout.

Exercise: Centring

Standing with your eyes closed, assume the yoga mountain pose (*tadasana*): feet hip width apart, back straight, shoulders back and chest open, and knees bent slightly. Bring your awareness to the soles of your feet and feel your connection to the earth beneath you. Now imagine a landscape that always beckons you. Imagine yourself within that landscape, experiencing its magnificence through all your senses. Take yourself there. What are you seeing? hearing? feeling? tasting? smelling? Now allow yourself to breathe in the landscape, inhaling and exhaling deeply, three times. Invite yourself back, now, to an awareness of your body and stance. Count backwards from three, then open your eyes. Welcome your centred self.

d) Stillness

As mentor-coach, it is essential that we are able to be still with ourselves, in relationships, and in conversations with others. Finding stillness can be particularly challenging in today's fast-paced, demanding world. However, it is critical for us as mentor-coach to approach each conversation with the mentee, having cleared the necessary space to allow us to show up fully, open, and receptive to whatever the mentee brings. This includes quieting our internal chatter, ongoing "to do" lists, and other urgencies. It also includes our capacity to be comfortable with silence within conversations and relationships. It is within this stillness that we open and hold the space for the mentee to show up fully as they step into their own work.

"Learn to love silence, the sort that flows from a mind that's perfectly still. Interior stillness promotes the wisdom that penetrates experience with meaning and fulfillment… It takes focus, intent, and silence to know and to be ourselves."

—*Sinetar, 1998, p. 63*

As we support the mentee through deep listening and inquiry, there is often silence while the mentee ponders and processes questions that provoke expanding awareness and clarity. It is important that we honour the space the mentee is seeking, by being comfortable with the silence and not rushing in with another question.

"I got to thinking about stillness… To read a book, one must be still. To watch a concert, a play, a movie, to look at a painting, one must be still. Religion, too, makes use of stillness, notably with prayer and meditation. Gazing upon a lake in autumn or a quiet winter scene—that too lulls us into contemplative stillness. Life, it seems, favours moments of stillness to appear on the edges of our perception and whisper to us, 'Here I am. What do you think?' Then we become busy and the stillness vanishes, but we hardly notice because we fall so easily for the delusion of busyness, whereby what keeps us busy must be important and the busier we are with it, the more important it must be. And so we work, work, work, rush, rush, rush. On occasion we say to ourselves, panting, 'Gosh, life is racing by.' But that's not it at all, it's the contrary: life is still. It is we who are racing by."

—*Martel, 2009, pp. 3–4*

Reflection: Stillness

In a discussion or journal, consider and respond to the questions below.

1. When are you still? How do you know? What difference does it make?

2. What draws you to stillness?

3. How does stillness nourish you?

4. When is it impossible for you to be still? How do you notice?

5. What helps you remember to access stillness in yourself?

6. How does stillness support you in relationships and conversations that matter?

7. How do you invite others to be still?

e) Engagement

Our level of engagement is profoundly impacted by how present we are and how others experience our presence. Full engagement brings and invites attention, intention, commitment, and contribution. Leaders and teachers know how critical it is to be able to deeply engage students and staff when facilitating capacity building and transformation.

As mentor-coach, our presence is greatly enhanced by our willingness to be purposefully engaged in "the now," interacting with energy, focus, and commitment. Operating from a place of full engagement is a powerful choice we are making when we partner with the mentee to support her or his learning and growth. When we are fully engaged as mentor-coach, leader, or facilitator, an energetic invitation is extended and others join us willingly. Risk taking and stretching beyond comfort zones are more forthcoming as everyone invests their whole selves in the dynamic.

> "Complete, creative engagement in all that we do is the natural response to our world; it need not be extraordinary at all. It is, in fact, the experience we have when we are at play."
>
> —Langer, 2005, p. 3

Reflection: Engagement

In a discussion or journal, consider and respond to the questions below.

1. When are you most fully engaged with others in relationship? in conversation? as a leader? as a teacher?

2. What fosters deep engagement in you? What sustains it? What's the impact?

3. When is it difficult for you to be engaged? stay engaged? What's the impact?

4. As a leader, how do you support others in engaging fully?

5. As a teacher, how do you support students in engaging fully?

f) Rapt Attention

Rapt—
to be engrossed, absorbed, captivated, enthralled

Attention—
from Latin, meaning "to reach toward"

Currently there is much research, particularly in neuroscience, regarding the impact of where we put our attention. How we choose to direct our rapt attention impacts what we see and how we feel, therefore controlling our responses and reactions.

> "At rest, the brain is noisy and chaotic, like an orchestra warming up, a cacophony of sound. When you pay close attention to something, it's like bringing the orchestra together to play a piece of music. Many neuroscientists now think of attention as being a type of synchrony, of the brain getting in tune and working as a unit."
>
> —Rock, 2009, p. 224

Mentor-coaching always involves paying attention and reaching toward, as the mentee becomes clearer regarding new awareness, choices, and desires. Our presence and success as mentor-coaches is greatly impacted by our capacity to bring deep focus, moment by moment, to each conversation. Our commitment to rapt attention not only increases our effectiveness, but also supports the mentee in keeping the spotlight on themselves, managing their attention, and zeroing in on what matters as they move forward.

Exercise: Rapt Attention

When we are deeply engaged in an activity we love, we often are completely absorbed, experiencing deep attention, energy, and focus in suspended time and space. We are "in flow." Think of a time when you were in flow—so deeply engaged in an activity that you were totally transported:

1. What is it about that activity that is so compelling to you?

2. What invites you in?

3. When you are in "the zone" what are you aware of? What is your experience of "rapt attention"?

4. What further opportunities are there for you to invite such deep attention into your life?

g) Openness

As mentor-coach, being open is a central aspect of our internal state or readiness. This means arriving with openness for the conversations and the relationship, as well as staying open throughout.

To be open entails

- clearing the space to arrive (literally and figuratively);

- arriving without preconceived notions of where the mentee will be or what he or she will be wanting from the mentor-coaching conversation or process;

- staying open to the constantly evolving meaning making and possibilities;

- giving the mentee a "fresh start each" day (Heathcote, 1984, p. 22), rather than interacting with the mentee based on previous experience or judgments; and

- inhabiting the intention of being and staying open as the conversation unfolds minute to minute, listening throughout and responding based on the immediacy of the responses and desires of the mentee.

Exercise: Openness

Before a coach-like conversation, practise taking time to let go of all that you have been experiencing. Prepare an open space for yourself to arrive into just prior to meeting with the mentee. As you navigate the conversation, notice what the intentionality allows in terms of your openness. Be mindful not to anticipate what the mentee may be bringing to the conversation in terms of agenda, concerns, attitudes, and so on.

h) Accessing Intuition

Intuition is coming to understand something or someone without engaging conscious thought. We believe that intuition encompasses our multiple ways of knowing and supports us and our presence in each moment. As mentor-coach, trusting and accessing our intuition as we interact in conversations and relationships can expand what we are able to see and hear in the moment.

As mentor-coach, we have access to our wider and deeper knowing when we call on our intuition. This expands our own presence and what we offer within the relationship, conversations, and process over time.

Reflection: Accessing Intuition

In a discussion or journal, consider and respond to the questions below.

1. How do you know when you are accessing your intuition? Where does it show up in your body?

2. How does your intuition support you in your life? your leadership? your teaching?

3. When has your intuition really supported you as a mentor-coach? as a mentee?

4. What opportunities are there as a mentor-coach to access your intuition in service of the mentee?

Cultivating Heightened Awareness Around Presence in the Mentee

Mentor-coaching is ultimately about enhancing our capacity to notice in the moment and to choose. Helping the mentee become aware of her or his capacity to be more present, mindful, and engaged is part of the ongoing work together.

Possible ways to heighten the mentee's awareness of their own presence include

- inviting the mentee to notice how present they are at the beginning of a conversation and to do whatever they need to be fully in the moment and engaged;

- supporting the mentee in fostering mindfulness; and
- inviting the mentee to read this section of the chapter and consider the exercises and reflections.

Being purposeful in supporting the mentee to build capacity in all aspects of presence furthers their growth and development as impactful change agents.

Practices That Develop Presence

We have found the following practices to be useful in expanding our capacity to be ever more present and in the moment:

- **breathing:** an internal anchor for us all to experience being and staying in the moment

- **meditation:** an invitation to be with ourselves as we are, cultivating meditative practices that build our capacity to be quiet and present

- **experiencing with all the senses:** a visceral experience of accessing our robust and multi-faceted senses

- **being in and with nature:** directly experiencing the rich, wondrous, and varied natural world

- **beauty:** engaging with and appreciating the immediacy of beauty; letting it in and responding

- **engaging deeply:** being actively involved in an art form, a challenging sport, reflection, or the like

- **rapt attention:** becoming engrossed through deep engagement, focus, and intent

- **being in flow:** full immersion within an experience, process, or activity; suspending time and outcome

- **being in relationship:** the experience of connecting deeply with another, being together in the moment, co-creating the dynamic

- **being in conversations that matter:** becoming energized through deep dialogue about what really matters

- **playing:** accessing our spontaneous, exploring, discovering, in-the-moment selves

- **curiosity:** being open and curious, inviting discovery, delight, and surprise

- **creativity:** accessing our creative energy pulls us into the moment, delighting in experimentation, discovery, and meaning making

- **movement and stretching:** engaging the body in movement or stretching to expand the energy field that lives in and around our physical selves

- **experiences that access our multiple intelligences** (intellectual, emotional, sensory, kinesthetic, social, spiritual, and intuitive): tapping into our multiple ways of knowing expands our awareness and our experience of the moment

- **improvisation:** agreeing to co-create together, responding to each other spontaneously; provides an opportunity to play as we continue to build our capacities to be in the moment as mentor-coach

Mindset: Fundamental Attitudes and Assumptions

Mindset refers to a particular perspective, a habit of viewing something through a preconceived set of attitudes and assumptions that are "set" in the "mind" of an individual and, thus, serve as a conscious or unconscious filter. We can think of mindset as a mental model that guides our attention, perception, expectations, and behaviour.

It is important to look at our mindset, since it has a powerful impact on how we see and interpret the world as well as who we *are* in relationship with ourselves and others. Furthermore, the beliefs and assumptions that we hold in our mindset directly impact our view of our potential, possibilities, strengths, limitations, successes, and failures as well as those of others.

> "Mindsets frame the running account that's taking place in people's heads. They guide the whole interpretation process."
> —Dweck, 2006, p. 215

The Mindset of the Mentor-Coach

Central to our presence is the mentor-coaching mindset, the fundamental attitudes and assumptions we hold as mentor-coach. The essence of this mindset is comprised of the following components:

- **assuming competence:** recognizing that the mentee's wisdom lies within and that they are resourceful, creative, and expert in their own life

- **inquiry based:** operating from an inquiring mindset rather than a directive or advising mindset

- **grounded in strengths, values, and vision:** working from an appreciative, rather than a deficit, frame or mindset, where we are looking to access "what is" within the mentee rather than "what is not"

- **it is the mentee's work:** inviting the mentee to step into the change they are wanting; resisting fixing, solving, and interpreting

- **mobilizing and building capacity from the inside out:** beginning within the mentee and with his or her internal resources, vision, values, and awareness

- **expanding awareness, reflection, growth, and movement:** grounding the process and conversations in opportunities for stretching oneself, generating valuable feedback

- **intentionality:** being forward focused and committed to movement toward the mentee's desired results

- **non-judgmental:** operating from openness and curiosity

- **collaborative:** engaging fully in a co-created learning relationship that is committed to the growth and forward movement of the mentee and, in turn, ourselves

Reflection: Mindset of the Mentor-Coach

In a discussion or journal, consider and respond to the questions below.

1. Which aspects of the mentor-coaching mindset feel most familiar to you?

2. What helps you notice your own mindset?

3. How will you support yourself in being more mindful and consistent in holding the specific aspects of this mindset?

DIG DEEPER

For further exploration of mindset as support for the mentee, see the Mentor-Coaching Toolkit.

4. Which aspects of the mindset will have the most impact on your intentions regarding your contribution as a mentor-coach?

5. Where is your growing edge as you step more fully into the mindset?

6. How might you use the notion of mindset to support the mentee in her or his work?

Stance: Positioning Within the Dynamic of the Process and Relationship

Stance is dynamic and relational, a concept that denotes an orientation toward self and others, a way we dance within process and relationship.

The Importance of Stance

The stance of the leader, educator, and mentor is often overlooked when educational institutions and organizations consider enhancing student or faculty achievement and capacities. Often the focus is on what needs to be done to attain the desired results, rather than on who we need to *be* to support the learning and growth of the other. Paying attention to our own stance within the ongoing relationship and conversations gives us the opportunity to position ourselves differently within them.

The Stance of the Mentor-Coach

When we are true to the guiding principles of mentor-coaching, we inhabit the mentor-coach stance. The six guiding principles (see Figure 5.2) position the mentor-coach within the stance and the dance of the relationship, process, and conversations. They help us, as mentor-coach, stay oriented and purposeful as we look, listen, and feel for the key ingredients that are critical for supporting growth and building capacity.

To consistently embrace and inhabit the mentor-coach stance, we need to become highly self-aware and rigorous in observing and managing ourselves within the dynamic of each moment. Ongoing reflection and rigour are required to increase our capacity to be conscious of the stance we inhabit as mentor-coach and to observe our stance in action within the conversations and partnerships.

In the Reflection below, we invite you to take another look at the six guiding principles as aspects of the mentor-coach stance.

Reflection: The Guiding Principles and Stance of Mentor-Coaching

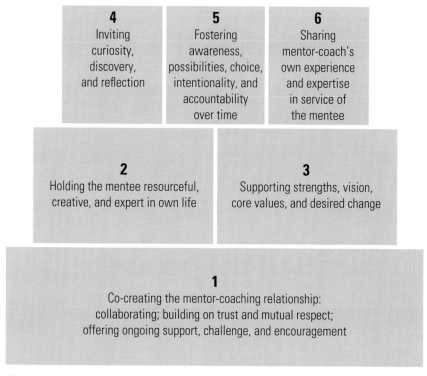

Figure 5.2 The Guiding Principles of Mentor-Coaching
The six guiding principles of mentor-coaching are the foundation of the mentor-coach's stance.

Consider the following questions about each guiding principle to help develop and ground yourself in the mentor-coach stance.

1. Co-creating the mentor-coaching relationship by collaborating; building on trust and mutual respect; offering ongoing support, challenge, and encouragement:

   a) What does "co-creating" look like within the evolving partnership? How does it show up minute by minute within the conversation?

   b) How am I doing in terms of building trust and creating or holding the space for risk-taking, growth, and stretching within the mentee?

   c) What helps me remember to offer ongoing acknowledgements, support, and challenges? How impactful are my offerings? What more is the mentee wanting in terms of support? challenges?

2. Holding the mentee resourceful, creative, and expert in own life:

   a) When is it easy for me to see the mentee as fully resourceful and creative? When is it most challenging?

   b) When and how do I honour the mentee as expert in his or her own life and experience? What is the impact? When am I apt to forget? What is the impact?

   c) How do I help myself notice when there is "slippage" in my capacity to see the mentee as capable? to notice the impact on how I am then holding the mentee and the process?

3. Supporting strengths, vision, core values, and desired change:

   a) How am I drawing on my strengths to support myself in being the best mentor-coach I can be?

   b) How am I doing in consistently holding mentor-coaching as a strengths-based process? When do I forget and what is the impact?

   c) What helps me keep the mentee's core values present in the conversations? What other opportunities are there for me to draw on her or his values in support of desired change?

   d) What helps me listen for vision and purpose? What is the impact of supporting the mentee in connecting vision and purpose to desired change?

4. Inviting curiosity, discovery, and reflection:

   a) What keeps me curious and out of judgment? How does being curious support the mentee's expanding awareness?

   b) What questions really foster discovering and uncovering in the mentee? How do I support the mentee in digging in and going deeper?

   c) How am I fostering reflection within each conversation? What questions invite deep reflection? How am I modelling being a reflective practitioner?

5. Fostering awareness, possibilities, choice, intentionality, and accountability over time:

   a) What helps me hold a big space for the mentee to explore new awareness and expanding possibilities?

   b) How do I help the mentee slow down to reflect and expand perspectives when they are in a hurry to get to action?

   c) What questions support the mentee in widening their perspectives and choices?

   d) When and how am I most impactful in supporting the mentee's intentionality and accountability over time?

6. Sharing mentor-coach's own experience and expertise in service of the mentee:

   a) How do I decide when to offer my own wisdom and expertise to the mentee? How do I know or discern that it will be in service of the mentee?

   b) How skilled am I in getting to the essence of the story (wisdom, experience)?

   c) How consistently do I remember to invite the mentee to make his or her own connections and meaning after I have offered up my experience or expertise?

Exercise: Metaphor for Being "Coach-like"

A metaphor can help capture many layers of meaning within an abstract concept, such as "being coach-like" (detailed below). By visualizing a concrete object, landscape, or collage of objects, the concrete and abstract come together to support expanding awareness and clarity. What feels elusive and hard to describe becomes more tangible and vivid.

Being Coach-like

- Presence: our internal state or readiness as mentor-coaches
- Mindset: the fundamental attitudes and assumptions we hold as mentor-coaches
- Stance: how we position ourselves within the mentor-coaching process and relationship, inhabiting the guiding mentor-coaching principles

Brainstorm a list of a variety of objects that represent the essence of being coach-like for you. Choose one object from the list—the object that feels most intriguing and rich in possibilities—as the metaphor. Mine it for as many layers of meaning as you can to develop further clarity regarding being coach-like and its implications for you as a mentor-coach. Record the metaphor and layers of meaning as a useful reminder for you to inhabit the mentor-coaching presence, mindset, and stance. You may also wish to find or create a concrete object or visual to represent your metaphor.

6 Critical Mentor-Coaching Skills: Being Present and Listening

"The ordinary stories of our ordinary lives have extraordinary gifts coded within them—for the one speaking and for the ones listening."

—BALDWIN, 2005, P. 31

PREVIEW OF CHAPTER 6

In this chapter, we will introduce and explore

- being in the moment, fully present

- listening deeply: distinguishing between "listening through" and "listening to"

- cultivating the inner conditions and stance for "listening to"

The Most Critical Skills of Mentor-Coaching

DIG DEEPER

See the mentor-coaching skills in action in the demonstration video on the *When Mentoring Meets Coaching* website.

Being present and listening deeply are the most critical skills that we, as mentor-coaches, bring to the learning relationship and process. They are what we use to facilitate the conversations that foster the mentee's development.

Being in the Moment, Fully Present

The skill of being deeply and consistently present is foundational—all other mentor-coaching skills require this skill to be in place. To maximize the experience of each conversation, it is also critical that we, as mentor-coach, support the mentee in being fully present throughout the conversation. We set the intention of being fully present throughout with the mentee—holding the process for the mentee to do his or her work.

> "When we are present, we stand as an invitation… [I]t is through this development of the capacity for presence in ourselves that we evoke the experience of presence in others."
> —Silsbee, 2008, p. 27

Being fully present is a visceral experience; we know in our bones when we are "here"…or not. And most of us also know when another person we are with is fully present…or not. Most of the time, people do not directly discuss or address this key element of conversations and interactions. To be consistently fully present, we must cultivate the practice of mindfulness, asking ourselves to be constantly aware of where we are and what we are paying attention to.

FROM THE FIELD

Mary Ann Tucker
Retired Director of Clinical Services, Thames Valley Children's Centre

As a leader in a children's rehabilitation centre, staff development and mentorship were key priorities. The team members, working

continued…

---

with the children with disabilities and their families, have a direct impact on the success of the families in ensuring the best quality of life for their children. Through a mentorship program, all therapists and support staff in the organization received coach training, shifting the organizational culture from a culture of therapist expertise to family expertise. The greatest gift for families was the coaching skill of "presence." Therapists trained in this coaching skill were able to be present and fully engaged with the families. The therapists listened deeply to the stories and met the families where they were, not where it was perceived they should be. In doing so, the therapists developed trusting relationships with the families that served as a conduit for co-creating solutions and strategies that fit with the families' values and lifestyle. In receiving this gift of presence, the families expressed that they felt heard, understood, respected, and valued as equal partners in their children's rehabilitation and well-being.

To be present requires us to be experiencing each moment as now. As we know, this is easier said than done. In our present-day world, with the ever-expanding roles and responsibilities of leaders and teachers and the demands of the digital devices that surround us, choosing where to direct our attention has become an ongoing challenge.

"It's not about how digital technology changes us, but how we change ourselves and one another now that we live so digitally… [O]ne of the primary impacts of thinking this way is to assume the rigours of digital time as our own. Our digital universe is always on…pinging, updates and email responses. There are so many incoming alerts competing for attention… [E]verything intrudes with urgency."
—Rushkoff, 2013, p. 73

We can manage this "all-at-once"-ness (Rushkoff, 2013, p. 209) and support our capacity for presence, by establishing internal and external structures that help us stay connected to the people and what matters in our day.

DIG DEEPER

For a detailed discussion on presence, see Chapter 5.

Reflection: Being in the Moment, Fully Present

In a discussion or journal, consider and respond to the questions below.

1. How do you support yourself in staying present and in the moment as a leader? as a teacher? as a mentor-coach?

2. What impact does being fully present have on you? on others?

3. What is the impact when you are not fully present?

4. How do you notice you are no longer present? What supports you in bringing yourself back?

Attunement—an exercise that invites the mentee and mentor-coach to be in the moment, aware of their own current internal state. It is an intentional way to create the space for arriving fully and able to engage in the conversation and process with an open and focused mindset.

Mentor-Coaching in Action

Tool: Attunement

As we all know well, we carry much with us throughout the day that can distract from our ongoing interactions and conversations. Thus, at the beginning of mentor-coaching conversations, it is helpful to do an attunement with the mentee to support the intention of being fully present and on purpose throughout the conversation. Consider using the following attunement tool:

I invite you to close your eyes and take a few deep belly breaths, in and out, on your own time, as I do the same.

[A few moments of silence.]

Now I invite you to notice any tension you are carrying in your body and release it in any way that works for you.

[A few moments of silence.]

Now take two more deep belly breaths.

[A few moments of silence.]

Now I invite us to open our eyes and together begin our mentor-coaching conversation today.

Listening Deeply: Distinguishing Between "Listening Through" and "Listening To"

When someone listens to us fully and deeply, we feel seen and heard. We feel as if the signals we send "are directly perceived, understood and responded to...in a dance of communication that involves mutual collaboration... [It] enables a vitalizing sense of connection that [is] at the heart of nurturing relationships" (Siegel & Hartzell, 2003, p. 80). This has an immediate impact on the mentor-coaching relationship, building trust and keeping the focus on the mentee's agenda and capacity building. In fact, the capacity to listen fully and deeply is the second most critical mentor-coaching skill.

Most educators have long made active listening a part of their practice. However, to further enhance listening, we have found it impactful for mentor-coaches to distinguish between

- listening through—being distracted in their listening, and

- listening to—truly listening deeply.

By simply recognizing these distinctions, participants in the mentor-coach training have consistently found that they begin to listen differently, more deeply.

> "Resilience research has established that *listening* is a simple but powerful 'turnaround' practice that adults can do in families, schools, programs, and communities to support and empower young people. Attentive listening incorporates all three protective factors—caring for, believing in, and inviting the participation and contribution of the one listened to. Moreover, the categories of resilience strengths...(social competence, problem solving, autonomy/identity, and sense of purpose and future)...are engaged and nurtured in the one listened to."
> —*Benard & Slade, 2009, p. 366*

DIG DEEPER

For an exploration of listening, see *Co-Active Coaching* (H. Kimsey-House, K. Kimsey-House, Sandahl, & Whitworth, 2011) regarding distinctions between listening through and to (Listening levels 1, 2, 3). This resource has been key in furthering our own understanding.

"Listening Through"

"Listening through" is what we experience internally as we listen. We listen through internal responses and experiences that we are having simultaneously that have a profound impact on our capacity to be fully present and focused on what we hear.

When we listen through, we filter what we hear, listening through the distractions of our own visceral experiences, lenses, emotions, assessments, experiences, stories, opinions, notions, conclusions, and judgments.

The curious thing is that we do not talk with one another about this interference in listening even though it happens constantly. If we are aware that it is happening, we usually do not comment, either as the one pretending to listen or as the one sensing we are not being listened to. The conversation proceeds "as if" the listening were happening. Thus, most of us have not developed much rigour around noticing interference in our listening.

By inviting ourselves to identify and notice the many ways in which internal and external factors interfere and compromise deep listening, it is possible to raise awareness and enhance our capacity to listen to the other person. By naming the interference, we are able to notice its impact on our listening and then we can consciously move it out of the way, so that we are once again fully present and in the moment, "listening to."

Noticing when we "have gone on a trip," and are thus "away," begins to heighten our capacity to notice when we are distracted as a listener. For example, since our minds are meaning-making machines, often as we listen we are making connections with our own experience, wisdom, current challenges, and so on. As we make these connections, we "leave" the conversation to recall, "connect the dots," and consider possibilities. This powerful desire to make meaning pulls our attention away from the speaker, and we are no longer listening. By recognizing when we are meaning making rather than listening, we can learn to "hold that thought" for later, when we are no longer required to listen to the other person.

As listeners and as mentor-coaches, cultivating the capacity to notice when we have left the conversation "on a trip" allows us to choose to go back "over there" with the other person, being fully present and listening deeply. The table below lists common sources of interference that pull our attention when we are listening.

Listening Distractions

External

- Other people
- Dialogue
- Surrounding environment, situation
- Smart phones, computers, and other technologies
- Sounds
- Visual distractions

Physiological Needs and Messages

- Comfort
- Energy
- Fatigue
- Wellness
- Sense experiences
- Hunger, thirst
- Temperature

Internal

- Internal state (e.g., not present, worried, excited, anxious, agitated, bored, frustrated)
- Making own meaning and connections
- Own unique interpretation of meaning of words, body language, silence, energy, breathing
- Connecting to own experience and memory
- Connecting to the wisdom and extrapolating from there
- Integrating into own experience, schemas
- Own filters and barriers influence what we can actually hear (e.g., values, beliefs, life experience, judgments, assumptions)
- Making lists (e.g., to do, responsibilities, future obligations and intentions)
- Internal responses (e.g., "Yeah, but…," "What if…?," judging, dismissing, embracing)
- Triggered (e.g., taking things personally, emotions, memories, visceral responses, amygdala activated [fight, flight, or freeze])

DIG DEEPER
For a detailed discussion of how our filters and barriers influence what we can hear in conversations, see p. 134.

Internal
• Anticipating
• Imagining
• Daydreaming
• Lack of trust
• Preoccupied with own issues
• Pace
• Own or other's expectations

Listening Distractions in Action

In the table above, there are almost three times as many types of internal distractions as external or physiological ones. As mentor-coach, our ability to notice internal interference and move it out of the way of our listening is critical. Consider the following examples of some of the most common internal distractions we experience as we listen in conversation:

a) Making Own Meaning and Connections

Mentee: There is so much to do and remember in terms of protocol and procedures. I am feeling overwhelmed.

Mentor-coach's internal interference: *Oh my...he's feeling overwhelmed again! Not a good sign! Thought we'd covered this territory already? Yikes!*

b) Connecting to Own Experience and Memory

Mentee: It is so important to me to somehow pull in the resisters... and I am finding it so hard!

Mentor-coach's internal interference: *Do I remember that! I can still see the triumvirate sitting in the staff room, heads together... Wonder what happened to them? ...Retired probably... Hope they're happier...*

c) Our Filters and Barriers Influence What We Can Actually Hear

> **Mentee:** You know that parent that we talked about last time…
> So much for our planning… I completely lost my cool when they
> started in on…
>
> **Mentor-coach's internal interference:** *What's with these
> helicopter parents? They drive me crazy!*

Reflection: "Listening Through"

In a discussion or journal, consider and respond to the questions
below.

1. What are you aware of in terms of internal interference in your
   own listening?

2. What distraction habits are you aware of as a listener?

3. How will you help yourself notice when you are "away" and no
   longer listening fully?

4. What opportunities can you create to practise noticing when you
   are "listening through"?

5. What are some examples of "listening through" in a variety of
   contexts in your life? When and how does "listening through"
   show up with colleagues, staff, parents, and students? with family?
   within your broader life?

"Listening To"

"Listening to" is intentional, focused listening. It means that the
listener is fully present, in the moment, and able to be "over there"
with the other person, listening deeply, with attention and intention.

When we are "listening to," we are present, curious, open, and
without judgment. We are aware of the speaker's words, energy, tone
of voice, body language and gestures, emotional expression, and
so on. And as we notice these elements, we stay with the speaker,

listening deeply, not leaving our listening to go on any "trips" to try to interpret what we think the speaker might mean.

As mentor-coach, "listening to" requires us to be "clean" as we listen, staying out of speculation and interpretation. Fundamental to "listening to" is the understanding that it is the speaker's thoughts and feelings being expressed, their wisdom and experience being shared. As mentor-coach, we hold the space for the mentee to think and feel out loud and then, through inquiry and reflection, expand their awareness, choices, and intentionality. To support this capacity-building process, it is critical for us to listen deeply and stay away from offering opinions, interpretations, and suggestions. It is the mentee's work—she or he is the one making meaning through the dialogue.

Listening deeply is listening with our ears, our eyes, our heart, and our gut. Neuroscience is helping us understand what many of us have intuitively recognized for a long time: we have access to information, memories, and understanding through vast neural networks in our heart and our gut as well as in our brain. It is critical to allow ourselves to be open to receiving signals from all these areas as we listen to the speaker's words, beyond the words, underneath the words, and to the silence between the words.

> "A committed listener helps people think more clearly, work through unresolved issues, and discover the solutions they have inside them. This often involves listening beyond what people are saying to the deeply held beliefs and assumptions that are shaping their actions."
> —Hargrove, 1995, p. 57

The mastery in all of this is the capacity to notice interference as it happens in our listening and, having noticed, invite ourselves back to deep listening.

In exploring how to cultivate the art of listening with educators over the years, many have spoken about the profound impact that distinguishing between "listening to" and "listening through" has had on their capacity to truly listen. By paying attention and being on purpose about "listening to," many have deepened their listening skills significantly, which in turn has enhanced their leadership, relationships, and capacity building.

Linda Beale
Principal and Mentor-Coach Training Program Facilitator

The single most important skill is listening. In my role of principal, I had many opportunities to listen deeply to students, parents, and teachers. By listening, I was able to become a truly collaborative leader in our school and in our community.

Val Fox
Co-founder, Digital Media Zone (DMZ) at Ryerson University; Chief Innovation Consultant, The Pivotal Point

The art of listening deeply is so much more than a space in which to receive someone's thoughts. Deep listening provides the platform for a mentee's internal gift of creativity to show itself in the form of strategic thinking and innovative problem solving.

With this, the mentee will experience the ability to develop his or her own deep listening skills, and with those skills, the bonus of learning and doing through curiosity, generosity, courage, and collaboration—the capacity-building traits of modern-day entrepreneurship and innovation.

Mentor-Coaching in Action

Creating the Conditions to "Listen To"

Use the following strategies to help you arrange the space, time, and place for "listening to."

- Make concrete changes in your office and meeting spaces— such as moving away from the computer, rearranging the furniture, putting up blinds, and closing the door—to create a more conducive environment for "listening to" and reducing interference.
- Practise being mindful and direct about negotiating the appropriate time and place for an in-depth conversation that requires deep listening, focus, and space.

"Listening To" in Action

What does "listening to" look like? Consider the following sample of a mentor-coaching conversation.

> **Mentee:** I could use your help. My "door is always open" policy seems not to be working very well right now.
>
> *Mentor-coach:* What's not working?
>
> **Mentee:** Almost everything...too many people taking up too much of my time, too frequently.
>
> *Mentor-coach:* Lots of "toos" there? What were you hoping for with the open-door policy?
>
> **Mentee:** It's who I am as a leader: available, supportive... That's who I am and that is the message I want to send.
>
> *Mentor-coach:* And remembering the "too...too...too," how do you see your way through all this?
>
> **Mentee:** ...Well, I think it's something about boundaries...and being able to close my door.
>
> *Mentor-coach:* Close your door?
>
> **Mentee:** ... Yes... I need to give myself permission to close my door sometimes.

Noticing Distinctions as You Listen

We invite you to become familiar with the distinctions between the two types of listening by practising within life's conversations. Notice when you are "listening to" and when you have been pulled away and find yourself "listening through."

"Listening through" is an essential part of being human, reflecting, making connections, and making meaning. We cannot banish "listening through," as these distractions are real and sometimes critical to understanding and gathering knowledge. However, we can learn to cultivate our capacity to notice when we have been pulled away, for whatever reason, and then invite ourselves back to deep listening. This rigour is essential to being able to consistently show up fully as a listener in mentor-coaching conversations.

Exercise: How Am I Listening?

1. Noticing "Listening Through" in the Moment

    a) As you begin a variety of specific conversations (at work, with family, or with friends), set an intention to be mindful of when you are distracted from "listening to." The challenge is to notice when you are "away" and then to invite yourself back to "listening to" immediately.

    b) Afterwards, reflect on your distractions and what helps you return to listening deeply. Notice the impact on yourself, on your capacity to listen deeply, and on the person you are "listening to."

    c) Heighten your awareness of distractions by sharing the listening distinctions with others and recruiting their support through feedback regarding their experience of you as a listener. To help you notice in the moment, you might raise your hand or put a mark on a piece of paper each time you notice you are "away."

    d) Try noticing as you are listening in a meeting, challenging yourself to be ever more aware of when you are "listening through" and inviting yourself back to "listening to."

2. Noticing "Listening To" in the Moment

    a) Challenge yourself to "listen to" someone you know who you are often distracted with, in your listening. Notice the difference.

    b) Switch to "listening to" when you notice you are judging someone. What does the shift make possible?

c) Underneath every complaint is a request. Challenge yourself to "listen to" a complainer with the intention of helping them become clear about what it is they want and what their part is in making it happen.

Reflection: "Listening To"

In a discussion or journal, consider and respond to the questions below.

1. How do you know when you are "listening to"?

2. What supports you in being fully present as a listener, in being able to "listen to"?

3. What is the impact on you as a listener, as you experiment with noticing when you are "listening through" and invite yourself back to "listening to"?

4. What is the impact on others when you are more consistently "listening to" rather than "listening through"?

Cultivating the Inner Conditions and Stance for "Listening To"

FROM THE FIELD

Teresa Hadley and Tracy Vanslyke
In-School Resource Teacher and Numeracy Coordinator, K–12, Hastings and Prince Edward District School Board

The mentor-coaching model has supported our work as learning partners by helping us refine the skills and the mindset critical to working collaboratively with others. By taking the stance of a learner and listener, we are hoping to thereby create a safe environment for learning and risk taking to take place. It is more than a strategy that is used. It is a stance that we try to genuinely live in.

In the preceding From the Field feature, the participants speak to the power that "listening to" can have, particularly in mentor-coaching classroom teachers. To consistently "listen to" the mentee, mentor-coaches cultivate the stance and mindset described below. We invite you to begin cultivating them by exploring the reflections, material, exercises, and practices that follow throughout the rest of the chapter.

Mindset and Stance for "Listening To"

Mindset: A mental model that guides our attention, perception, expectations, and behaviour

- Noticing when "listening through"; inviting self back to "listening to"
- Consistently holding the mentee as resourceful, creative, and expert in own life
- Recognizing that each of us has a unique view of the world, shaped through our experience, frame of reference, values, assumptions and beliefs, personal agenda, leadership, and teaching priorities
- Remembering we cannot truly know the lived experience of another

- Listening with the intent to understand rather than the intent to reply (Covey, 1989)
- Being comfortable with silence; recognizing that reflection takes time and space
- Being unattached (e.g., to the direction of the conversation, to the outcomes)
- Sharing own wisdom, expertise, and experiences only when in service of the mentee

Stance: An orientation toward self and others; a way we dance within process and relationship

- Being present and in the moment; centred and available
- Being open, curious, and non-judgmental
- Co-creating a conducive relationship and environment for deep listening

- Heightening own capacity to notice the mentee: language, tone of voice, body language, energy, between the lines, silence
- Noticing own impact on the mentee
- Accessing own intuition, other ways of knowing

Reflection: The Mindset and Stance of the Mentor-Coach

After considering the above lists, reflect on the following questions.

1. What allows you to be consistently present as a listener, centred, and available?

2. What gets in your way?

3. How do you stay curious as a listener?

4. How do you notice when you are in judgment as a listener? What supports you in letting go of judgment as you listen?

5. How will you help yourself remember that the mentee is resourceful and creative, especially when they do not remember that themselves?

6. What helps you remember that the mentee's lived experience is not the same as yours? How do you refrain from making assumptions based on your own unique experience?

7. How comfortable are you with silence? How will you enhance your capacity to be silent as you listen?

8. Identify the one critical factor regarding the stance of the mentor-coach that will have the greatest positive impact on your capacity to "listen to."

9. How will you be intentional about stepping into this growing edge as a listener?

Learning to Notice Our Filters and Barriers

Being aware of our filters and barriers is a critical aspect of learning to "listen to" consistently. The filters and barriers that we create, or hold, between ourselves and others are so much a part of who we are and how we see the world that they are often hard to notice. And if we do not notice them as we listen, they influence what we *can* hear and how we feel about and respond to what we *do* hear. Our filters and barriers allow only selected words and ideas to enter our consciousness as they screen out less familiar or uncomfortable words and messages.

Sometimes, it is not so much the filters and barriers that obstruct our deep listening, but the emotions associated with them, such as judgment, anger, worry, fear, frustration, perceived threat, indignation, and desire. Building our capacity to navigate our emotions, so that we can listen deeply, then becomes the **learning edge** or challenge.

Learning edge— also called "growing edge"; the threshold between knowing and competence and not knowing and experimentation

Building authentic relationships and fostering meaningful collaboration are critical aspects of leading and teaching from the inside out. Thus, it is important to realize that our filters and barriers can become obstacles for our capacity to genuinely connect with others and to "listen to" them deeply.

If we increase our ability to identify our filters and barriers as they show up and, as a result, recognize how they affect what and how we hear, we can significantly enhance our capacity to "listen to" consistently. The list below summarizes common external and internal filters and barriers that you can use as a starting point for inquiry.

Possible Filters and Barriers That Influence Our Listening

- age
- gender
- race
- culture
- ethnicity
- sexual orientation
- status
- education
- values
- core beliefs
- mindset
- mental models by which we operate
- our past experience and stories
- stereotypes, labelling
- appearance
- expectations (of self, of others)
- personal agenda
- knowledge and expertise
- perceived relevance
- competence
- confidence
- time
- physical state/energy
- mental and emotional state
- distractions: internal and external
- language; unique connotative understanding of words used

Filters and Barriers in Action

The following examples highlight the possible consequences of being "unaware," as mentor-coach, versus "aware" of our own filters and barriers.

a) Expectations

Mentee: I know we agreed that I would go in to observe Jillian in her classroom this week to support me in getting more of a sense of what else I can be doing in terms of classroom management, but there always seems to be too many other things that need my attention in my prep time…

Mentor-coach's internal filter: Oh my…here we go again… She never seems to be able to find the time to get in to observe Jillian in action! She needs to get in there now!

Mentor-coach's question is then influenced by the filter: *You didn't get in to observe her in her classroom? Sounds like you could use my help in setting priorities.*

OR

Mentor-coach notices "listening through" own filter, chooses to move it out of the way and then asks a question that comes from "listening to" the mentee instead: *What support are you wanting around this?*

b) Personal Agenda

Mentee: I am excited about this new opportunity for me to contribute as a member of the district-wide Parent Engagement Committee. My master's thesis was in this territory and it's close to my heart…

Mentor-coach's internal filter: She doesn't have the time to add this to her plate. She needs to stay focused on all her challenges. Besides, the chair of that committee will drive her crazy.

Mentor-coach's question is then influenced by the filter: *Are you sure you should be adding this to your plate?*

OR

Mentor-coach notices "listening through" own filter, chooses to move it out of the way and then asks a question that comes from "listening to" the mentee instead: *Say more about "close to my heart"…*

c) Our Past Experience and Stories

Mentee: I left a note for one of the tech teachers to come and see me regarding standard safety issues that I noticed he was ignoring in his classroom the other day, but he has not come to see me yet. Not sure what to do now?

Mentor-coach's internal filter: Oh my...a note in the mailbox from the VP. I remember when I tried that... Can still see Stuart standing in my office, yelling at me about lack of respect and my obsession with useless rules.

Mentor-coach's question is then influenced by the filter: Oh, I remember when I did that as a new VP too... Not so useful a strategy, I found. How can I help?

OR

Mentor-coach notices "listening through" own filter, chooses to move it out of the way and then asks a question that comes from "listening to" the mentee instead: What is critical for you in dealing with this now?

Reflection: Impact of Filters and Barriers

In a discussion or journal, consider and respond to the questions below.

1. Which filters and barriers are the most challenging for you to notice in yourself?

2. What is the impact of them on your listening?

3. How will you heighten your ability to notice, in the moment, a filter or barrier to your listening?

4. Having noticed a filter or barrier to your listening, how will you move it out of the way and invite yourself back to "listening to"?

5. How will you help the mentee notice her or his own filters and barriers?

"Listening To" the Language of the Mentee

DIG DEEPER

See Chapter 7 for details and support around questioning within these areas.

The language that the mentee uses within mentor-coaching conversations is a rich resource for both the mentor-coach and the mentee. Since the choice and meaning of the words are unique to the mentee, it is important for us to honour their words and meaning by remembering to use their language as the catalyst for further exploration. For the mentee, hearing their own language used to deepen the conversation helps to establish that we are listening deeply, and enhances their trust in the relationship.

Being able to hear more in what is said or implied in what the mentee shares is a skill that we need to develop as mentor-coach. The following table can help build this capacity by highlighting some of the ongoing themes, strengths, values, and longings that sit beneath the words of the mentee.

The Mentor-Coach Listens For...

The mentee's...	Definition
Strengths	Gifts and capacities the mentee has within
Values	Core operating principles that serve as the bedrock of who the mentee is
Assumptions	Beliefs and perspectives held by the mentee
Discovery	New awareness and insight on the part of the mentee
Metaphors	Concrete images used to describe abstract concepts
Energy	The body language and energy present or shifting within the mentee
Commitment	How deeply what is being discussed matters to the mentee
What they want	What the mentee is truly wanting; desired result
What they do not want	What the mentee is *not* wanting
Obstacles/"Yeah, but…"	What stands in the way for the mentee
Inner critic	The internal voice that is critical of the mentee
Inner ally	The internal voice that supports and honours the mentee
"Ought to"	The internal "rules" that seek to guide behaviour
What is not being said/what is between the lines	An opportunity for the mentee to notice what is not being said
Growing edge	The rich challenge or stretch for the mentee

The Mentee's Language in Action

The following excerpts of mentor-coaching conversations illustrate how deeply "listening to" the language of the mentee can allow the mentor-coach and mentee to "mine" areas within the mentee for expanded awareness, choice, and clarity together.

a) Strengths

Mentee: I am frustrated with that group of students we talked about before. I have spent time with them exploring their options and encouraging them...and not much has changed... Now what?

Mentor-coach: Clearly you have brought your encouraging self to them. What other strength of yours might you recruit?

b) Assumptions

Mentee: Nothing I say or do is going to make a difference in how this parent views this school!

Mentor-coach: Strong language. "Nothing"...?

c) Metaphor

Mentee: The VP and I are an ocean apart on this, that is clear.

Mentor-coach: Say more about the "ocean"...

d) Energy

Mentee: So my plan is to jump in with both feet; no need to wait any longer. The time is right. I can feel it!

Mentor-coach: I can see you have lots of energy around this. How will it feel to jump in with both feet?

e) Obstacle

> **Mentee:** I am excited about the opportunity to collaborate with my colleagues as we continue to grow our instructional strategies, but I never feel like I know enough…
>
> ***Mentor-coach:*** *What helps you navigate when you feel you don't have enough expertise?*

f) Inner Critic

> **Mentee:** I keep telling you… I feel useless at structuring my day. Every day this week I have arrived determined to navigate the day differently, as we discussed, and each day I get side-swiped by all the demands on my time. I am hopeless.
>
> ***Mentor-coach:*** *"I am hopeless." I am curious about this judgment. Where is your inner critic in this?*

Impact of "Listening To" the Mentee's Language

"Listening to" and using the mentee's language within the mentor-coaching conversation have the following impacts:

- building a trusting relationship
- creating a space in which the mentee is heard and seen, in service of expanding awareness and trust in self, strengths, and capacities
- generating impactful questions that grow out of the mentee's language and insights and serve to expand the mentee's awareness, choices, and action
- accessing the mentee's strengths and gifts as powerful resources for accessing energy, commitment, and intentionality
- inviting heightened awareness of energy, tone, and internal state
- supporting the mentee in discovering and clarifying what really matters

- acknowledging and challenging the mentee

- celebrating learning, growth, and successes

- reflecting back: values, strengths, claiming growth, perspectives, limiting beliefs, and assumptions

- building on the mentee's metaphors and images as windows on meaning

- inviting the mentee to shift perspective: to see the "metaview" as well as the details; to view a "failure" as a critical experiment within the learning

- increasing the capacity of the mentee to notice own filters and barriers

- increasing the mentee's capacity to notice the presence or impact of his or her inner critic and "ought to" tapes, internal monologues, rules, and so on

- supporting the mentee in increasing their awareness of the internal support offered by their inner ally

FROM THE FIELD

Barbara Bower
Professional Learning Facilitator, The Bishop Strachan School

In co-piloting a mentoring program for incoming teachers, I learned very quickly that the most important thing I needed to do was to listen carefully to my colleagues. As a mentor-coach, I had to provide a quiet space for conversations, filter out extraneous distractions, and consciously "check" my own experiences and wise counsel in favour of listening and coaching my colleagues as they worked their way through issues and problems. Prior to conversations now, I consciously remind myself to focus on the other person—to listen, attend to body language, and refrain from shifting attention to myself in any way.

Reflection: Impact of "Listening To" the Mentee's Language

In a discussion or journal, consider and respond to the questions below.

1. What strengths do you bring to your capacity to listen to the language of the mentee? What are your challenges?

2. How will you challenge yourself to "listen to" more of the mentee's language?

3. What are the opportunities, as you further your impact as a deep listener?

4. What is important to you moving forward?

7

Critical Mentor-Coaching Skills: Asking Questions, Focusing on the Mentee's Agenda, and Self-Managing

"Human systems grow in the direction of what they persistently ask questions about."

—COOPERRIDER & WHITNEY, 2005, P. 9

PREVIEW OF CHAPTER 7

In this chapter, we will introduce and explore the skills of

- asking impactful questions

- focusing on the mentee's agenda and commitment to learning, growth, and development

- rigour in self-managing: staying out of fixing, solving, and interpreting—it is the mentee's work

Three Critical Skills of Mentor-Coaching

DIG DEEPER

See the mentor-coaching skills in action in the demonstration video on the *When Mentoring Meets Coaching* website.

As mentor-coach, we ask questions to provoke and invoke reflection, inquiry, action, and growth within the mentee. We continually focus on the mentee's agenda, and we resist any pull to solve problems for the mentee to help keep him or her moving forward on the journey. These three skills—along with those of being present and listening deeply from Chapter 6—are critical for facilitating the relationship and process.

Asking Impactful Questions

"Questions can be dangerous. They can take us right to the edge of what is known and comfortable…can lead to new ways of perceiving…to new explorations of our world…to the perilous, growing edge of our minds."
—Markova, 2000, p. 28

As mentor-coaches, "inquiry is both [our] primary tool and [our] state of mind" (Reynolds, 2014, p. 33). The current shift toward conversations propelled by inquiry, rather than by direction or advice, places a higher value on learning and an awareness that learning demands more on the part of the mentee than simply receiving direction or advice. As mentor-coaches, adopting an inquiry stance invites us to ask questions that truly support the mentee's learning and growth.

By letting go of always having to have the "right answer" and adopting the more open stance of "thinking partner," we can call on our depth of experience to ask questions that provoke the mentee to inquire, reflect, and stretch beyond their perceived limits and choices.

Dr. Heike Bronson
Vice Principal and Mentor-Coach Training Program Facilitator

Asking questions that allow the teacher to think aloud have been my greatest area of learning. I used to feel that I should make suggestions and offer support such as "That sounds good" and "Oh yes, I've used that..." I noticed that when I became too involved in creating choices, it interrupted the creative flow of ideas from the teacher.

The training through the mentor-coaching model has been invaluable in showing me the importance of being present as a curious learning partner in a way that serves the teacher. I feel I accomplish this by asking thought-provoking questions that will support creativity, really holding the space open for the teacher to do the thinking. Holding this space is what fosters creativity and often teachers will be truly amazed with what they come up with.

So What Are the "Best" Questions to Ask?

To assess the value of questions we ask, we need to focus on the impact of the questions on the mentee's awareness, choices, and action. We can do this by watching the mentee's body language and energy levels and, of course, by listening to what the mentee says.

> ### Value of Question = Impact on Mentee's Awareness, Choices, and Action

In the article "The Art of Powerful Questions," Vogt, Brown, and Isaacs (2003) position the impact of questions as "catalyzing insight, innovation, and action" (p. 1). For us, this is a helpful way to look at the key role, value, and skill of asking questions in the coaching process. Vogt et al. believe that questions are used to accelerate the generation of insights, innovation, and action without altering the nature of the "reaction" occurring within the client.

Catalysis—
1) the causing or accelerating of a chemical change by the addition of a substance, which is not permanently affected by the reaction;

2) an action between two or more persons or forces, initiated by an agent that itself remains unaffected by the action (Random House dictionary of the English language, 1966)

The traditional mentor role is often about knowing, telling, answering, fixing, solving and, thus, effectively factoring "self" into the substance that undergoes "chemical reaction." Our approach is to become the "catalyst" through a very different means: listening, inquiring, reflecting, expanding, and navigating the relationship and conversations with questions. By resisting the tug to take on, fix, and solve, mentor-coaches serve as the catalyst for change and growth instead. This is a mindset and skill that grows with attention, intention, and practice.

Our Guide to "Best" Questions

The "best" questions to ask are...

Simple, Clean, and Clear	Results Oriented
Simply constructed, unencumbered questions are easy to understand, and grow directly out of the content, intent, and meaning of what the mentee has just said. **Examples:** • What stands out? • How can you keep this simple?	Goal-, vision-, or results-oriented questions dial up the crispness or power of the mentee's connection with what they want. Forward-moving questions support the mentee, as they step further into choice, action, and accountability. **Examples:** • What will success look like for you? • How will you know you are making a difference?
Poignant and On Target	**Creating Space and Perspective**
Poignant or relevant questions grow out of "listening to" the mentee and speak to the immediacy of expressed concerns. Such questions "touch people with new possibilities and choices and lead to new skills and capabilities" (Hargrove, 2007, p. 255). Keeping the focus on the mentee rather than on the problem also increases the poignancy and traction of the question. **Examples:** • What will this require of you? • Where is the opportunity in this for you?	Effective questions create space. They invite the mentee to examine their own thinking, step back, and access a broader perspective by going up to the 10,000-metre level for a higher perspective, or by reaching forward and imagining success. Such questions can help to reposition the mentee within their frame of reference and provide an opportunity to "look at" what they had previously only been able to "look through" (Kegan & Lahey, 2009, p. 53). **Examples:** • Stepping back, what do you notice? • How else can you look at this?

continued...

Energizing and Emotive	Relationship Building
When we ask the mentee questions that intrigue or feel relevant, there is an energetic or emotional response. Emotions live around things that matter, as do the "best" or the "right" questions. **Examples:** • Where is the energy in this for you? • How will connecting to this emotion support you?	Powerful questions build relationships. Questions that speak to the immediacy and reality of the mentee's experience or concern build connection, trust, and strength in the mentor-coaching relationship. Feeling seen and understood brings people together. **Examples:** • How does your strategic self feel about this? • What sits at the heart of this for you?
Provocative	**Challenging**
Questions that provoke and evoke generate more awareness and further inquiry. They help the mentee dig deeper as they see and feel more. **Examples:** • How can you dig deeper? • What really matters to you in this?	The "best" questions can be challenging for the mentee to respond to, as they can provoke or invite a range of responses: deep reflection and silence, candidness, honesty, regret, courage, excitement, sadness, willingness not to know, or vulnerability. **Examples:** • Noticing the silence… What is critical here? • When will it be time?

Exercise: Creating "Best" Questions

Use "Our Guide to 'Best' Questions," above, to practise creating questions to navigate the conversation with your mentee.

The Impact of Powerful Questions

The diagrams that follow (adapted from Gallwey, 2000, shown in Figure 7.1) illustrate what happens when we ask powerful questions that extend or expand the mentee's capacity to move toward their desired result or change.

Awareness

Choice   **Trust**

Figure 7.1   As an educator, Gallwey offers this diagram to illustrate the relevance and interconnectedness of three fundamental aspects of learning and growth: awareness, choice, and trust. What has inspired us is the notion that, through inquiry, the mentor-coach supports change in the mentee by expanding these three critical and interconnected pieces.

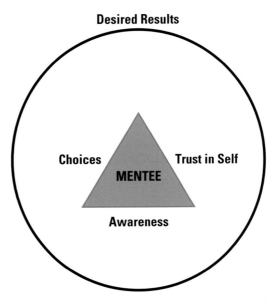

Desired Results

Choices   **Trust in Self**

MENTEE

Awareness

Figure 7.2   The triangle represents the mentee and the agenda they bring to the conversation. The base of the triangle represents the mentee's level of awareness regarding the focus of the agenda; the left side, the choices that they believe exist as a result of their level of awareness; and the right side, the trust they have in themselves to move or step into the required choices.

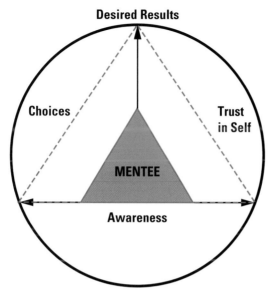

Figure 7.3 When we use the inquiring stance to support the mentee in expanding their awareness, there is an equal and proportionate increase in the mentee's choices and trust in self. With inquiry at the core, the mentee's awareness, choices, and trust in self all expand out toward the mentee's desired results.

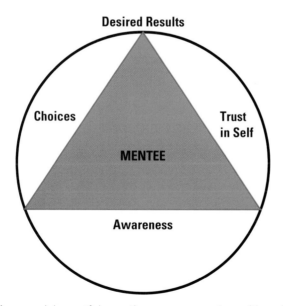

Figure 7.4 As we ask impactful questions, we co-create—with and within the mentee—an expanded frame of reference that supports the mentee in growing toward their desired result.

Figures 7.2 to 7.4 highlight not only the impact we want our questions to have, but also that mentor-coaching conversations create new awareness and understanding. Through our questions, we work with the mentee to access, engage, and expand their capacities in service of the desired result or lasting change that they are wanting. We are helping to create greater attention and intention within the mentee, one conversation at a time.

DIG DEEPER

For more on impactful questions to support expanding awareness, see Chapter 8.

Mentor-Coaching in Action

Questions to Expand Awareness

Mentee: I have been really looking forward to this session. I need to figure out how I'm going to handle having my close friend Nikita on staff. I guess that's what happens when you return as administrator to a school where you used to teach.

Mentor-coach: *Where do things stand currently?*

Mentee: We are both avoiding the topic, to be honest. She's busy doing her thing in the gym, and I'm trying to keep my head above water in the office.

Mentor-coach: *What's been possible as a result of that unofficial agreement?*

Mentee: It's letting me stay focused on more pressing issues. The reality is we're old friends and I know she can see how hard I'm working.

Mentor-coach: *So what are you wanting?*

Mentee: …Well, I think it's something about boundaries… I guess I want her to know that I really value her presence on staff and that I have a job to do this year. I know she'll get that.

Mentor-coach: *What do you want to be sure she understands?*

Mentee: …I need her to know that it's hard being one of her bosses and that I want us to keep the communication doors open.

Mentor-coach: *Open? …What is that going to require of you?*

continued…

Mentee: A settled state of mind…and some time, away from school, for us to have a chat about all this.

Mentor-coach: *What might get in your way?*

Mentee: My bad habit of obsessing over getting things off my "to do" list… That I'm going to jump into the conversation while at school, rather than off site.

Mentor-coach: *So where are you now, as you think about this conversation you're wanting to have?*

Questions to Extend Choices

Mentee: I guess I'm realizing how important it is for me to handle this conversation with love and care. And, that Nikita keeps me grounded, amidst all the unknowns and variables that come with the job.

Mentor-coach: *What will serve to ground you in your conversation with her?*

Mentee: I want to get clear about what I need, in order to feel comfortable having my good friend on staff.

Mentor-coach: *And what do you need?*

Mentee: To not have our friendship compromised by this and to connect with her…and find out what she's thinking.

Mentor-coach: *What else?*

Mentee: I need to trust that the relationship is solid enough to handle this. And not treat it like it is something on my "to do" list…like the leaky faucet in the boys' washroom…

Mentor-coach: *Anything further to consider here?*

Mentee: Stop thinking about it! Just have the conversation! We're meeting this Friday at our favourite coffee spot. We always have the best conversations there.

continued…

Questions to Extend Trust

Mentor-coach: *How are you feeling now about "handling" the conversation with Nikita?*

Mentee: Clear. I need to be sure we have the whole conversation and that I don't let myself get distracted.

Mentor-coach: *What will help you do that?*

Mentee: I will ask her, when we begin, to help me keep this conversation focused, until we get ourselves sorted out. I know I can ask her to do that; I often make this request because we always have lots to talk about.

Mentor-coach: *I am struck by your forthright approach and also by your commitment to your friendship. I also notice how your trust in yourself has increased as you explored how you want to handle this conversation. I know you will handle it with love and care.*

Types of Questions to Ask

Consider the list that follows as a resource and invitation to explore a variety of perspectives in conversation with your mentee.

Opening up the mentee's agenda with questions that invite them to examine themselves and their circumstances from multiple perspectives is a rich, engaging experience. Weaving various types of questions into the conversation is most impactful when the questions grow directly out of what the mentee is saying and the language they are using.

As you review the list, think about your questioning "habits" and which types of questions might be new for you to use. Feel free to take this list with you to your next conversation.

Questions that support the mentee's agenda...

- invite the mentee to get clear about what they want to focus on

Examples:
1. What do you want to focus on today?
2. Say more about the broader meaning of this agenda.

---

continued...

3. Where are you in this?
4. How is this serving what you want?
5. What matters most for you in this?

Questions that expand awareness...

- encourage the mentee to look more widely and deeply at their understanding of present circumstances
- help them to identify what they want
- help them notice the words and metaphors they are using
- help them recognize their strengths, challenges, obstacles, hopes, and goals

Examples:
1. Stepping back, what do you notice?
2. Let's go to 10,000 metres... What do you see?
3. Where are you now?
4. What ground have you claimed?
5. What's emerging? What else?
6. What sits at the centre for you?
7. Where's the energy in all this for you?
8. Let's unpack this... What are some of the key pieces?
9. What else?
10. What's missing?
11. What feels most critical?
12. How is this feeling?
13. If you were to only take the most critical piece forward, which might that be?
14. Where are you in this?
15. What could you leave out?
16. What would travelling light look like?
17. What's taking shape?
18. Where is the edge in this for you?
19. What is the result you are wanting?
20. What strengths do you bring?
21. Where do you want to be?
22. Who do you need to be in this?
23. What do you need to access in yourself?
24. What will it take?
25. What impact are you wanting?
26. How will this serve you?

continued...

Questions that are open-ended...

- encourage the mentee to unpack their level of current understanding, detail, and meaning to increase clarity
- expand awareness, possibility, and new learning, which eventually leads to more effective action

Examples:

1. What do you really want?
2. What will it take to make that happen?
3. What are your assumptions here?
4. What will this get you?
5. What haven't we considered? What's crystal clear for you now?
6. Tell me about…?
7. How was that for you?
8. How can I support you?

Questions that explore current conditions...

DIG DEEPER

For more on impactful questions to explore current conditions, see Chapter 8.

- ground the mentee in the reality of the current conditions vis-à-vis their lived experience and goals or agenda

Examples:

1. Where are you now?
2. What do you know for sure?
3. What questions have you been asking yourself?
4. What would you like to learn more about?
5. What feels like a challenge for you in this?

Questions that surface and challenge the mentee's beliefs and assumptions...

- invite the mentee to notice their underlying beliefs and assumptions

Examples:

1. What belief are you operating from?
2. What assumption are you holding?
3. What is the truth about that?
4. What assumption sits behind what you just said?
5. You "know" you won't be able to do this? …What's the belief that sits underneath that?

continued…

Questions that invite reflection...

- help the mentee see, feel, hear, and observe themselves by "holding up the mirror" and invite the mentee to explore the reflection
- encourage self-generated feedback to enhance relevance and impact

Examples:

1. When you reflect on your experience, what do you notice about yourself?
2. Who are you at your best?
3. Where were you challenged?
4. How has your own thinking contributed to the results?
5. What feedback would be most valuable for you right now?
6. In looking back on it now, what stands out?
7. What do you hear yourself saying as you reflect?
8. How did you feel during the process? ...What's in that for you?
9. If I'd been a fly on the wall, who would I have seen you being? What would I have seen you doing? What feedback would you like to offer yourself?

Questions that serve the mentee's vision and larger purpose...

- touch on the mentee's vision and sense of purpose for themselves and their work
- help the mentee stay connected to the larger idea or drive, amidst all of the "doing"
- access purpose in order to offset "stuckness" or feelings of apathy and lack of motivation

Examples:

1. What is your vision for this?
2. What is the deeper purpose for you in this?
3. What's taking shape here for you?
4. How would this choice align with your vision?
5. If you were to be "purposeful" (act in service of your purpose), what would you do?
6. What is the deeper current running beneath this idea?
7. What does your vision for this look, feel, sound, and smell like?
8. How can you get there?
9. What's the desired change?

Questions that support forward movement and change...

- help to move the mentee forward, a fundamental aspect of mentor-coaching
- support intentionality and concrete action

Examples:

1. What would it take to create change on this issue?
2. What's possible now?

DIG DEEPER

For more on impactful questions to support exploration of vision and purpose, see Chapter 8.

continued...

3. What needs your immediate attention going forward?
4. What's the boldest step you can choose?
5. What conversation can we start today that will ripple out and engage others?
6. What seed, if planted today, will make the biggest difference for you?
7. How will you know when you get there?
8. What are your first steps?
9. How can you be sure that this is going to happen?
10. What strengths will support you? What support do you need?
11. What might get in your way?
12. Where is the challenge in this for you?
13. How is this going to move you forward?
14. What is the title of the song you will be singing?

Questions that generate possibilities...

- invite the mentee to generate a broad range of possibilities to access the most effective action
- broaden perspectives and choices to generate an increased sense of resourcefulness and energy

Examples:
1. What options have you considered?
2. What have you not considered?
3. What's another perspective?
4. What else?
5. If you could do this any way you wanted…?
6. Big picture, what else is possible?
7. What if…?
8. What choice is most aligned?
9. What choice is most compelling?

Questions that stretch and build capacity...

- invite the mentee to stretch into new territory, ideas, and possibilities rather than look back at what they already know

Examples:
1. Where are you in this?
2. What do you want to access in yourself?
3. What strength or gift of yours can you call on?
4. How do you want to show up?
5. Who do you want to be in this?

continued…

6. What's the next level of thinking that you need to access?
7. What's hard in this for you?

Questions that explore the learning edge...

- help the mentee explore their learning edge, the stretch, their capacity "not to know," being a beginner, "learning to swim," and resisting the premature rush or tug for "certainty" and "knowing"

Examples:
1. Where is the edge in this for you?
2. What if you were guaranteed success?
3. What support do you want?
4. What part of yourself have you forgotten?
5. Where does the opportunity for learning begin?
6. Where is the stretch in this for you?
7. What threshold have you arrived at?

Questions that access creativity...

- invite the mentee to own the opportunity before them
- invite the mentee to access their creative spirit and energy
- invite new connections and divergent thinking to stimulate new perspectives, unearth potential, and identify previously unimaginable choices

Examples:
1. What perspective have we not touched on?
2. If you could do this any way you wanted…?
3. What if…?
4. What ideas sit out beyond the realm of right and wrong…?
5. What have you not considered?
6. What's another perspective?
7. Where is the energy in this initiative for you?
8. What does your creative self have to say about this?
9. How can we recruit your creativity here?

Questions that separate the person from the problem... (Epston, 1996)

- support the mentee in naming and clarifying the problem or challenge they are facing and recognizing that it is external to who they are

"Naming and exploring the wider context in which experience takes place changes the way we see and define problems."
—McCashen, 2005, p. 12

continued…

Examples:

1. If you could name the issue…?
2. How would you describe the problem, keeping yourself out of the equation?
3. What do you know for sure about the problem?
4. How would you like the problem to be different?
5. What are you wanting for yourself relative to the issue?
6. What's the new story you are wanting to tell?

Questions that invite the mentee to generate their own questions…

- invite the mentee to identify and step into the question that has been missed, avoided, or not asked
- mine the mentee's creativity, resourcefulness, wisdom, and expertise

Examples:

1. What is the most powerful question I could ask you right now?
2. What are we not talking about?
3. What have we missed?
4. And the question you want to ask yourself right now is…?

How Do We Know Our Question Had Impact?

As mentor-coaches, we know a question has been "effective" when it

- invites new perspective
- generates energy and appetite for forward movement
- invites creativity and deeper insights
- invites stepping back and examining the obvious with fresh eyes
- promotes shifts in mindset, awareness, perspective
- fosters reflection
- surfaces underlying assumptions
- secures the mentee's learning
- calls on the mentee's resourcefulness
- reveals new solutions
- supports adaptation
- shifts the emotion surrounding the mentee or the situation

- stays with the mentee

- generates new choices

- increases the mentee's capacity to create powerful choices and possible action steps

- increases the mentee's depth and breadth of awareness, which increases the depth and breadth of resources available to the mentee to support engagement and capacity building

- "travels well"—when the question spreads beyond the place where it began into larger networks of an organization (Vogt, Brown, & Isaacs, 2003, p. 10)

FROM THE FIELD

Teresa Hadley and Tracy Vanslyke
In-School Resource Teacher and Numeracy Coordinator, K–12, Hastings and Prince Edward District School Board

Another key element of the mentor-coaching program that goes hand in hand with listening and has been essential to our role is *questioning*. Our first reaction when someone comes to us with a problem or a question is often to help them solve it by providing a solution. We know that this doesn't build capacity or honour the strengths of the individual and often doesn't get to the underlying questions the person is really asking. Questions can be a very powerful tool to promote thinking and problem solving, so we have given it a great deal of thought. We have spent time as a team reflecting upon the types of questions we are asking in order to refine and improve this skill in service of supporting others.

Reflection: What's My Type?

In a discussion or journal, consider and respond to the questions below.

1. Which types of questions are you most likely to ask?

2. Which types are you least likely to ask?

3. To extend your capacity to support the mentee, which types of questions do you want to ask?

4. What questions seem the most impactful to use with your mentee?

"Judge a man by his questions rather than his answers."

—*Voltaire*

5. Where is the growing edge for you in your capacity to ask impactful questions?

6. How will you continue to build your skill as a questioner?

Types of Questions to Avoid

Questions that grow out of our judgment, interpretation, or agenda for the mentee...

Examples:
1. This sounds challenging… Is this staff member competent?
2. What if we started with your leadership goals? I think you need to pay attention to them.

Questions that are in service of our curiosity rather than the mentee's agenda...

Examples:
1. How have you found that new social worker in your school?
2. What on earth were the students thinking?
3. How exactly did you make that happen?

Questions that are closed...

- often begin with verbs such as *do, did, does, can, will,* and *are* and can be answered with a "yes" or "no" response
- seldom lead to any new learning for the mentee

Examples:
1. Are things going any better?
2. Do you think you are prepared?
3. Will you be practising regularly?

Questions that are leading or suggestive...

- reflect where we think the conversation should go, rather than inviting the mentee to do her or his own work

Examples:
1. Sounds like some change is required?
2. Have you thought about inviting them in for a conversation?
3. How can you get more teachers involved immediately?

continued…

Questions that are intended to advise or fix...

- can suspend the capacity building and undermine the mentee's competence and confidence

Examples:

1. How about getting someone else to lead the meeting?
2. Clearly the budget is a problem. What about initiating some fundraising?
3. You sound confused. Why don't you think this through again?

Questions that are stacked...

- ask several questions at once

Examples:

1. How do you think it's going to go? ...Are you nervous? ...What support do you need?

Questions that ask "Why?"...

- should be used sparingly as they typically invite a defensive response

Examples:

1. Why did you do that?
2. You aren't going to send the email? Why not?
3. Why do you continue to let that get to you?

Questions that ask for unnecessary detail...

- take up precious time and space without moving the mentee forward and are often in service of our personal curiosity or puzzlement that has nothing to do with the mentee's focus

Examples:

1. What did the parent say?
2. What happened at the meeting?
3. How did you let him know?

Questions that are problem focused...

- can be a slippery slope toward venting, justification, and details, so we need to proceed with caution. Regaining traction and forward movement can be extremely challenging once we start down this line of questioning.

continued...

> - Conversations about challenges need to be positioned as an opportunity for gathering the learning in service of next steps rather than an analysis of the failure or challenge.
>
> **Examples:**
> 1. What is it about this problem that has you all fired up?
> 2. What is stressing you out?
> 3. How long has this been going on?

Generating Questions from the Mentee's Language

The ability to stay connected to the mentee and anchored in his or her frame of reference and language rather than in our own is essential to creating impactful questions. Thus, increasing our attention and intention to listen to the mentee's words and use them in our questions is a practice that will increase our impact as mentor-coaches.

The practice of listening deeply to the mentee's words supports staying in the moment. As mentor-coaches, this shift releases the grip of worrying about the next, "best," or "right" question and lets us connect with the mentee and the emotions, intentions, and subtleties embedded in her or his words.

Building our questions out of what we hear, feel, and notice dials up the level of relevancy. This invites the mentee to lean further into the conversation.

Below are some examples of questions growing out of the mentee's language.

- When you say "rolling along," how does that speak to your intentions?
- "Fine"—what does that mean?
- "Amazed," because…?
- You are "jazzed"… What's "jazzing" you?
- You "have to"? What does that mean for you?
- You're saying "great" and your body language seems to be saying something else.

From the mentee's perspective, hearing their language reflected back in a question confirms that they have been heard. In turn, this supports the building of the relationship and trust. It also supports the mentee in expanding their awareness as it invites them to reflect further on the meaning and significance of their words, thoughts, and feelings.

From a neuroscience perspective, the feelings of safety and fairness that emanate from a conversation with someone who can "relate" to us, invite the brain to release the pleasurable neurochemical oxytocin. This is "the same chemical reaction that a small child experiences when he or she makes physical contact with his or her mother at the moment of birth and onward—this is known as the neurochemistry of safe connectivity" (Rock, 2009, p. 162). The human brain thrives in an environment of trustworthy relationships and safe connections to people. Thus, using the mentee's language in our questions generates a "toward" emotional state that makes the mentee more open to new ideas and more willing to collaborate and connect to the opportunities available.

Questions That Grow Out of "Listening For"

As mentor-coach, we "listen to" the mentee. We also learn to "listen for" moments when the mentee is, or is not, referring to or accessing particular parts of themselves or their situation, such as strengths, values, core beliefs, assumptions, their inner critic, and commitment. The example questions in the table below provide a useful tool to support your enhanced capacity to "listen for" and generate impactful questions.

"Questions can be an invitation, a request, or a missile. What impact do you want your questions to have?"

—Adams, 2011, p. 1

"Listening For" in Action

What does generating impactful questions from "listening for" look like? Consider the examples in the table below.

DIG DEEPER

Note that the table below builds on the "listening for" table offered on p. 138.

"Listening For" Questions

Listen deeply to mentee language for evidence of...	Example Questions Generated from "Listening For"
Strengths	• How can your curiosity [the strength the mentor-coach notices] support you with this difficult conversation?
Values	• I can hear that working independently is important to you. How can you leverage that value of yours in your work with your colleagues?
Assumptions	• What assumptions are you making as you anticipate the conversation with this person?
Discovery	• What are you discovering in yourself through all of this?
Metaphors	• "A mountain of work"? Where are you in that?

continued...

Energy	• Where's the energy in all this for you?
Commitment	• How committed are you to this?
What they want	• How can what you are hoping for inform moving forward?
What they do not want	• So, what do you want?
Obstacles/"Yeah, but…"	• Feels like the "but" is looming large; what's in the way?
Inner critic	• What's your inner critic saying to you right now?
Inner ally	• Great to hear from your inner allies… What else do they have to say?
"Ought to"	• What would shift this from "have to" to "want to"?
What is not being said/ what is between the lines	• Feels like your energy just shifted. What's happening?
Growing edge	• What support do you need as you step further into this challenge?

Reflection: Explore Your Inquiry Mindset

In a discussion or journal, consider and respond to the questions below.

1. How have impactful questions provoked or invoked change or action in your life? in building your capacity?

2. How does using questions and an inquiry mindset show up in your leadership right now? in your practice right now? What difference is it making?

3. "Asking" rather than "telling" is critical, as we support others in building their capacity. What supports you in operating from an inquiring stance?

4. When is a directive mindset likely to take over? How do you support yourself in remembering to stay with an inquiring mindset?

5. Where do your best questions come from? (Consider who you are being or not being, what you are doing or not doing, your mindset, and your intention.)

Exercises: Build Your Capacity to Ask Impactful Questions

1. **Capturing Effective Questions of Impactful Interviewers**
   Some interviewers know how to ask questions that invite the interviewee to go deeper and discover and uncover. Listen to the questions asked by such skilled interviewers on TV, the radio, or

the internet. Record these questions to expand your repertoire, noting the impact of particular questions.

2. **"Instant Replay": Feedback on Your Questions**

   Asking permission to record mentor-coaching conversations and listening to your questions afterwards is an effective way to build your capacity in asking impactful questions. You will find that it is easier to hear yourself and your questions by listening to the recording.

   With your mentee's permission, record your next mentor-coaching conversation, or jot down the questions you ask and note any major shifts or responses from the mentee (e.g., changes in body language, energy, level of engagement, or awareness/perspective).

   After the conversation, ask the mentee for feedback on the impact of the key questions that you asked or any questions that stood out for them. Also, consider the following questions to help you reflect on the responses they provoked and the types of questions you are asking:

   a) What happened to the mentee's

      i)   body positioning?

      ii) energy?

      iii) tone?

      iv) emotion?

      v)   level of engagement?

   b) What new awareness did this question provoke?

   c) How did this question help support forward movement?

   d) What two or three questions could I have asked that would have had a greater impact than those I asked during our session?

   e) Which types of questions am I *not* asking in my conversations?

3. **Questions from Curiosity**

   As mentor-coaches, operating from a place of curiosity supports being in the moment with the mentee and not worrying about what the next question should be. Curiosity also helps as an antidote to any judgments or filters to listening. Creating the space for the compassion and understanding that can accompany genuine curiosity helps us see, hear, and feel more.

In your next mentor-coaching session, try operating from a place of open curiosity—not to satisfy your own interest, but to see where else the conversation can go. Let go of the need to ask any particular type of questions and simply allow yourself to generate questions from a curious mindset. Posting this intention in a subtle place as a reminder can help to support this exercise. Sample questions include:

- Who is this person?

- How might she/he surprise me today?

- What's different about her/him?

- What is she/he paying attention to?

- What matters?

- Where is she/he at?

After the conversation, reflect on the questions below.

a) What is it like for you to ask questions from a place of curiosity?

b) How does curiosity support your ability to access impactful questions?

c) How are your "curious" questions different from other questions?

d) How does being curious help you stay in the moment and listen deeply?

"In coaching, the ideal is to ask truly curious questions with a curious frame of mind. The curious coach doesn't have all the answers. When you are curious, you are no longer in the role of expert. Instead, you are joining clients in a quest to find out what's there. You are exploring their world with them, not superimposing your world on theirs. It is like looking at their world through the wondering eyes of a child."
—Whitworth, H. Kimsey-House, K. Kimsey-House, & Sandahl, 2007, p. 71

4. "Open Sesame": Open Questions Versus Closed Questions

Open questions invite the mentee to explore his or her own experience, situation, or story. Open questions access meaning, relevance, understanding, new perspectives, feelings, and learning. Open questions can also precipitate silence because new connections are often being created, requiring reflection.

Closed questions are useful for checking facts, accessing specific information, and asking for clarification. However, they seldom lead to any new learning for the mentee. Consider, for example, the following closed question:

- Are you satisfied with your work?

Here's how the same question can be asked as an open question:

- When have you been satisfied with your work?

- What is it about your work that satisfies you?

- How would you describe the most satisfying aspects of your work?

- Where do you derive satisfaction in your work?

In your next conversation, or for the rest of the day, notice the closed questions you ask. Retract them in the moment, and tweak them so that they become open questions.

Afterwards, reflect on the questions below.

a) What closed questions did you ask?

b) How were you able to tweak them?

c) What's the difference for you? for the receiver?

Be patient to all that is unsolved in your heart,
And try to love the questions themselves.
Do not seek the answers that cannot be given you,
Because the point is to live everything,
Live the questions now.
Perhaps you will gradually, without noticing it,
Live along some distant day into the answers.
—*Rainer Maria Rilke*

Focusing on the Mentee's Agenda and Commitment to Learning, Growth, and Development

One of the most important characteristics of the mentor-coaching relationship is that the agenda comes from and stays with the mentee. This ties in to the mentee's commitment to growth and development over time as well as to the agenda for each unique conversation.

The intention of the relationship, process, and conversation is for the mentee to work with us, as mentor-coaches, to focus on what is important to them; to collaborate and co-create new learning and new possibilities; and to maximize what they already have within them-selves (e.g., capacity, resourcefulness, strengths, and expertise).

At the beginning of each conversation, our responsibility is to support the mentee in articulating what they want to focus on during the time together. Becoming clear and focused on the agenda upfront sets up the conversation for success. This allows the mentee to co-navigate throughout the conversation, in service of what she or he wants regarding expanding awareness, choices, and possible action. It keeps the conversation on purpose.

Clarity around focus helps ensure that each conversation is about what matters: becoming clear, going deep, and moving toward rich possibilities for action and transformation. It establishes a relation-ship and process that honours the mentee's desires and intentions as the mentee continues to build capacity.

Mentor-Coaching in Action

Becoming Clear About the Mentee's Agenda Upfront

DIG DEEPER
Setting the agenda is the first step in a mentor-coaching conver-sation. See Chapter 8 for an in-depth discussion of the structure.

Mentor-coach: *What would you like to focus on today in our conversation?*

Mentee: I need help with managing my workload; I have so many things that get added to my plate each day that I am feeling snowed under. I arrive in the morning with a plan re priorities, navigating et

continued...

cetera,...and then all sorts of new and often urgent pieces get added. So hard to attend to it all! ...And then there is my ongoing wish to make a difference each day for the students and staff. Sigh!

Mentor-coach: *What is the difference you are wanting to make each day?*

Mentee: There is so much in that for me... My commitment to the kids, period. The energy and focus required of us all, as educators, to foster learning and growth in our students and in ourselves, the excitement I feel as we build a collaborative and caring culture together. And sometimes it feels like I have little time in the day to be purposeful around any of that!

Mentor-coach: *I can hear your deep commitment to making a difference each day. Where would it be most useful for us to look, then, given our time together?*

Mentee: How do I navigate more effectively each day, so that the critical pieces are attended to, and my leadership is making a difference?

Mentor-coach: *Feels like there are two big pieces in this for you: navigating each day more effectively and your leadership making a difference. Where shall we look?*

Mentee: Well, I do have a clear sense of our emerging culture and my role in fostering the growth and development of staff and students. It's critical to me that I connect each day with kids, staff, and parents. But then it feels like there is too much else to attend to... which takes me away from what is most important. And then I can get grumpy and, suddenly, it has all turned into a "to do" list. Not very inspiring! ...I need to look at my navigating.

Mentor-coach: *Navigating it is, then. How can you help yourself hang on to "inspiring" as you navigate?*

Reflection: Setting the Agenda

In a discussion or journal, consider and respond to the questions below.

1. What questions help the mentee become clear about what they want to talk about?

2. What helps you hear what the mentee is really wanting?

3. Which questions have helped clarify the mentee's agenda and its importance? [Capturing some in conversation is helpful to use as reference.]

4. What helps you hold the agenda throughout the conversation? What makes it difficult for you?

5. How are you learning to support the mentee in staying focused and intentional as they explore new awareness and possibilities?

6. What are your strengths and challenges in keeping the conversation about what matters deeply to the mentee?

Rigour in Self-Managing: Staying Out of Fixing, Solving, and Interpreting—It Is the Mentee's Work

Our job, as mentor-coach, is to hold the space for the mentee to explore their chosen agenda, expand awareness, consider choices, and set intentions as they move forward. To hold the space and the process, we must remember that

- it is the mentee doing the work,

- the mentee is creative, and

- the mentee has access to their full resources (even if they do not feel that way in the moment) and has the insights and answers within.

Therefore, as the mentee explores his or her agenda, it is critical that we resist any temptation to step in with suggestions and solutions. Rigour is also required for us not to impose our own interpretation on what the mentee is exploring or uncovering. We must keep in mind that the work is always in service of building capacity in the mentee.

> "If we move in too quickly with solutions, we can make it harder for others to be in touch with their own competence and inner resources, and we unwittingly rob [them] of the opportunity to feel what they are feeling and express it to us. Learning to be an attentive, caring listener and a skilled questioner can empower others to search for their own solutions."
> —Lerner, 2001, p. 46

Furthermore, as mentor-coach, we must cultivate our capacity for non-attachment and not become attached to the mentee's insights, choices, and actions—or our insights and interpretations. This can be particularly challenging if we share similar experiences, have "solved" similar challenges, and so on.

Finally, it is important to continually build our capacity to notice when we are "triggered" as mentor-coaches. This involves, as examples, learning to notice strong emotional responses and compelling personal recollections as we have them in the moment—and, once we notice them, being able to let go of these responses and return to the conversation with the mentee.

FROM THE FIELD

Brian Jones
Leadership Officer/Principal on secondment to the Leadership Development and School Board Governance Branch, Ontario Ministry of Education, and Mentor-Coach Training Program Facilitator

Traditionally, administrators have the "fix it" chromosome and seem conditioned to default to offering advice. However, through trusting the coaching relationship with mutual respect combined with rehearsing the foundational coaching skills, the success rate is high. Our mentor-coaching administrators are reminded to hold the "client creative, resourceful, and whole" and to always invite curiosity to the conversation.

FROM THE FIELD

Ida Kmiec
Former Business Analyst at the Ivey Business School, Western University

As a business analyst at the Ivey Business School, I was brought in to different business areas to solve problems, improve processes, and increase productivity. This process was often threatening to the staff. I found that using a coaching approach, valuing them as important and critical solution builders in the process, increased

continued...

trust and ultimately achieved the best sustainable outcome. The challenge for me was staying true to honouring and trusting the process and not jumping in to offer quick fixes. The magic that happened was that they became empowered and creative and, as a result, a continuing learning culture emerged.

Self-Management in Action

The following is a scenario that came to us from a participant in our program and a few mentor-coaching conversations that stemmed from it. As you consider them, note the possible outcomes of the mentor-coach using (or not using) rigour in self-management.

Mentor-Coaching in Action

Scenario from a Principal in the Field

A mentee (principal) brings forward a dilemma about a performance appraisal. The issue is that the mentee has been working with a teacher on staff to upgrade his teaching practice by incorporating instructional strategies that have been the focus of discussion at the meetings of a professional learning team. The teacher talks a good line in the meetings with the team, but there is little evidence of follow-through in the classroom. The mentee is looking to the mentor-coach for advice on what to do.

Mentor-Coaching Conversations

a) The Pull to Fix, Solve, and Give Advice

Mentee: What should I do to correct this situation? I have to do this teacher's appraisal in the next month and I don't know what to write. He's not doing a good job, but there's not enough reason to assign him a below-standard assessment. I know, with your experience, you'll be able to advise me on what to do.

Mentor-coach getting pulled in:

Mentor-coach: *I have been there, too. Believe me! You need to wade in here immediately. What I know for sure is that you want*

continued…

to be out loud and upfront about your expectations re integrating instructional strategies and the lack of evidence in his practice. Otherwise, it will only get worse. Trust me.

OR

Mentor-coach resisting the tug:

Mentor-coach: What is most critical in all of this for you?

Mentee: I want him to really change his practice. And it feels to me that he is just paying lip service. How do I get him to truly engage in having a real look at best practices?

Mentor-coach: What are you asking of yourself as you approach him around all this?

Mentee: I need to be clear and direct around expectations. And I know I need to believe in him…that he has it in him…build on his strengths. If I don't, how can I expect him to engage and take risks?

b) Staying Out of Interpreting

Mentee: So, I need your direction around handling a colleague who's giving our team a lot of push back around implementing the three-part math lesson. Wondering what we can do to get him to buy in? to join us in experimenting with our kids?

Mentor-coach interpreting:

Mentor-coach: In my experience, teachers who don't buy in often lack a sense of competency in that particular area. Wondering if this teacher struggles with math instruction generally?

OR

Mentor-coach not interpreting:

Mentor-coach: What is most critical for you in this?

Mentee: We need to pull him in… His resistance or reluctance is slowing us down. And, of course, his students must be missing out.

Mentor-coach: So what if it wasn't about "pulling"?

"Mentors should avoid directing the actions of novice principals but facilitate their learning through reflective questions… [T]he goal is to move new principals from 'dependence to independence.'"

—*Wallace Foundation, 2007, p. 12*

Exercises: Building Rigour in Self-Managing

1. **Resisting the Tug to Give Advice, Fix, and Solve**

   a) Have a five-minute conversation with someone who has a challenge or problem they are willing to share with you. Ensure you do not give any advice or offer to fix or solve the problem in any way. Afterwards, debrief with them to see how you did. What did you notice about yourself? the process?

   b) Invite a colleague to share a challenge they are currently having as a leader or teacher. Your job is to ask questions only, no "telling" allowed. Hold the intention that all the questions you ask are to support your colleague in accessing their own strengths, wisdom, clarity, and resources. In contrast, now ask the same colleague to pick another current challenge for the two of you to tackle. This time, let yourself get pulled into offering advice, fixing, and solving. Notice any differences in the way the two kinds of interactions feel. Afterwards, debrief the conversations together: what impact did each have?

   c) When colleagues or students seek your help and advice, practise asking only questions that will support them to build their own capacity.

   d) When friends and family ask for advice, try *not* to give it and to be coach-like instead by asking questions to support them in stepping into their strengths, wisdom, and solutions.

2. **Practising Self-Management Through Role-Playing**
   Enlist colleagues to role-play the following scenarios with you to practise self-management. Be sure to observe the following "rules" of the exercise: invite colleagues to practise in a safe place; when in role, "think" and "feel" as you imagine the person you are playing would; and keep it spontaneous and "real." After each role play, debrief the exercise together, noting the challenges for the mentor-coach in self-managing: staying out of problem solving, fixing, and giving advice.

Scenarios

- A staff member or parent has made an appointment with you, determined to solicit your problem-solving skills and advice with regard to her or his pressing issue.
- You are a mentor-coach who has been working with your mentee for six months, when your mentee arrives and is excited about a new initiative that he or she is stepping into. The mentee wants reassurance and input from you (e.g., your experience, wisdom, and advice). Your job is to remember it is the mentee's work and resist the tug.
- You are a mentor-coach who has been working with your mentee for one year. Your mentee arrives, requesting your help with a previously discussed plan that has been implemented and now feels like a failure. Your job is to remember it is the mentee's work and that the mentee is resourceful and creative (even if they cannot remember that now).

3. **Don't Interpret—It Is the Mentee's Work**

   a) When you are about to interpret what the mentee is saying, challenge yourself to keep silent, leaving space for the mentee to interpret for themselves.

   b) As you listen, learn to notice the urge in yourself to interpret the mentee's words, facial expressions, gestures, body language, and so on. Resist the tug and ask questions instead, such as *What do you mean by that? What are you noticing? What is happening in your body?*

   c) Stay curious and ask questions to support the mentee in exploring their meaning of the words they use and the thoughts and feelings they share.

Best Practices for Sharing Experience and Wisdom

When to Share

Before sharing experience and wisdom, it is helpful to ask ourselves whether our contribution will be in service of the mentee:

- Will sharing my experience serve either to support the mentee in expanding her or his awareness or in moving forward with intention?

- Is this a time to support the mentee in digging within for further perspectives, possibilities, clarity, or resourcefulness?

- Will a succinct sharing of my experience enhance the mentee's awareness at this point?

If so, ask the mentee directly whether sharing wisdom, experience, or a personal recollection is what she or he wants right now to determine whether to share in the moment.

How to Share

Since the focus of sharing is the learning journey of the mentee, it is critical that what we share is timely, relevant, laser focused, and succinct. It is equally important to share it respectfully with authenticity and humility. Following up with a question invites the mentee to make their own meaning and connections to their circumstances: *...of that, what resonates for you, if anything?*

Note how the mentor-coach shares within the sample conversation below.

Mentor-Coaching in Action

Sharing Wisdom and Experience

Mentee: I need your help around how to position things with this very challenging parent I am meeting with this afternoon. I've mentioned her before. Seems we never do enough for her son and now she is threatening to pull him out of the school. I haven't had to deal with this before.

continued...

Mentor-coach: What are your immediate concerns?

Mentee: Well, I do not want to arrive annoyed or get defensive. I believe we have really tried hard to do the best for this student.

Mentor-coach: Would my experience be helpful here?

Mentee: Yes indeed. Not clear how I should be handling this one.

Mentor-coach: In my experience, you need to be sure you have covered all the bases. There is a procedures outline for your reference I will point you to, if you have not already looked there. Also, how you present yourself and the student's teachers is critical. In my experience, it's useful to remember... What, if anything that I've shared, is helpful for you, given where you are in your own thinking?

Mentee: Actually, I have already reviewed the procedures and am up to speed there. I think I need to think about how I can best connect with this woman. I know that if I keep us focused on the best outcome for her child, she will stay engaged. However, in previous conversations, despite my best intentions, I became defensive.

Mentor-coach: What strengths can you draw on to build the connection and commitment that you are wanting?

When the Mentee Asks for Advice or Expertise

Mentee: I keep going back and forth in my mind about what is the best approach. I would appreciate your wisdom around this.

Mentor-coach: In my experience, it is very helpful to involve all the key players. For me...

Is this a "mentoring moment"—a time for the mentor-coach to share relevant information, wisdom, and experience? After all, the mentor-coaching approach encourages the mentee to ask for these things directly.

In moments like this, the challenge for us is to be discerning. If the requested advice or expertise feels premature, we then invite the mentee into further inquiry by asking impactful questions, to support the mentee in digging deeper.

However, when advice or expertise is what the mentee wants, it is critical for us to share according to the best practices discussed in the previous section. We need to be mindful not to overuse the word *I* from a declarative stance, as this can diminish the mentee's trust if they start to feel that it is all about the mentor-coach now. To create an openness and willingness to follow through, we need to keep the spotlight on the mentee.

Remember that we do not want to be attached to our own wisdom or experience. When sharing advice, we can position it as only one of many possible perspectives to create space for the mentee to take the offering in any way they want:

- It seems to me…

- It has been my experience that…

- My feeling is…

- What worked for me was…

"Words are how we think. Narrative is how we link."

—Baldwin, 2005, p. 10

Another approach we can use is to share wisdom through a relevant personal story. Sometimes, sharing a story that relates directly to what the mentee is wondering about can add to the mentee's wisdom and understanding. The challenge here is to distill the experience, and share the essence, in service of the mentee. Remember to invite the mentee to make their own meaning and connections to your story within their own context.

At other times, we might share

- moments of our passion for the work as a way of contributing to intrinsic motivation and support;

- relevant contacts, inviting the mentee to connect with other people who can also support their learning objectives; or

- procedural paths to support effective action and free up energy that would otherwise be wasted in uncertainty and fear going forward.

8 The Mentor-Coaching Conversation: Navigating with Depth, Breadth, and Intentionality

"Truth is an eternal conversation about things that matter, conducted with passion and discipline."

—PALMER, 1998, P. 104

PREVIEW OF CHAPTER 8

In this chapter, we will explore

- mentor-coaching: cultivating conditions for change, one conversation at a time
- a model for navigating the mentor-coaching conversation
- navigating common challenges of mentor-coaching conversations
- seven dimensions of awareness: areas of inquiry to support co-creating awareness

Mentor-Coaching: Cultivating Conditions for Change, One Conversation at a Time

> "Human conversation is the most ancient and easiest way to cultivate the conditions of change—personal change, community and organizational change, planetary change. If we can sit together and talk about what's important to us, we begin to come alive. We share what we see, what we feel, and we listen to what others see and feel."
>
> —*Wheatley, 2002, p. 3*

Conversation—
from the Latin prefix *con*, which means "with," and the verb *vertere*, which means "to turn." Based on this derivation, the definition of conversation is "to turn together, to turn to one another"

At the beginning of all of our mentor-coach training sessions, we read the above passage from Margaret Wheatley's book *Turning to One Another* to the participants. For us, it captures the essence of what is possible when people come together in **conversations** about what matters.

Structured with rich conversations like these, mentor-coaching provides a frame to intentionally "cultivate the conditions" for deep change. Through being together over time, talking about what matters, the mentee continuously steps into intentionality, learning, and growth, supported by the mentor-coach.

Mentor-Coaching Conversations Foster Connection and Relationships

"Substantive change doesn't happen in one hit-and-run conversation... It is the direction we're moving that matters, not the speed of our travel."

—*Lerner, 2001, p. 62*

We are social creatures, hardwired for connection (Lieberman, 2013). Conversation allows us to be present together, in the moment, each with a voice and an experience of being witnessed for who we are and what we stand for.

Siegel and Hartzell (2003) use the term "contingent, collaborative communication" (p. 82) to describe that special experience in a conversation, when each person feels seen and heard, listened to deeply, and fundamentally understood. According to Siegel and Hartzell, in such conversations, we "expand our own minds by taking in others' points of view and seeing our own point of view reflected in their responses" (p. 80).

"...this focus on the mind of another person harnesses neural circuitry that enables two people to 'feel felt' by each other. This state is critical if people in relationships are to feel vibrant and alive, understood and at peace. Research has shown that such attuned relationships promote resilience and longevity."

—*Siegel, 2007, p. xiii–xiv*

Connection through conversation is fundamental to cultivating such relationships. Scott (2002) challenges us to see conversation as the centrepiece of our relationships, suggesting that "the conversation is the relationship" (p. 5). Scott elaborates on this idea, noting, "If the conversation stops, all the possibilities for the relationship become smaller and all of the possibilities for the individuals in the relationship become smaller" (p. 6).

In mentor-coaching, relationships are built one conversation at a time, and the quality of the conversations determines the quality of the relationship. Over many conversations of shared stories and experiences, a common language grows. This often spawns a "shorthand" of shared metaphors, key words, and a specific set of gestures that become part of the ongoing collaborative conversation. As these threads develop, they extend the connection between the mentor-coach and the mentee and take the cognitive, emotional, and social processes to a deeper level. This helps to build purposeful and ongoing mentor-coaching conversations.

DIG DEEPER

For more information on learning in relationship, see Chapter 3.

Reflection: On Conversations

In a discussion or journal, consider and respond to the questions below.

1. In your experience, how does conversation "cultivate the conditions of change—personal change, community and organizational change, planetary change" (Wheatley, 2002, p. 3)?

2. With whom have you had the experience of "feeling felt," of being listened to deeply, of being fundamentally understood?

3. What is it about the person or relationship that allows this to happen?

4. What is your experience of "the conversation is the relationship"? What impact does it have?

Mentor-Coaching Is Collaborative Conversation, Accessing Voice, and Bearing Witness

As mentor-coaches, educators, and leaders, we know how vital it is to show up fully and authentically in conversation—to participate with an open mind (and heart). This allows us to look to understand, to find our own voice, and to share our lived experience. True dialogue is spontaneous and co-created, and it allows participants to uncover new meaning and understanding from individual and collective wisdom and experience.

Bearing witness— being present and listening deeply while another shares a life experience

Another critical aspect of mentor-coaching conversations is the experience of **bearing witness** and being witnessed. Sharing deeply with one another and our feelings of reciprocity and care are sacred. As we listen to the stories, life experiences, and intentions of another, we bear witness. We look through a window on the substance and unique experiences of another and, thus, our worldview expands.

Reflection: On Bearing Witness

In a discussion or journal, consider and respond to the questions below.

1. When have you had a strong sense of bearing witness?

2. What was the impact?

Just as bearing witness has impact, so does being witnessed— saying things out loud, in front of another. When the mentee declares a challenge that they are taking on, or an intention that they are setting for themselves, they are no longer mulling things over. They are asking themselves to step up and make it happen—and they have the built-in support of another, the witness, to help hold them accountable.

DIG DEEPER

For more detail regarding the observer self, see Chapter 9.

Saying things in conversation can also enhance self-observation. We often hear ourselves more clearly and, thus, are able to expand our self-awareness as we notice our language, meaning making, assumptions, and choices. This enhanced capacity to observe ourselves in conversation is a critical piece within mentor-coaching that deepens self-awareness.

Reflection: Observing Yourself

In a discussion or journal, consider and respond to the questions below.

1. When is it easy to observe yourself in action?

2. When is it challenging to observe yourself in action?

3. How might accessing your observer self on a more consistent basis support you?

> "...I speak here of 'response-ability'— that is, the ability to observe ourselves and others in interaction and to respond to a familiar situation in a new and different way."
>
> —Lerner, 1985, p. 14

Noticing Our Internal Conversations

As we navigate mentor-coaching conversations, it is important to look at our internal conversations. Typically we do not notice, let alone acknowledge, these conversations.

In 2007, I heard psychologist Dr. Stephen Madigan speaking at the NASAP (North American Society of Adlerian Psychology) Conference and was intrigued when he suggested that more than 90 percent of the conversations that we have in our lifetimes are with ourselves. Very provocative!

From Jeanie

Since our internal dialogues are a consistent, persistent presence in our daily lives, they have a strong influence on our internal state of being, our feelings about ourselves in the world, our perspectives, and our assumptions. When we are unaware of them, we do not have the opportunity to choose what we are talking about, listening to, or being influenced by.

Sometimes, the variety of our internal voices is referred to as "the committee." Some of these voices have been identified and named, such as the inner critic, the inner ally, and the inner child.

Much attention has been paid in our culture to the inner critic, as it seems to have the biggest, noisiest, and most persistent voice on the committee. The inner critic's messages often include direct attacks on our capabilities, self-image, and self-worth, fostering shame and disappointment in ourselves and affecting who we are *being* and how we show up in the world. We often speak to ourselves more directly, negatively, and harshly than we would ever consider speaking to others (Brown, 2010). By naming our inner critic and helping ourselves notice its presence, we can become aware of its messages and their impact on us. In turn, this awareness can open up the possibilities, in the moment, of being able to choose to listen or to make "changes in how we listen" (Andreas, 2012, p. 5).

Our inner ally—the voice that believes in our gifts and strengths—supports us in our endeavours and helps us remember who we are at our best. If we develop the capacity to hear our internal conversations, we can learn to acknowledge and recruit our inner ally to help us stand tall.

Our inner dialogue also consists of the many stories we tell ourselves about ourselves. Again, being aware of the stories as we tell them can help us choose whether we want to listen, embrace, or change particular stories. Dawna Markova (2000), an international expert in learning and perception, calls some of these stories "rut stories" and "river stories." The "rut" metaphor invites us to notice the stories we are telling ourselves that keep us stuck and no longer serve us, as we endeavour to move forward in our lives. The "river stories" are the stories we tell ourselves that support our evolving self, carried along within the energy and flow of the river.

"When we become aware that we are telling ourselves stories, we begin to have a choice about what stories we are telling, and that is the true beginning of authoring our own existence. *Rut or river* [emphasis added], these strategies of our imagination tell us who we are, what our purpose is, and how we connect, or don't, to the whole... To be in a life of our own definition, we must be able to discover which stories we are following and determine which ones help us grow the most interesting possibilities."
—Markova, 2000, p. 125

Thus, both as mentor-coach and mentee, it is important to be aware of our own internal dialogue of stories and voices. With this awareness, the work then is to support ourselves and each other in cultivating a heightened capacity to notice their presence, influence, and impact in the moment and then to choose to listen or not listen.

Reflection: Your Internal Conversations

In a discussion or journal, consider and respond to the questions below.

1. What is your reaction to the idea that 90 percent of the conversations we have in our lifetime are with ourselves?

2. What challenges do you have with your inner critic?

3. How does your inner ally support you?

4. How do you notice your own rut and river stories?

5. What is the rut story you want to let go of right now in your life?

6. What is the river story that is beckoning you?

"Once you have understood the basic principle of being present as the watcher of what happens inside you—and you 'understand' it by experiencing it—you have at your disposal the most potent transformational tool."

—Tolle, 1999, p. 41

Conversation Is Central to Learning

"True dialogue cannot exist unless the dialoguers engage in critical thinking…thinking which perceives reality as process, as transformation, rather than as a static entity—thinking which does not separate itself from action."

—Freire, 2000, p. 4

Rich dialogue lies at the heart of learning, providing the immediacy of shared energy, curiosity, experimentation, and meaning making. As a result, conversations that foster depth, breadth, integration, and sustainability support transformational learning and growth.

With capacity building as the focus, mentor-coaching conversations hold a large space, inviting the mentee to a deeper level of thinking and awareness. This means moving beyond what Kahneman's (2011) formative work refers to as System 1 ("fast… intuitive…and emotional") thinking into System 2 ("slower…more deliberate…and effortful") thinking (p. 13). Optimizing cognitive abilities and pre-empting our tendency to slide into what is most accessible requires intentionality and consistency. Typically, this is not something we can do on our own—having a "thinking partner" such as a mentor-coach can literally help us think better.

It is also important to have a broad definition of "conversation." More possibilities open up when mentor-coaching conversations include a range of strategies to access the mentee's many ways

DIG DEEPER

See the Mentor-Coaching Toolkit for more examples of strategies to expand mentor-coaching conversations.

of knowing (e.g., kinesthetic, sensory, emotional, social, spiritual, creative, imaginative, and intuitive) to further expand awareness. As mentor-coach, we may invite the mentee to select a card (images or text); experience a visualization or meditation; explore metaphors (words, images, and objects); expand understanding or recollection through writing, drawing, collage, movement, or reading; and so on. We may also have a "walking session" with the mentee, accessing the physical realm to further expand the conversation and the emerging awareness.

Reflection: On Learning in Conversation

In a discussion or journal, consider and respond to the questions below.

1. Recall a conversation that had great impact on your learning. What aspects of the conversation and the relationship were critical?

2. What did the conversation foster in you?

3. When are you at your best as a leader or teacher in conversations that support capacity building and learning in others?

4. What does it take in you?

A Model for Navigating the Mentor-Coaching Conversation

DIG DEEPER

See navigating a mentor-coaching conversation in action in the demonstration video on the *When Mentoring Meets Coaching* website.

Since the mentor-coaching conversation is always about expanding awareness and possibilities for learning and growth, specific aspects are critical for success. We provide the following model for you to use as you navigate the conversation with the depth, breadth, and intentionality that best supports your mentee's transformational learning, capacity building, and growth.

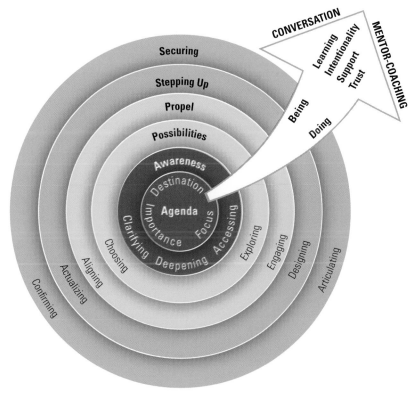

Figure 8.1 Navigating the Mentor-Coaching Conversation
This model provides an overview of the critical layers within the mentor-coaching conversation. The keywords in each layer outline the focus and purpose of the layer.

Six concentric circles with an arrow running through them, from the innermost circle to the outermost circle, represent the model for navigating the mentor-coaching conversation. The arrow represents the relationship and the conversation between the mentee and us, as mentor-coach. The circles represent the layers of the conversation, expanding in size to illustrate the evolving depth and breadth of the conversation, as the mentee's awareness and possibilities grow out toward their desired change.

Each layer plays a critical role in helping the mentee, or student, move from the agenda zone, where they begin, to the securing zone, where they want to be. The keywords in each layer are signposts for the focus and purpose of each step.

Starting with the mentee's agenda in the centre, exploring the possibilities outward, and securing the desired results, is a useful way to describe the structure of the conversation:

- The STOP/Red Zone creates the necessary focus and space for clarity regarding the agenda, followed by in-depth exploration and expansion of awareness.

- The PROCEED WITH CAUTION/Yellow Zone allows for exploring possibilities, resulting in a compelling choice for moving forward.

- The GO/Green Zone steps up and into designing effective action and securing accountability.

This model encompasses all of the guiding mentor-coaching principles outlined in Chapter 1, embodying the following three in particular:

- holding the mentee resourceful, creative, and expert in own life

- supporting strengths, vision, core values, and desired change

- fostering awareness, possibilities, choice, intentionality, and accountability over time

Thus, the model serves as a critical reminder that we are facilitating a process and conversation that is focused on leveraging the mentee's strengths, competencies, expertise, resources, experiences, and talents.

In our experience, it is helpful to refer to this over-arching structure as you co-navigate the ongoing conversations with your mentee. The challenge in this, however, is to avoid using or interpeting the model as a linear, fixed set of steps. Because each conversation is co-created in the moment, spontaneity is vital. As the conversation unfolds, you may need to circle back to particular layers, to clarify or expand, in order to proceed with the necessary energy and commitment.

The model also helps to secure a reflective stance in the mentee, which is critical within this "age of accountability" (Hopmann, 2008, pp. 417–456) and our culture's current focus on external or evidence-based measures. Thus, it balances the outside-in approach of evidence-based accountability with the inside-out approach of mentor-coaching.

Exploring the Layers of the Mentor-Coaching Conversation

In this section, we invite you to explore the mentor-coaching conversation, layer by layer, considering the type of inquiry required at each layer and possible questions to ask.

The STOP `Red Zone`

Agenda: The mentee identifies the **"agenda"** for the conversation. Together, with the mentee, we clarify what the mentee wants to **focus** on and link it to its **importance** for the mentee, at this particular point in time, and the desired **destination** of the conversation.

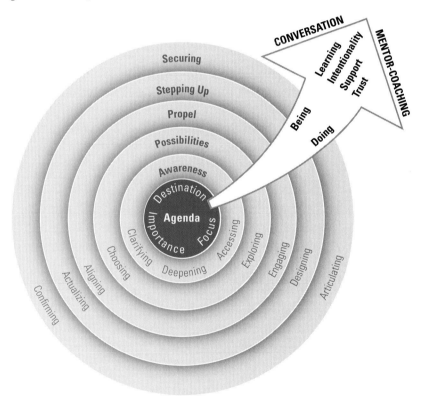

Figure 8.2   Navigating the Mentor-Coaching Conversation
Agenda: Focus, Importance, Destination

By becoming clear together upfront, the conversation has a focus throughout, which helps in co-navigating the conversation:

Focus: Identifying the agenda
Possible questions:

- What would you like to focus on today?

- Say more about the broader meaning of this agenda.

By articulating the deeper meaning, or relevance, of the focus of the conversation, the mentee can connect with what matters to them and what they want for themselves through this process:

Importance: Linking to what really matters
Possible questions:

- What is critical right now about considering this?

- What matters to you in all of this today?

As mentor-coach, by asking the mentee where they want to be by the end of the conversation, we support them in clarifying the purposeful orientation of the conversation:

Destination: Articulating possible outcome
Possible questions:

- Where would you like to be by the end of this conversation?

- What are you hoping to accomplish by looking up close at this today?

In the Conversation

- If the mentee identifies an agenda that seems too big or multi-layered, it is helpful to invite the mentee to narrow the topic by identifying the piece that feels most valuable to focus on and carry forward. It is also useful to ask questions to help the mentee sort and prioritize.
- If the conversation drifts or loses focus, invite the mentee to reconnect with the agenda to clarify where they are now and what needs to happen as they continue.

Awareness: As mentor-coach, in this layer of the conversation, we help the mentee expand their **"awareness"** of the agenda, uncovering and/or clarifying what they want and what really matters. We ask questions that support the mentee in **accessing** internal and external resources, **deepening** their awareness by expanding their understanding of themselves, and **clarifying** intentions and desired focus.

DIG DEEPER

For an in-depth look at expanding awareness, see "Seven Dimensions of Awareness" on p. 210.

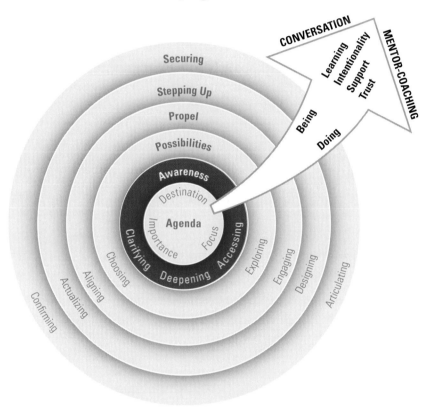

Figure 8.3 Navigating the Mentor-Coaching Conversation
Awareness: Accessing, Deepening, Clarifying

This process helps the mentee see "more" and zero in on what matters to them within their agenda, as new insights emerge through the conversation.

During this part of the conversation, ensuring that the mentee is operating from an optimal depth of awareness is our primary responsibility as mentor-coach. Daniel Kahneman (2011), renowned psychologist and winner of the Nobel Prize in Economics, warns of the pitfalls that overconfidence, framing, biases, and our old stories or "anchors" (pp. 119 ff.) can pull us into. He also tells us that we cannot necessarily override these pitfalls on our own. We *need* an outside

"The main obstacle is that subjective confidence is determined by the coherence of the story one has constructed, not by the quality and amount of the information that supports it."

—Kahneman, 2011, p. 209

perspective. Recognizing that we are operating from a limited perspective or awareness is challenging. So, as mentor-coach, we need to provide the place, space, and structure to help the mentee notice when this occurs and support him or her to step beyond.

In our experience, asking the mentee *Where shall we begin?* is a useful way to start the awareness exploration. Often the mentee has a sense of where to start digging, to uncover new understanding. This also ensures that the work is staying with the mentee.

Accessing: Wisdom, gifts, support
Possible questions:

- What prior wisdom or experience can you draw on here?

- What strengths do you know you have?

Deepening: Expanding and enhancing insight and understanding
Possible questions:

- What sits at the heart of this for you?

- What really matters deeply here?

Clarifying: Intentions, desired focus, and results
Possible questions:

- What's critical in all of this for you, right now?

- Given all we have explored, what stands out for you now in terms of what you are wanting?

DIG DEEPER

For a more extensive discussion of effective feedback and its important role in the mentor-coaching relationship, see Chapter 9.

In the Conversation

- If it feels like it will serve the mentee, we can contribute our own observations and feedback to help expand the mentee's awareness and insight.

The PROCEED WITH CAUTION Yellow Zone

Possibilities: As we continue to progress from the inside out, the focus of the conversation moves from expanding awareness to considering **"possibilities"**—**exploring** and **choosing** possibilities for moving forward based on the new understanding and clarity uncovered in the previous zone.

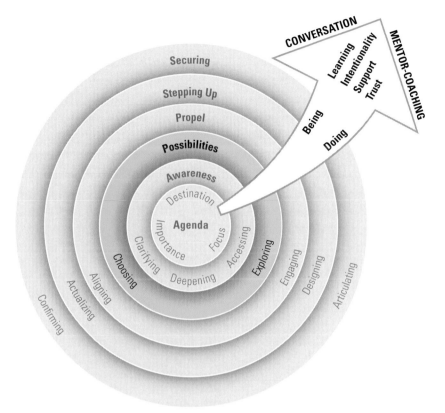

Figure 8.4 Navigating the Mentor-Coaching Conversation
Possibilities: Exploring, Choosing

Together with the mentee, we identify and generate a variety of possibilities for moving forward. The new and expanded awareness, accessed in the previous layer of the conversation, provides a wide perspective from which to spot possibilities. However, if not enough time or attention was invested in the awareness layer, or if the new awareness is not fully leveraged to generate possibilities, the choices that the mentee sees will be limited, or worse, tired and uninspiring. That is why the inside-out approach of the mentor-coaching conversation is important. As shown in Figure 8.4, each layer of the conversation grows out of the previous layer. This allows for due consideration to happen and the cumulative effect of the layers to build.

"How is my behavior opening up possibilities? How is my behavior shutting down possibilities?"
—*Cashman, 1995, p. 115*

"A person stands in the great space of possibility in a posture of openness, with an unfettered imagination of what can be."
—*Zander & Zander, 2002, p. 19*

Expanding Awareness = Expanding Choices

In generating possibilities, it is important to keep the mentee's agenda present in the conversation. The interaction between the possibilities and intention will help to keep the mentee's awareness, choices, and desired action aligned. As mentor-coach, our job is to help prevent the mentee from wandering off the path or losing sight of her or his end goal: the desired change.

Nevertheless, exploring options may prompt the mentee to change, or make necessary shifts in, his or her intention. This interaction between the possibilities and intention is part of what makes the conversation vital and alive. As we have all experienced, sometimes when we share our choices or intentions with others, we realize that a tweak or change of course is in order. Having the space and opportunity to expand or refine our choices or target is often the difference between success, moderate success, and failure.

As mentor-coach, we want to provide the mentee with the space and support necessary to explore the possibilities for moving forward. This means helping the mentee continue to articulate, and stay firmly connected to, the relationship between what they are choosing to *do* (or *be*) now and the intended destination. For example, if a mentee's goal is to increase their ability to offer honest, valuable feedback to their direct reports and they are considering taking a course to learn more, we could ask: *How does this course align with your end-goal of offering honest and valuable feedback? …How else could you increase this ability you want? …What haven't we considered?* Creating the opportunity for the mentee to identify a direct link between a choice they are making and the capacity they want to build is time well spent.

As mentor-coach, we may offer to brainstorm ideas or provide relevant feedback during the process of generating possibilities, remembering to ask permission before giving suggestions or observations. Above all, it is important to create a safe environment for putting ideas forward. Holding a big space for the process by being fully present, listening deeply, and welcoming all ideas without judgment has a powerful impact and invites the mentee into a place of thoughtful consideration and exploration.

In the Conversation

- If the mentee is restricted by self-limiting assumptions and beliefs, it can be helpful to ask *What if...* to counter any objections that might arise from these self-imposed limitations.
- If the conversation feels restricted or the mentee is not engaged, inviting them to reach out, beyond, or underneath what is in the way, can open up the dialogue.

Considering the possibilities and what will be required to pursue them is an important part of the conversation that helps the mentee evaluate the various options. Exploring the benefits and costs of each can also help refine the journey forward as the mentee identifies her or his most compelling next step.

Once all the possibilities have been explored, the conversation focuses on choosing the option that feels the most enticing and making the commitment to its requirements.

Cautionary Notes

- As mentor-coach, we need to be careful not to become attached to the mentee's choices or intentions throughout the process, as difficult as this might be.

- If we feel that the mentee is putting themselves or others at risk, asking permission to share observations is recommended.

- We need to watch for—and resist—the pull to interpret through the lens of our own experiences what the mentee shares and chooses.

The following questions are helpful to ask in the "possibilities" layer of the mentor-coaching conversation.

Exploring: Opening up a wide range of possibilities
Possible questions:

- What are the possibilities here?

- What else...? What else...?

- What do you really want to achieve? What will help make this happen?

- In stepping back, what other options can you see?

- Big picture, what else is possible?

- If you made this easy, what would your choices be?

- If you could do this any way you wanted…?

- What possibilities have you not considered?

- What if…? [to counter limiting assumptions or beliefs]

- How else can you look at this? What does that new perspective provide you with?

Choosing: Considering which possibilities resonate and intrigue; selecting an option that will bring desired results

Possible questions:

- Which possibilities do you find most intriguing?

- Which of the choices do you have the most energy around?

- Standing back, which choice(s) will have the greatest impact?

- Which choice is most aligned with what you are wanting?

- Which option will "propel" you forward?

"Let yourself be silently drawn by the stronger pull of what you really love."

—*Rumi*

"Commitment is the key not the lock."

—*Kate Sharpe*

Propel: In this layer of the conversation, the mentee calibrates the "pull" that their choice has for them, in order to notice their energy and commitment level as they consider being mobilized or, **"propelled,"** by their choice into effective action. As mentor-coach, we listen and watch for **engagement** and **alignment** to see whether the choice truly evokes the energy and forward focus of the "best" or "most impactful" next step.

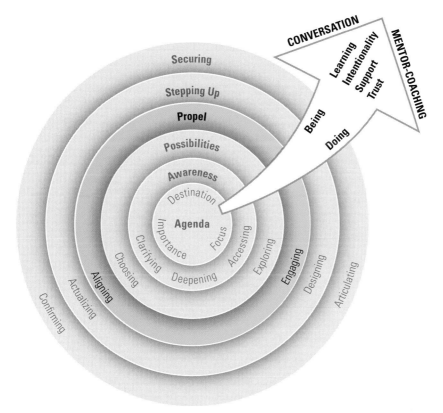

Figure 8.5 Navigating the Mentor-Coaching Conversation
Propel: Engaging, Aligning

As always, in our inquiry-based stance as mentor-coach, we offer a selection of open-ended questions to support the mentee as they reflect on their choice. We listen deeply and watch the mentee's body language, emotions, facial expressions, and general demeanour as they respond. These externalizations provide an initial read on the mentee's level of commitment to moving forward, and are often more revealing than their words.

As mentor-coach, we can also play a fortifying role at this critical stage in the conversation by asking questions that create the space for the mentee to connect with and articulate their trust in their own resourcefulness and capacity to be successful. This is not the typical territory that leaders or teachers explore in conversations with staff or students, yet it is the lifeblood of action.

Engaging: Energy and commitment
Possible questions:

- How is this feeling for you?

- What's important to you about this choice?

- On a scale of 1 to 10, how much energy do you have around making this choice happen?

- What strengths will support you in embracing this?

Aligning: Growing out of new awareness and desired results
Possible questions:

- How does this choice align with your intentions?

- What is the relationship between your choice and your desired result?

- How will stepping into this choice serve you?

The GO   Green Zone

Stepping Up: In this layer of the conversation, having identified the choice that feels most aligned with his or her intention, the mentee is purposefully **"stepping up"** into action. By **designing** compelling action, **actualizing** resources to act, and clearing obstacles, the mentee is setting up for success.

It is helpful to keep this phase of the conversation as concrete as possible: *What will be happening? When? Where? Who will be involved? How will you structure the…?* (e.g., conversation, space).

Remembering to go deeper and help the mentee become clear on who they need to *be* as they *do* whatever has been identified as crucial. In our experience, it is often who the mentee is *being* (e.g., courageous, focused, tenacious, or committed) that drives effective action. For this reason, creating the space for the mentee to become clear on their part in the process is vital for actualizing to happen.

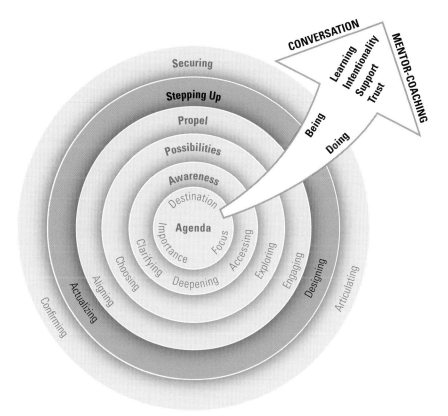

Figure 8.6   Navigating the Mentor-Coaching Conversation
Stepping Up: Designing, Actualizing

Designing is creating a concrete plan of action that includes

- the specific action(s) the mentee is stepping into (what, where, when, who, and how), and

- the nature of the action (Is it internal or external? Who will it require the mentee to *be?* What will it require the mentee to *do?*).

It is important to make the time for the mentee to articulate an action plan for "stepping up." Playing the plan through and visualizing, drafting, recording, outlining, or sketching a design of the process provides yet another opportunity for refinement, realignment, or correction. Resisting the mentee's tug to "get going" without a concrete action plan is essential.

As mentor-coach, it is useful to notice the mentee's planning style and gauge the depth and detail of the questioning, so that it aligns with what the situation requires. If we see that the mentee is planning with too broad an outline, asking questions that invite attention to critical details can be extremely helpful. Our wisdom and expertise is an invaluable resource, particularly at this point in the design stage.

Through this process of articulating a plan, the mentee is compelled to draw on their commitment as they consider the action's viability. This is when we can hear confirmation or see cracks in the mentee's resolve made in the "propel" layer. Uncertainty or tentative language is our cue, as mentor-coach, to ask the mentee whether they want to circle back and reconsider, tweak, or change the choice or action they have identified. Our primary commitment is to the mentee's success, so encouraging them to customize their plan whenever necessary is a critical part of our role.

Actualizing is accessing internal and external resources and making a plan happen. It includes

- accessing key resources and support; addressing possible obstacles

- securing a concrete action plan (including both *doing* and *being*)

- scheduling or clearing space so the action is possible

- checking in on how the plan is feeling for the mentee

In the "stepping up" phase of the conversation, our focus is to help the mentee reach the point where they feel they have their arms (planning) and their head/heart (viability) around the steps they will take when they leave the session.

Supporting the mentee in accessing key resources in their life and work helps them "step up," as they consider how they will actualize their action plan. The more resourced the mentee feels, the more they will trust themselves and feel propelled forward. We want to encourage them to tap into their internal resources (energy, strengths, experience, values, beliefs, and gifts) and external resources (training, finances, reading, courses, software, peer group, curriculum guides, and leadership frameworks).

At this point in the conversation, we also have an opportunity to invite the mentee to identify possible obstacles and scan for signs of doubt or fear. Legitimizing doubt (Kahneman, 2011) by giving it a voice creates the space to address it, get it out of the way, and create a better plan.

As mentor-coach, our objectivity and questions can help to uncover anything that may have been missed or stepped over.

It is important to recognize that "action" is a broad term that may include reflection, learning, making space or time, researching, having a conversation, and so on. Ensuring that the mentee has clarity around what an action will "actually" look like is critical. However, it is important to assess the mentee's needs. If it feels like the mentee is crystal clear on their action plan, and that spelling things out is unnecessary, we can move on to "securing" accountability.

Designing: Creating a concrete plan of action
Possible questions:

- How will you "step up" to make this choice a reality?

- What specific actions are you stepping into?

- What are your first steps?

- What's the boldest step you can choose?

- How will you make it happen?

- What belief sits underneath all of this?

- What matters most in all of this for you?

- Who do you need to be in this?

- What will it require of you (*doing* and *being*)?

Actualizing: Accessing internal and external resources and making it happen
Possible questions:

- Which strengths will support you in this?

- What past experiences can you leverage?

- What further support and resources will you need to access?

- What might get in the way? How will you manage the interference?

- What does "stepping into action" look like for you now?

- What are the key pieces in the plan?

- How do you see the plan unfolding?

- What does the timeline look like?

- How will you know when you get there?

- How are you feeling as you move forward?

Securing: In the current culture of accountability, the notion of **"securing"** accountability may seem unnecessary. However, current research tells us that being encouraged to articulate what we want (purpose), what we will do to get it (autonomy), and how it will contribute to our level of competence (mastery) motivates people (Pink, 2010). Therefore, **articulating** and **confirming** accountability for action and desired change in this layer of the conversation increases motivation. Furthermore, as with all mentor-coaching conversations, it happens in an appealing way.

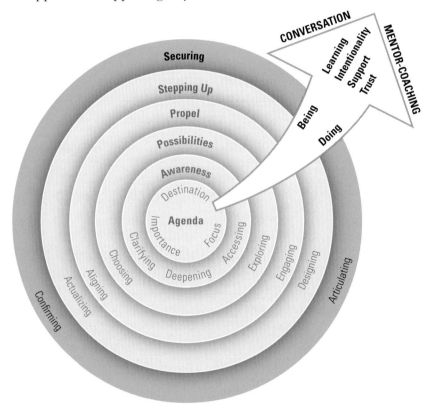

Figure 8.7 Navigating the Mentor-Coaching Conversation
Securing: Articulating, Confirming

Together with the mentee, we clarify how the mentee will secure their own accountability for the action they have committed to take. It is important to remember not to take on the responsibility for accountability. As mentor-coach, our job is to help the mentee become clear on how best to ensure action. We serve as the mentee's "accountability partner" (Hayashi, 2011, p. 128). We are present, at regular intervals, to share in and secure the mentee's learning and progress. The mentee owns and confirms the action, results, and accountability. This clear delineation of roles and responsibilities keeps the capacity building front and centre.

If it will serve the mentee, we can offer to receive updates regarding actions or goals met. Since the mentor-coaching process happens over time, the mentee may find it useful to report on her or his progress at the beginning of the next conversation.

Articulating: Responsibility
Possible questions:

- How will you hold yourself accountable?

- How would you like to keep track of your progress?

- What do you want to be watching for?

- How will you measure or capture your success?

Confirming: Making sure the action happens
Possible questions:

- How will you be sure that this happens?

- What further support, if any, do you want, in terms of holding yourself accountable?

- What is this going to take in you?

Completing the Conversation: In the final layer of the conversation, it is important to check in with the mentee about what you have co-created and whether the conversation has met their needs. Linking back to the initial agenda and supporting the mentee in recognizing where they started and where they are now anchors the learning and growth and helps them notice movement. Inviting the mentee to acknowledge themselves and how they have shown up in the conversation is often a powerful way to complete the conversation.

DIG DEEPER

For a template and digital model of navigating the mentor-coaching conversation, see the Mentor-Coaching Toolkit.

The Arrow Runs Through

As mentor-coach, our work in navigating the conversation is described inside the arrow (see Figure 8.8)—and it comes to life in who we are **being** and what we are **doing** to facilitate the process.

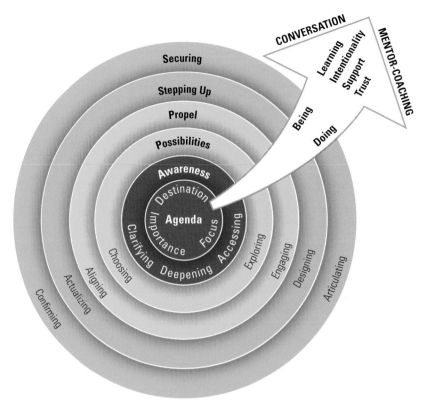

Figure 8.8 Navigating the Mentor-Coaching Conversation: Being, Doing, LIST

We continue to secure learning, intentionality, support, and trust (**LIST**) throughout the conversation, as noted in the tip of the arrow. Checking in with the mentee to see how each of these elements is showing up for him or her as the conversation unfolds helps us maintain a purposeful orientation within the conversation.

Securing: The learning, intentionality, support, and trust
Possible questions:

- What's new for you here?

- Where is the learning edge in this for you?

- What ground have you claimed?

- What's your broader intention around this?

- How do you want this to play out?

- How supported are you feeling (internally and externally)? What do you want to dial up or down?

- What resources (internal and external) do you want to draw on or access?

- On a scale of 1 of 10, where is your trust in self? [If low, investigate support and resources and what more may be wanted.]

Navigating Common Challenges of Mentor-Coaching Conversations

What If the Conversation Feels Too Superficial?

It is important to connect upfront with what matters to the mentee about addressing the particular "agenda" for the conversation. This helps the mentee connect with her or his deeper wants as the exploration begins.

If it feels like the mentee is speaking only to what is superficial, it can be helpful to reflect back what we are noticing and ask questions that invite the mentee to go deeper.

As always, we need to begin by asking permission to share our observations:

- Would it be helpful to share what I'm noticing?

  If the mentee says yes, we can continue:

- It feels like you are speaking to what's on the surface of this issue for you. What sits underneath? What forces are at play here? What other details would be helpful to share?

- Where are you in this?

- Where's the heart of this for you? Given that, where would you like us to focus our conversation?

- What feels central in all of this for you?

- It feels like we're dancing along the top of this issue for you. What matters for you in this? What would help you stay connected to that?

It can also help to reconnect the mentee with their larger goal or purpose:

- Where are you trying to get here? Given that, how are you doing?
- What will it take in you?

What Do You Do If All the Mentee Wants to Do Is Step into Action?

As mentor-coach, our goal is to ensure that the mentee is positioned for success. Inviting them to take the time to identify their target in relation to where they are now and where they will need to be to hit it, can help mitigate the sense of urgency and excitement.

Providing a moment to pause helps ensure that the intentionality central to the process is alive and well. Then we can ask questions that create breathing space to reground the mentee in deeper (less reactive) thinking. Spending time expanding awareness and going deeper will lead to new possibilities and a richer sense of the change that the mentee wants and what it will take to make it happen.

What Do You Do If the Agenda Changes as the Conversation Evolves?

It is not uncommon for the agenda to morph as the mentee processes an issue and peels back the layers. As mentor-coach, it is our job to keep the conversation focused on the most vital pieces. Thus, if we notice a shift in focus or agenda, it is important to reflect this back to the mentee. Then they have a chance to clarify where they are now in the conversation and identify a revised focus. This may then involve circling back through the red and yellow layers of the conversation to open up their awareness and identify their revised choice before stepping into action.

What Do You Do If the Mentee Arrives with No Agenda?

As mentor-coach, our success depends on our ability to meet the mentee exactly where they are. If they are unclear or arrive without a focus for the session, we want to be with them in their uncertainty and ask questions that will help them to become clear on their agenda as they continue to journey forward. From a process perspective, beginning by inviting the mentee to step back and orient themselves is valuable.

Offering the mentee an attunement that invites the mentee to go inside and notice their internal state may support them in arriving mentally and physically, and being fully present. Letting go of, or articulating, distractions that may have happened prior to the session is often very helpful. Attunements can include picking a card, scanning the past week for "noteworthy landmarks" (e.g., successes, learning, new awareness, and challenges), or looking out the window to find an object that beckons, and these can often inform the rest of the session.

DIG DEEPER

For more information on attunements, see Chapter 6 and the Mentor-Coaching Toolkit.

Another strategy to help the mentee clarify their agenda is to invite them to scan their recent challenges and successes, and identify one that feels valuable to explore. You can also look back together at the initial agreed-on objectives of the mentor-coaching process and ask the mentee to identify what feels relevant or what thread they would like to pick up.

What Do You Do If the Conversation Doesn't Unfold Sequentially?

Remember that mentor-coaching conversations do not always flow sequentially or remain forward-focused. Watch for opportunities when layers need to be revisited, streamlined, or revised. As mentor-coach, our primary commitment is to the mentee's success and to work from the inside out in navigating the conversation. To that end, checking in with the mentee to ensure that we are on track is important.

Above all, we want to ensure that we are

- moving forward relative to the mentee's focus or goal; and

- following the basic structure of the mentor-coaching conversation: helping deepen awareness, invoking new possibilities, and realizing desired and aligned action.

The movement and path within the structure depend on the situation and larger intention of the mentee.

What Do You Do If the Mentee Is Stuck and Can't See Any Choices or Other Alternatives?

Feeling stuck, with little sense of the capacity to change anything, is a challenging place to be for any of us. If the mentee feels stuck as they explore their agenda, it is important for us, as mentor-coach, to notice and then to remind ourselves that, despite the mentee's present sense of not being able to move forward, they are resourceful and creative. By expanding awareness, the mentee may be able to become "unstuck" and access possibilities for action.

When we notice that the mentee is stuck, we may want to reflect this back to them. As mentor-coach, we need to be careful not to get pulled into their "stuckness," as it can be contagious. We may suddenly find ourselves offering suggestions and giving advice, having lost sight of the mentee's resourceful and creative self.

It is useful to remember that feeling stuck is often a by-product of mindset or perspective. Asking questions that prompt the mentee to access the reality of what he or she is (or is not) seeing, feeling, or hearing can sometimes help to create a provocative dissonance that mobilizes the mentee.

Possible questions for expanding awareness when stuck:

- Look around, where are you? How would you describe your current perspective or mindset? What are you seeing? What are you not seeing? What would you like to be seeing?

- Where would you like to be? What's in the way? What do you need? Where can you get it?

- What's on offer here? What's taking shape?

- What do you know about "stuck"? What wisdom or experience can you access here?

- What typically helps you get unstuck?

- What part of yourself are you not accessing?

- What strengths, creative gifts, or talents can you call into action here?

Sometimes, the mentee can be too close to an issue, so helping them step back or up can be helpful.

Possible questions for accessing a broader view when stuck:

- Inviting you up to 10,000 metres: what can you see from here? What do you notice? Where are you now? Where do you want to be? What's in-between?

- What choices do you have? How do those choices feel?

- What's not on that list? What choices would you like on the list?

- How can we open things up for you?

- Freeing you up from the concrete for a moment, what's the larger objective behind all this? What's the deeper want?

Identifying the "Yeah, buts…" and what is getting in the way (limiting beliefs and assumptions) can also help the mentee see their way through. Naming the situation they feel they are in—being stuck—then imagining their success or change as realized and considering how they might make that happen is another helpful strategy. Calling on past successes and capacities to "move through" can create space and a sense of resourcefulness. It also helps to build a greater sense of self-efficacy.

What Do You Do If You Don't Get Through All the Layers of the Conversation?

Navigating the mentor-coaching conversation takes time, space, and intentionality. There will be times when the conversation is almost over and the mentee has not yet arrived at a clear articulation of what "stepping up" will look like.

Shortly before the end of the conversation, regardless of where the mentee is in the process, we always want to honour the mentee and their movement in the mentor-coaching process and conversation. We can do this by inviting them to a relevant place of action through any of the following questions that support forward momentum:

- Where are you now?

- What are you taking from this conversation?

- What piece of this do you want to pick up or focus on between now and next session? How will you do that?

- What inquiry do you want to carry forward from this conversation?

- What thinking/reading/reflecting/digging/drafting will you be doing when you leave here?

Seven Dimensions of Awareness: Areas of Inquiry to Support Co-creating Awareness

"Real change only happens when people see things they haven't seen before"
—Rock, 2009, p. 218

Expanded awareness is important in all layers of the mentor-coaching conversation.

To support deepening awareness and understanding within the mentee, we invite you to consider seven possible areas of inquiry and to explore them, as needed, as each unique conversation unfolds.

We need to have awareness of the following:

1. Current reality relative to the goal or desired change

2. Own strengths and gifts

3. Internal and external resources

4. Own values

5. What gets in the way

6. Vision and purpose

7. Mindset

As mentor-coach, we can share the seven dimensions of awareness with the mentee when

- it feels like further depth or resources are required in a conversation; or

- it seems that the mentee is operating from a constricted perspective, and is stuck, wavering, or uninspired.

Considering the following questions provided for each dimension will help with digging, deepening, and expanding awareness.

1. Awareness of Current Reality Relative to the Goal or Desired Change

The first dimension of awareness explores the accuracy of the mentee's perception and understanding of their current reality, the conditions surrounding them, and their desired goal.

For the mentee to maximize mobility and available choices, they must be aware of the reality that they hold and, without unhelpful judgment, explore whether it serves them as they move forward. For some, the idea that the beliefs they hold about their current conditions and "reality" can be altered to better suit their objectives is revolutionary.

Being well anchored, with a strong sense of their current reality, helps to offset the pull of old stories or past experiences that can derail or inhibit the mentee. Working in the territory of "what is" versus "what was," "what is not," or "what should be" provides firm ground from which to step forward. If the current reality is difficult or upsetting, it is important to note that this territory can be unsettling for the mentee. As mentor-coach, we need to stay unattached and not get hooked by strong emotions that may surround the situation for the mentee. Our capacity to support the mentee as mentor-coach depends on our ability to maintain this objective stance and our ability to hold the mentee as resourceful, creative, and expert in their own life.

Open-ended questions to support expanding awareness of current reality relative to goal or desired change:

- What's happening?

- What stands out?

- What do you notice when you look at…?

- How do you feel about the situation?

- What do you understand about…? What don't you understand?

- As simply as possible, what's the underlying challenge for you in this?

- How would you define the task at hand?

- What are the critical variables in this situation?

- How do they relate to one another?

- What standards and time frame have you accepted around this?

> "Only when people begin to see from within the forces that shape their reality and to see their part in how those forces might evolve, does vision become powerful."
>
> —Senge, Scharmer, Jaworski, & Flowers, 2004, p. 132

> We need to train ourselves to challenge the stories we tell ourselves about ourselves and the world…and "be present with what [we]…actually experience."
>
> —Markova, 2000, p. 41

2. Awareness of Own Strengths and Gifts

"Instructions for living a life: Pay attention. Be astonished. Tell about it."

—Oliver, 2008, p. 37

DIG DEEPER

For a more extensive discussion on the role of a strengths-based approach to capacity building, see Chapter 2.

The second dimension of awareness is about providing the mentee with opportunities to articulate and lay claim to their strengths and gifts, which will support them in moving purposefully forward. This awareness increases the mentee's sense of resourcefulness by reconnecting them with their whole self. It can also help to offset a bias, unhelpful perception, or mindset toward overemphasizing or becoming attached to what is lacking, weak, or missing.

Strengths are "large muscle groups" that we can engage to support the heavy lifting that sustainable growth and change require. They are the competencies, gifts, and talents that we know in ourselves, and can easily recruit to support us. Accessing them early in the conversation and recruiting them throughout to help build capacity is central to the mentor-coaching process.

Open-ended questions to support expanding awareness of own strengths and gifts:

- What strengths do you bring to this?
- What strengths of yours can we recruit to help?
- Where do you feel strong?
- What's the biggest tool in your kit? How can you bring it into play?
- What gifts or talents do you know you can call on?
- Who are you at your best? How can we recruit that person in this situation?
- Where can you work your magic?

3. Awareness of Internal and External Resources

Internal resources can easily be assumed or stepped over by the mentee, especially as the mentee focuses on something that seems external. For example, when a leader receives a new role, challenges around particular responsibilities are often framed in terms of expertise or training that is lacking. When this happens, inviting the mentee to work from the inside out and identify the internal resources that can best support their current goal can increase their level of self-trust as they will feel more resourced to step into the learning and growth that is required.

Internal resources include strengths and gifts, as discussed above, as well as wisdom that the mentee has from past experiences, previous training, memories, and so on. Specific capacities that one has developed, such as resilience, interest, creativity, self-regulation, "grit" (Duckworth, Peterson, Matthews, & Kelly, 2007, pp. 1087–1088), adaptability, imagination, patience, core values, and sense of humour, are also vital ingredients that fortify and nourish the process of change and growth. Having these gifts and capacities present and accessible in the conversation shifts the stance, energy, and engagement level of the mentee.

Without access to their strengths and gifts, the mentee may feel like they are working outside themselves, which in essence they are. As mentor-coach, we may need to invite the mentee to become aware of their physical, mental, and spiritual capacities, which they will need to access to actualize the desired change. Ensuring that the mentee can sustain the energy, focus, emotional connection, and fortitude required for change and growth is an essential part of the conversation because it speaks to how the mentee will *be* amidst all their *doing*.

External resources may be more obvious. However, as mentor-coach, we want to ensure that we recruit them as we continue to access, expand, and deepen the mentee's self-awareness as she or he works toward the desired change. External resources include support from people, mentors, friends, family, community, books, and the immediate environment. Physical resources, such as the mentee's home environment, office, tools, and virtual support can also be a helpful place to look when the mentee feels under-resourced. In our experience working with both individuals and teams, people always bring more to "the job" than they realize. Accessing and building on what is already there, when it feels relevant, is prudent and can serve as an antidote to inertia or reluctance, increasing the mentee's level of engagement.

Time and money are two high-profile external resources with extraordinary influence over people's sense of what is and is not possible. As with all external resources, asking questions that help the mentee become grounded and work with, rather than against, the available time and money is valuable in invoking new perspectives. Time and money may also be part of the "current reality" conversations that occur in the first dimension of awareness.

"Imagination is more important than knowledge. For while knowledge defines all we currently know and understand, imagination points to all we might yet discover and create."
—*Albert Einstein*

Open-ended questions to support expanding awareness of internal resources:

- What past successes have supported you?

- What wisdom do you bring to this?

- What previous training or experiences can we recruit here?

- How can your creative talents and gifts contribute?

- Where is the interesting part in this for you?

- How do you help yourself be patient? *or* What supports patience within you?

- How can you support your physical self in this process?

- What helps you stay resilient?

- Where do you go for inspiration?

- How can we continue to create space for your imagination in this?

- What core values do you want to be sure you are honouring as you go forward?

- Who do you want to be in this?

- What does your wise self (creative self, and so on) say?

- What helps you stay focused?

Open-ended questions to support expanding awareness of external resources:

- Who would be a valuable resource to access?

- [Magic-wand question] If you could call on anyone right now, who might that be? What would they likely tell you?

- What resources do you know you already have and can access?

- What can we build on?

- If you were to stand on the shoulders of pre-existing work, what might that be?

- What books or programs might support you?

- What further learning, knowledge, skills, or practice do you want?

- If you were to spend your time and money as efficiently and productively as possible, what might that look like?

4. Awareness of Own Values

Our values represent what is most important to us—our core essence. They serve as the foundation for what we hold to be of worth in our lives. They are also necessary preconditions for fully engaging ourselves as a learner, leader, partner, and so on. Values are not chosen. They are unique and intrinsic to each individual. Becoming clear about what we value helps us to better understand ourselves and to create a good fit between our personal values and those of organizations we join or work in.

> "Values are like directions on a compass. They're never 'achieved,' but in each and every step they influence the quality of the journey. Values dignify and clarify our life course...they are ongoing and perpetually generative."
>
> —Hayes, 2007, pp. 46–52

Over time, as mentor-coach, we can help the mentee access and clarify what they value most. Once a mentee identifies his or her core values, the mentor-coach and mentee can begin to see how these core values are expressed in the mentee's work and relationships, and consider how the mentee's values show up, how their values are showing up (or not) in their choices or decisions, and the impact this is having.

As the mentor-coaching partnership and conversations continue, the mentee's values are woven in, or referenced like the directions on a compass, to ensure that the "best" route has been chosen. Operating within this matrix of well-understood personal values also increases the mentee's ability to navigate difficult decisions or choices.

Living and leading in alignment is what it means to be true to oneself. This is where our most powerful, undivided, and committed selves show up. When our leadership is grounded in our core values, we lead authentically, we "walk our talk," and we are consistent. If, as many suggest, authenticity *is* the central core of effective leadership, then creating space for our values to inhabit the mentor-coaching conversation and process is essential.

In my work with students, I have explored personal and class values as part of the healthy relationships and bullying prevention programming that I have developed. Creating space early in the program for the students to identify, both individually and collectively, what is important for them in how they are being and how they are interacting with one another, has proven to be a very valuable process, particularly in classes where the students have had a tough time getting along and accepting each other's differences. As the coach-facilitator-teacher in the room, I have become part of the process, sharing my values, too, and together, we have identified the "non-negotiable" collective values, which they then agreed to help keep front and centre, as they navigated the relationships, work, and conversations.

By identifying the values shared by the class, the students have a clear idea of "what's OK" (acceptable) and "what's not OK" (not acceptable) and are, therefore, more apt to manage and regulate themselves and one another.

From Kate

Open-ended questions to support expanding awareness of own values:

DIG DEEPER

For tools to access core values, see the Mentor-Coaching Toolkit.

- What values are important to you as a learner/educational leader/ leader?

- What does…mean to you?

- What's important to you about…?

- What do you have when you honour this value? What does it make possible?

- Where and when have you lived this value?

- Who are you when this value is present?

- Which values do you want to honour more consistently?

- Given what you just said, what values stand out?

- What values will help you feel more aligned?

5. Awareness of What Gets in the Way

As mentor-coach, we want to help the mentee find *their* path of least resistance. Mining the mentee's knowledge of what can get in their way and how best to mitigate or circumvent familiar obstacles, old habits, and unhelpful beliefs helps to keep the mentee unencumbered.

Remember, it is important to proceed with caution in the territory of challenges and obstacles. Mentees can get pulled in by obstacles and spiral downward if they lose sight of, or connection to, their larger goal and agenda for the conversation. To avoid this, it can be helpful to invite the mentee to identify what might get in the way, and consider what it will require of them to keep that obstacle out of the way.

The wisdom of the mentee and her or his ability to self-manage and self-regulate are extremely valuable resources to access, expand, and deepen, particularly when we want to help them manage potential obstacles, such as the following:

- limiting beliefs and assumptions
- inner critic
- stale patterns or habits
- becoming overwhelmed
- lack of interest
- lack of trust in self or others
- doubt/not believing
- other priorities
- speculation
- distraction
- old unhelpful stories
- analysis paralysis
- impatience
- insufficiency
- lack of time
- lack of energy

> "The emotional tail wags the rational dog."
> —Haidt, 2001, pp. 814–834

- relationships
- strong emotions (e.g., anger, jealousy, fear, sadness, excitement)

Open-ended questions to support expanding awareness of what gets in the way:
- What might get in your way?
- How might that belief/assumption be restricting you?
- What impact is your speculating having on you?
- What can help you stay in the "here and now" and be less future focused?
- Who are you when you are not distracted? What's different?
- How does that old story speak to who you are now? What's the new story?
- What does "enough" look like?
- Where are you patient in your life? How might that apply here?
- What if this was enough?
- How would you like this relationship to feel differently? Where is your place in that?

6. Awareness of Vision and Purpose

Vision

"In the beginning of the creative process there will be a discrepancy between what you want [vision] and what you have [current reality]. This discrepancy forms a tension. Tension seeks resolution. The tension is a wonderful force because, as it moves toward resolution, it generates energy that is useful in creating. I call the relationship between the vision and current reality *structural tension*."
—Fritz, 1991, p. 27

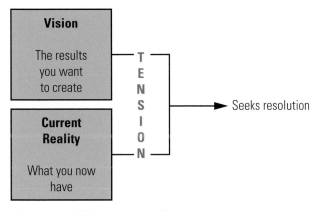

Figure 8.9 The Role of Vision in Mobilizing
The difference between your vision and current reality can create tension that drives you toward achieving your goals.

Robert Fritz's (1991) work around the power of creative tension, as illustrated in Figure 8.9, features the role of vision in the mobilizing process. The structural tension created between the mentee's current reality, as discussed in the first dimension of awareness, and the vision or results they want to achieve, draws the mentee onward and pulls them toward the desired result.

As mentor-coach, providing the mentee with an opportunity to clearly articulate their vision so they can see *and* feel it and why it matters is a crucial piece of expanding awareness. It is also helpful to invite the mentee to create the vision concretely in a medium that resonates with them, such as drawing, creating a collage, selecting a song, or identifying a metaphor. Capturing the essence of the desired result or vision concretely can access somatic and neurological markers that trigger a deeper drive within the mentee. The mentee can then keep the concrete image, object, or piece of music within their immediate environment or field of vision, to support their intentionality as a totem.

It is important to emphasize that the conversation regarding vision does not need to be long or complicated. It can be as simple as having the mentee identify what they "want." The simple question *What do you want?* can open up a more intentional or purposeful flow in the conversation, and the more detailed, compelling, and visceral the mentee's description of what they want, the more clarity they will have in regard to their vision.

"It's not what the vision is, it's what the vision does."
— *Holmes & Senge, 2009*

In the world of sports psychology, the power of visualization is a key part of the training and goal-setting process. It serves to create the structural tension that mobilizes the athlete as he or she prepares to compete. Many athletes work tirelessly for years with a picture of a gold medal in their mind's eye (or taped inside their locker) to keep them focused and clear on what they are striving to achieve. Such stories speak to the success of the power of visualization.

Open-ended questions to support expanding awareness of vision:

- What do you want? How might this speak to a larger vision?
- What possibilities are you reaching for, as you step into your leadership vision?
- What's pulling you forward?
- What are you creating?
- Where are you in that picture?
- What do you see at the end of this?
- What song do you want to be singing when you arrive?
- What image comes to mind that captures this for you?
- What would a metaphor for this be?
- If I met you in three months, what would you like to be saying?
- Going big, what's possible?
- What if…?

Purpose

"Purpose is a constellation not a destination. It is a pattern that helps us to find our unique path to serving others, which, ultimately, is the only way we can serve ourselves. It's not a solution, a decision or an event. It's not necessarily what we do for work, although work can be a vehicle for its expression. Rather, purpose is the current of a river hidden underneath the ice. It defines the energy with which we can commit to something, but not the outcome."

—*Markova, 2000, p. 140*

The mentee's awareness of when and where their determination and resolve are most apt to show up provides immediate "backstage" access to "purpose territory." As mentor-coach, we can help expand awareness of **purpose** by listening and watching for the telltale commitment, motivation, and focus that inhabits purposeful activity and movement. For further deepening and clarifying, we can ask questions about the places where the mentee's energy never seems to run out:

- What draws you toward…? [the mentee's purpose]
- What engages you in…? [things the mentee does]
- I notice you care deeply about… What sits beneath that?

Open-ended questions to support expanding awareness of purpose:
- Where is your commitment coming from?
- What matters to you in this?
- Where is the energy in this for you?
- If you could do this in a purposeful way, what would be different?

Purpose—
an individual's sense of what really matters overall, where they want to focus their energy and resolve

"Is the life I am living…the life that wants to live in me?"
—*Palmer, 2000, p. 2*

7. Awareness of Mindset

Helping the mentee step back and recognize how they "see" things, or the impact that their mindset has on their attention, thoughts, feelings, behaviour, choices, and actions is a simple way to deepen awareness and provoke new choices that can mobilize and boost performance. The sequence outlined below represents a chain of events that is precipitated by mindset and the extent to which our mindset drives what we pay attention to, what we think, how we feel and behave, and in turn, our impact and results.

> **Mindset→Attention/Thinking→Emotion→Behaviour→ Performance/Action→Results**

When we are not satisfied with our results, we typically unpack the situation by retracing the sequence of events back one or two steps. We will look at what we "did" (performance/action) or how we behaved, and focus on generating alternate actions for moving forward, rather than digging deeper to consider how our mindset could be impacting or driving our thinking, feeling, ineffective action and, in turn, unsatisfactory results.

Our role as mentor-coach, in such situations, is to invite the mentee to get a clear picture of what they were seeing (or not seeing), what they were paying attention to (or not), and what they were noticing in the situation (or not), so they can begin to determine whether and where new awareness of these events will be valuable.

As mentor-coach, we want to be listening for evidence of the mentee's mindset—their assumptions as well as their foundational beliefs about others, themselves, and their situation—to ensure that it is aligned with their desired result. When the mentee's mindset is at cross-purposes with their goals, reflecting it back or sharing our observations is vital feedback. Likewise, when we see that the mentee's mindset is supporting their journey forward, it is important to secure that awareness so that they can lock it in.

During the mobilizing process, asking questions that increase the mentee's awareness of their mindset expands mental complexity, choices, and desire for purposeful and meaningful action. Thus, exploring mindset is essential in the awareness-building portion of the mentor-coaching conversation.

The challenge with mindset is that it is often so much a part of us and our way of looking at ourselves, others, and the world that we are not aware of it. Part of the power of mentor-coaching is that it invites the mentee to notice their mindset and be "in a place to choose" whether it is serving them.

> "One of the difficulties of stretching ourselves is that we tend to see ourselves as our limitations, not as our potential."
>
> —Rock, 2006, p. 55

DIG DEEPER

- For more on the mindset of the mentor-coach, see Chapter 5.

- For tools to access mindset, see the Mentor-Coaching Toolkit.

- For more types of questions to support increased awareness, see Chapter 7.

Open-ended questions to support expanding awareness of mindset:

- What's the hook in this for you?

- How do you see the opportunity/situation/challenge? What are you not seeing?

- Stepping back, what do you notice?

- What has your attention? What doesn't have your attention?

- If you had to characterize the mindset you are operating from, how would you describe it?

- What mindset or frame would you like to be operating from?

- What do you see?

- What's easy in this for you? What's hard?

- How are you holding or positioning that person?

- What other perspectives are there? What can you see from there?

FROM THE FIELD

Jean Zu
Professor and Chair, Department of Mechanical & Industrial Engineering, University of Toronto

Through being coached, I have significantly increased my awareness of several important areas of development in my leadership, thus enhancing my capacities and effectiveness.

Two distinct areas of expanding awareness highlight how the coaching has been so helpful for me in my leadership. One is my previous tendency to make assumptions and speculate about surrounding matters and people. I was totally unaware of this habit before I started my leadership coaching. In fact, I was proud of my "ability" to be able to "know" and "predict" what was going on; I assumed my speculation was the truth and acted upon it. However, over time, my coach supported me in expanding my own awareness of when I was making assumptions, and the impact that was having, by asking questions and occasionally directly helping me notice. After exploring this new understanding in depth, I am now able to be consciously and diligently aware of choosing not to speculate or make assumptions.

Coaching has also shifted my stance as a leader. I have come to recognize that a coach-like leadership style can effectively change the behaviour of people in a positive way. Rather than continuing to be directive as a leader, I have learned to ask questions, listen deeply, and resist the urge to fix and solve. I have become increasingly aware that coach-like leadership really supports the development of people and the achievement of desired results.

9 Offering and Inviting Feedback: Nourishing Growth

"What we see is what we decide to observe."
—TUROK, 2012

In this chapter, we will explore

- offering and inviting feedback
- facing the feedback challenge
- shifting the feedback frame
- three approaches for offering impactful feedback
- challenging the mentee
- role-playing scenarios: practising giving feedback in a safe place

As authors Stone and Heen (2014) observe in *Thanks for the Feedback*, "we swim in an ocean of feedback" (p. 1). A never-ending stream of information about ourselves and who we are in the world comes to us constantly, through other people and ourselves as we notice and process our experiences. Though not all of it may be welcome or even helpful, learning and growing is deeply nourished, from the inside out, with **feedback** that is relevant, accessible, and forward focused.

Feedback— "information provided by an agent (e.g., teacher, peer, book, parent, experience), regarding aspects of one's performance or understanding" (Hattie & Timperley, 2007, p. 81)

Offering and Inviting Feedback

> "My synthesis of more than 900 meta-analyses (2009, 2012) shows that feedback has one of the highest effects on student learning… [S]tudents welcome feedback that is just in time, just for them, just for where they are in their learning process, and just what they need to move forward."
> —*Hattie, 2012, pp. 18, 20*

Feedback is essential to learning. We build capacity by noticing our growth and challenges in the moment, in anticipation, and after the fact. We learn to gather our own feedback and reflect, integrating the information that supports us in becoming clear about what we need to pay attention to and where we want to look for continuous growth and improvement. We constantly receive feedback from others around us as well, either directly or indirectly, and it has a strong influence on how we see ourselves and our evolving learning, confidence, and competence.

Feedback increases our sense of connection to our learning, our work, and others in our lives. Without feedback, we operate from "rote"; as routines become established, the status quo sets in, and resistance to newness develops.

Wheatley (2005) challenges us to think about feedback as life sustaining, providing essential information about how to maintain one's existence. Feedback can also indicate when we need to adapt and grow.

In considering feedback for learners, Hattie and Timperley (2007) suggest that effective feedback must answer the following three major questions, in a holistic manner.

"Feed up: Where am I going?"

- What will success look like?
- What matters to me most about achieving my goals?

"Feed back: How am I going?"

- Where I am on the journey?
- What progress am I making?

"Feed forward: Where to next?"

- Where do I need to put my effort and attention in order to continue to move forward?
- What needs to happen to further enhance my progress?

Hattie and Timperley (2007) invite educators to be mindful in providing impactful feedback to learners around these questions and to encourage them to ask these questions of themselves. The simplicity of their frame and focus for feedback is intriguing as the questions relate to all those involved in learning: teachers, leaders, students, mentees, and so on.

In mentor-coaching, which focuses on building capacity and creating desired change, feedback is vital. Cultivating a dynamic within the mentor-coach and mentee relationship that encourages offering and receiving feedback requires us to develop a particular set of skills outlined later in this chapter. The first step is to consider feedback that we have received in the past:

What has been your experience of receiving feedback?

We always ask this question at the beginning of the feedback section of our training sessions. This allows us not only to work from the inside out, but also to cut to the heart of the topic by inviting participants to consider how they have felt when they have been on the receiving end of feedback. We believe that to build capacity as mentor-coaches—to offer feedback that is going to nourish growth—we need to begin by going inside ourselves and remembering our own experiences and feelings around receiving feedback.

The responses we receive to this question are almost always the same:

As leaders, we hardly ever get any and, when we do, it's rarely positive or useful.

Then when we ask:

Do you want more feedback?

We consistently get the same answers:

YES! ...Only if they learn how to give it.
...Only if it's useful.
...Only if they take the time to come more than once and see what I have actually been doing.
...It also depends on my relationship with the person.

Sound familiar? In *Thanks for the Feedback,* Stone and Heen (2014) note the following finding from their research about what helps people learn and what gets in the way:

> "When we give feedback, we notice that the receiver isn't good at receiving it. When we receive feedback, we notice that the giver isn't good at giving it."
>
> —*p. 3*

Facing the Feedback Challenge

There is a systemic challenge around giving and receiving feedback in our world today. When feedback is offered, the person giving it often begins with "positive feedback," in the hope that the receiver will hear it and that the positive feedback will soften the blow of the "constructive criticism" that is coming next. So often in anticipating the criticism, the receiver is unable to truly hear the acknowledgement of their gifts and strengths—the receiver hears the positive feedback as platitudes offered en route to the "real" message about weakness, failure, or deficit.

In mentor-coaching, we have the opportunity to change this frame, so that feedback is offered and received in true service of learning and growth. To do this, it is critical to establish a relational dynamic with the mentee that invites rich acknowledgement of gifts and strengths, stimulates expanding awareness, and uncovers opportunities within challenges and learning edges. We also need to consider the challenges we face in giving and receiving feedback:

- How do we navigate the experience together to honour the integrity of the individuals, the ongoing relationship, and the growth process?

- How do we support ourselves in being able to hear and process feedback so that it fosters continuous learning and growth within us?

- What skills do we need to cultivate as educators/leaders so that, when we offer feedback, it is experienced as relevant and inspiring?

- What kinds of feedback conversations does the school/ organization/culture foster?

"If our goal as leaders is to improve people's performance, then lots of feedback is essential, whatever has happened. Without feedback we cannot learn. However we need to move away from the current paradigm of constructive performance feedback, a nice way of saying 'politely tell people what they did wrong!' In its place, respectfully ask people what they learned, and how you can best help them to improve even further."
—*Rock, 2006, p. 215*

The Brain's "Negativity Bias"

Neuropsychologist Rick Hanson (2013) highlights a further challenge regarding feedback by explaining that "*to help our ancestors survive, the brain evolved a negativity bias*" (p. xxvi). This means that our brain is vigilant, constantly scanning for danger, threats, inconsistencies, losses, and disappointments so that we can protect ourselves from harm and pain. Often, this scanning results in perceived danger that unconsciously triggers the amygdala of our brain's limbic system, sending us into "fight or flight," releasing cortisol and adrenaline.

"The default setting of the brain is to *over*estimate threats, *under*estimate opportunities, and *under*estimate resources both for coping with threats and for fulfilling opportunities. Then we update these beliefs with information that confirms them, while ignoring or rejecting information that doesn't… [Our] brain is like Velcro for negative experiences but Teflon for positive ones."
—Hanson, 2013, pp. 24, 27

The following acronym encapsulates our understanding of this bias and can serve as a useful reminder when fear and worry present themselves:

"Fear is only as deep as the mind allows."
—Japanese proverb

FEAR = False Evidence Appearing Real

Considering the brain's negativity bias, it is easy to see why feedback is so challenging and why we often anticipate receiving it with anxiety and fear. As feedback is offered to us, our brain is looking for any evidence that we are not meeting the mark.

"When we focus on what went wrong and why, we might find lots of reasons for failure, but finding these is unlikely to move us towards future success. And bear in mind that we are deepening the circuits that caused us to fail in the first place."
—Rock, 2006, p. 210

By acknowledging this negativity bias, we encourage educators, leaders, and learners to be mindful and purposeful about cultivating the capacity to notice our strengths, our gifts, and opportunities to "[let] in the good" (Hanson, 2013, p. 1).

We also invite all of us, as learners, to hear and generate feedback around our areas of growth, to see the challenges as genuine opportunities to dig in and grow our own capacities. We want to invite and offer feedback as a gift given truly in support of learning and growth.

"Growth" and "Fixed" Mindsets: Impact on Experiencing Feedback

Growth mindset— human qualities, including intellectual skills, are developed over time; the framework of growth

Fixed mindset— human qualities are static, already formed; the framework of judgment

As we consider the challenges inherent in feedback, it is useful to look at Dweck's (2006) work around mindset. In looking up close at how children approach puzzles of increasing complexity, Dweck identified two mindsets that shaped their responses to feedback: the **growth mindset** and the **fixed mindset**.

According to Dweck (2006), the growth mindset is "based on the belief that your basic qualities are things you can cultivate through your efforts" and that "[e]veryone can change and grow through application and experience" (p. 7). The growth mindset is about the transformative power of learning and effort—to "grow" your ability and thus continually develop yourself as a person. Within this mindset, feedback is consistently seen as a source of useful information, with vital implications for learning and constructive action.

By contrast, the fixed mindset views human qualities as fixed. The problem with this mindset, Dweck (2006) points out, is that "believing that your [intelligence and personal] qualities are carved in stone...creates an urgency to prove yourself over and over... [Everything is about performance and thus] a direct measure of... competence and worth" (pp. 6, 8).

With a fixed mindset, Dweck (2006) says, ability is "expected to show up on its own, before any learning takes place...[which] does not allow you the luxury of becoming. You have to already be" (pp. 24–25). With such a mindset, feedback is experienced as evaluative and critical, concerned about how you are or will be judged.

Current research regarding neuroplasticity shows that our brains are always changing their structure, as we learn and grow. Thus, there is now evidence to support the reality of the growth mindset, and it has significant implications for leaders, teachers, and students regarding learning and feedback.

Dweck (2010) and others are involved in research focused on teaching students to embrace the growth mindset and become increasingly aware of how learning and stretching builds new connections in their brains as they build their capacities.

These findings about how we learn invite us to co-create learning environments that foster risk taking, stretching, not knowing, and leaning into new challenges in service of deep learning and growth.

Within this context, offering and receiving feedback is framed as an opportunity for more learning and growth.

> "If education is going to be transformative, it's going to be uncomfortable and unpredictable… I always like to tell my students, 'If you're comfortable, I'm not teaching and you're not learning. It's going to get uncomfortable in here and that's okay. It's normal and it's part of the process.' …The big challenge for leaders is getting our heads and hearts around the fact that we need to cultivate the courage to be uncomfortable and to teach the people around us how to accept discomfort as a part of growth."
>
> —Brown, 2012, pp. 198–199

Reflection: Facing the Feedback Challenge

DIG DEEPER

See Chapter 5 for more on the mentor-coaching mindset.

In a discussion or journal, consider and respond to the questions below.

1. What has been your experience of receiving feedback?

2. Recall a specific instance when receiving feedback supported your learning and growth (consider specific qualities of the feedback, how it was offered, and the person offering it).

3. Recall a specific time when receiving feedback was counter-productive (consider specific qualities of the feedback, how it was offered, and the person offering it).

4. What does "taking a stand" on the quality of feedback look like for you?

5. What helps you arrive for feedback with a growth mindset as the receiver? as the giver?

6. How do we support mentees and students who are holding a fixed mindset toward feedback and their own learning and growth?

Shifting the Feedback Frame

Given the challenges that surround and undermine feedback, we need to shift the frame around it, so that we can offer feedback generously and receive it gratefully. The feedback frame in mentor-coaching does just that to support the mentor-coach and the mentee's learning and growth.

Dr. Heike Bronson
Vice Principal and Mentor-Coach Training for Educators Program Facilitator

Using the mentor-coaching model I was really able to create an environment where the teacher was guiding the process. Valuable feedback was exchanged that would support the teacher as well as help me become more informed about the challenges of practice. I felt like I was invited into the heart of "what matters" in the classroom.

Feedback as a Gift

We believe that the best and most impactful feedback is offered and received as a gift. As mentor-coach, we offer rich, concrete, and specific feedback, in service of the mentee and what they are wanting and growing toward. The input then becomes part of the mentee's expanding awareness of their strengths and learning edges. Self-generated feedback is also a rich aspect of the learning dynamic, growing out of the expanding awareness of the mentee as they observe themselves as learners. Thus, the feedback serves to "feed forward."

Emma Nishimura
Sessional Instructor, Ontario College of Art and Design University

As a printmaking instructor, when I talk to students about their work, whether in the form of individual meetings or group critiques, my emphasis first and foremost is to connect with them and create a meaningful dialogue. When I have students present their work, I ask them to first discuss what ideas they are investigating and how they are exploring that within the piece. At this time, I also always encourage them to focus on what is working and not to dwell on what they are disappointed with. I work to

continued...

keep the emphasis on what has been learned along the way, as
we address the successes and challenges and have a discussion
about how they will move forward. By asking questions, offering
insight and knowing when to remain silent, I encourage students
to think about how they can apply their learning to current and
future projects. In this way, the feedback conversation is able to
really support the students' learning and growth.

Since the mentor-coaching process and relationship are co-created
and reciprocal, it is critical that the mentor-coach invites feedback
from the mentee as well.

Feedback also supports increased metacognition, thus helping the
receiver "see" more clearly. When we receive feedback from others, or
through our own reflective practices, we gain access to a perspective
that otherwise may be unavailable to us. We are able to "think about
our thinking" with more awareness. This can help the mentee recognize the mindset they are operating from, making what was implicit
or "out of sight," explicit and "in sight." This expanded awareness
increases their level of metacognition, a key piece in building capacity.

"No problem can be solved by the same consciousness that created it. We
need to see the world anew."

—*Albert Einstein*

Linking Feedback to Desired Results

The importance of aligning feedback with the desired result cannot
be overstated. For feedback to feel relevant and in service of nourishing the mentee's desired growth or results, it needs to speak directly
to the individual's intentions. When we know the feedback we are
receiving is going to help us be successful, we are far more likely to
integrate it into our *being* and *doing* as we move forward.

Building capacity from the inside out and growing talents and
skills toward desired results offers a variety of opportunities for
specific feedback to foster new learning. Using the signposts in the
individual/red zone, collective/yellow zone, and results/green zone

of the mentor-coaching model, the mentor-coach helps keep the mentee's attention, movement, and intentions aligned. We may also use the questions provided for each signpost (see Chapter 4, p. 96) as springboards to specific areas of feedback to help unpack the depth and breadth of the mentee's experience, learning, and growth.

Requirements of Impactful Feedback

Characteristics of rich, powerful, feedback:

- It is offered as a gift to support capacity building, growth, and transformation.

- The feedback is based on the underlying assumption that the mentee is resourceful, creative, and committed to reflection, learning, and growth.

- It serves and aligns with what the mentee wants—and links to intentions, purpose, values, longing, commitment, and contribution.

- Feedback is offered as a powerful reflection strategy, inviting further consideration and increased awareness, choice, and action.

- It grows out of a trusting partnership, a learning relationship based on the mindset of experimentation, growth, and opportunity versus weakness, deficit, and gaps.

- It fosters openness, capacity building, and opportunity rather than judgment.

- It is shared in an atmosphere that supports risk taking and experimentation, welcomes the willingness not to know, and embraces "failure" as an essential part of the learning process.

- The giving of feedback is often permission-based.

What feedback requires of the mentor-coach:

- Be honouring and authentic.

- Create space for rich dialogue and reflection.

- Be in an open and ongoing conversation that is grounded in a deep caring for the mentee and his or her strengths, success, growth, and development.

- Offer feedback respectfully, with an open heart.

- Believe in the mentee and support the mentee in believing in themselves.

- Invite the mentee to become more self-aware, rather than evaluating performance.

- Offer balanced and concrete observations that are in line with the mentee's desired results.

- Invite feedback from the mentee regarding the effectiveness of the mentor-coaching relationship and the processes.

- Take responsibility for co-creating an effective process and being ever mindful of the impact of the feedback on the mentee.

- If there is a power imbalance, be aware of the further challenge in how the feedback is experienced.

What feedback requires of the mentee:

- Ask for/be open to receiving, processing, and integrating feedback.

- Acknowledge personal strengths and gifts as well as stretching in terms of possibilities, intentions, actions, and reach.

- Choose to receive feedback as an opportunity for ongoing growth and development rather than hearing feedback as judgment and shutting down.

- Feel seen and heard.

- Take responsibility and experiment with new possibilities for "stepping up" to maximize potential.

How the Mentee Responds to Feedback Is Critical

Further to the lists above, Wiliam (2012) references the work of Kluger and DeNisi (1996), which looked at research on feedback from 1905 to 1995. In particular, Wiliam notes the finding that "the effects of feedback depended on the reactions of the recipient. The nature of the feedback itself was less important than the kind of responses triggered in the individual" (p. 2).

Thus, it is important, as mentor-coach, to be mindful of how the feedback is "landing" for the mentee (being viscerally received) and to be open and flexible, inviting feedback from the mentee in terms of what they want more of, and less of, from you in terms of the feedback process.

What feedback requires to "land":

- align with what the mentee wants; thus, it should be oriented toward overall goals and vision and not be evaluative
- be balanced: it should speak to strengths and gifts as well as challenges and growing edges
- take the mentee beyond his or her own awareness and way of operating, inviting new perspectives and stretch
- attach to what the mentee cares about, inviting her or him to dig in, to leap
- speak to who the mentee is *being* not just what the mentee is *up to*
- be honest and concrete, grounded in evidence-based observation and specific to the context
- be experienced as meaningful, real, relevant, and useful
- feel possible and doable, while at the same time inviting stretch and challenge
- be timely, ongoing, and consistent
- help to clarify, simplify, and focus

Reflection: On Feedback

In a discussion or journal, consider and respond to the questions below.

Receiving Feedback

1. What feedback is most useful to you as a leader or teacher?
2. What helps you hear the feedback and integrate it as you move forward?
3. What are your requests of the person who gives you feedback?
4. What is an example for you of receiving impactful feedback as a gift?

Offering Feedback

1. What feedback have you been offering as a mentor-coach?

2. What feedback has the greatest impact on the mentee? on others?

3. What are your strengths in offering feedback?

4. What are your challenges in offering feedback?

5. What are some possibilities with regard to how you will *be* and what you will *do* differently, when offering feedback as a coach-like leader? as a teacher? as a mentor-coach?

Three Approaches for Offering Impactful Feedback

To provide a clear feedback frame that serves the mentor-coach and the mentee, we have identified the following three approaches. While these approaches attempt to capture the essence of feedback within mentor-coaching, they are by no means an exhaustive list.

DIG DEEPER

See the mentor-coaching approach for offering feedback that supports learning and growth in the demonstration video on the *When Mentoring Meets Coaching* website.

1	**Acknowledging: INSPIRE** This is the skill of noticing and sharing with the mentee who they are *being* in order to do what they are *doing*.
2	**Holding Up the Mirror: INSIGHT** The mentor-coach holds up the mirror, inviting the mentee to reflect and notice.
3	**Sharing Observations: INCITE** The mentor-coach shares observations without judgment or interpretation, for the purpose of raising awareness and provoking further reflection in the mentee.

Figure 9.1   Three Approaches for Offering Feedback: Inspire, Insight, Incite

Mentor-coaches can use these three approaches to provide impactful feedback.

Let us look more closely at each approach.

1. Acknowledging: INSPIRE

Acknowledging is noticing and reflecting back to the mentee who he or she is *being* in the moment. We see the strengths and capacities, the "shining" and growth in the other person, and we reflect back what we see as feedback. It is critical that the acknowledgement is authentic and comes out of who the mentee is *being* in the moment or within the experiences and stories shared.

Offering this kind of acknowledgement is a powerful form of feedback that has a deeper impact on the mentee than praise or compliments. When we praise or compliment someone, we are usually recognizing their actions, appearance, initiatives, and so on. However, when we acknowledge someone, we are digging deeper, speaking to what it took in them to do what they did—their presence, gifts, strengths, and qualities of character. We are inviting them to see the person we see—who they are, who they are becoming, or where the growth in them is occurring.

Our skill in offering powerful acknowledgements depends on our ability to notice who the mentee is *being,* or *has been,* as they share their thoughts, feelings, and experiences within mentor-coaching conversations.

In our experience, there is a sacredness within acknowledgement; it is about beauty seen within and shared authentically.

Providing an acknowledgement has the potential to expand the mentee's self-awareness and self-trust. The power of the acknowledgement increases when we are able to identify, or get at the heart of, where the growth has occurred. This can secure the learning and increase the mentee's capacity to move forward powerfully. Often this growth or capacity is not yet recognized by the mentee or is dismissed. Identifying and claiming the growth are critical components of this process. Sometimes, this may include inviting the mentee to acknowledge themselves, to look in their own mirror and see the growth, gifts, and qualities that are evident to us, as mentor-coach.

Once we have offered an acknowledgement, we should notice the impact on the mentee. This is a way for us to determine whether the acknowledgement truly resonates.

It takes much experience, experimentation, and practice for the mentor-coach to be able to consistently "see" and authentically articulate acknowledgements. Furthermore, many of us are not used to being acknowledged and find it challenging to have our gifts and strengths highlighted aloud. We encourage you to forge ahead… mentees and others will learn to let in the light.

> "If we want to transform people's performance we need to master the skill of acknowledgment. This means building a new mental wiring around seeing what people are doing well. It means watching out for how people are challenging themselves, growing, learning, and developing. And it means noticing the new wiring others are developing, and being able to feed back what we see in ways that make a difference."
>
> —Rock, 2006, p. 62

Mentor-Coaching in Action

Providing Acknowledgement: Opportunities and Examples

Opportunity: Who the mentee is *being* amidst their *doing* (e.g., committed, courageous, tenacious, connected, fully present, creative)

Mentor-coach: *I would like to acknowledge how much courage it took for you to have this difficult conversation with your colleague. You are truly standing in your current commitment to out-loud clarity.*

Opportunity: Speaking to the mentee's presence, qualities of character, efforts, gifts, and strengths

Mentor-coach: *What I notice in you is your deep caring and commitment to the children and their well-being and success.*

Opportunity: Recognizing where and how the mentee is honouring her or his core values, vision, purpose, intentions

Mentor-coach: *I hear your determination and clarity around the importance of making it happen…and trust that your gift of connection will support all of you as you move forward.*

continued…

Opportunity: Recognizing what it took in the mentee to achieve their goal, their intention, their vision

Mentor-coach: *You have been very intentional around holding your vision for the students throughout this difficult and challenging process. I want to honour your deep commitment and integrity throughout.*

Reflection: On Acknowledgements

In a discussion or journal, consider and respond to the questions below.

1. What is your experience of having others acknowledge your gifts, strengths, and qualities? What does it access in you? How does it support your learning and growth?

2. How skilled are you in noticing other people's gifts, strengths, efforts, capacities, and qualities of character, in the moment? How often do you share what you see in others out loud?

3. How will you challenge yourself to be able to notice, in the moment, these gifts and qualities in the mentee and others?

4. How will you support yourself in being more intentional about speaking to these aspects of the mentee? of others in your life?

5. What is the impact on others when you acknowledge them deeply? What is the impact on you?

6. How will you invite the mentee to acknowledge themselves?

Exercises: Practice in Offering Acknowledgements

1. Set an intention to listen deeply in a variety of conversations to identify who the person is *being* in order to do what they are *doing*. Practise sharing with them who they are *being*.

2. Practise listening for gifts, strengths, and qualities of character as the mentee and other people tell their stories and share their experiences. Challenge yourself to share with them what you are noticing, in the spirit of honouring and building capacity.

3. Notice when it is easy, and when it is more difficult, for you to listen for and articulate gifts, strengths, effort, and qualities inside conversations and relationships. How will you continue to grow your skill?

4. Notice the impact when you acknowledge the mentee authentically and deeply. What is it fostering in terms of the growth and development of the relationship? of the mentee? of the mentor-coach?

5. What do you want to acknowledge in yourself as you continue to grow as a mentor-coach?

2. Holding Up the Mirror: INSIGHT

In this approach to feedback, we hold up the mirror, asking questions that invite the mentee to notice himself or herself in the moment, observe after the fact, and so on. This form of feedback is offered in the spirit of self-reflection, heightening the mentee's capacity to notice and to choose. This ability to observe oneself is critical in expanding awareness and possibilities.

Mentor-coaching is essentially about expanding the mentee's capacity to notice, to observe oneself in the moment. This is often a challenging area for the mentee, as it requires them to be in the experience and observe it at the same time. By inviting the mentee to pause and reflect on who and what they see in the mirror, the mentor-coach is supporting the mentee in observing themselves and raising their awareness of their own thoughts, feelings, perspectives, beliefs, assumptions, energy, behaviours, interpretations, and so on.

> "*Observation* is the ability to perceive the self even as we are experiencing an event. It places us in a larger frame of reference and broadens our perspective moment to moment... Observation offers a powerful way to disengage from automatic behaviors and habitual responses; we can sense our role in these patterns and begin to find ways to alter them."
> —Siegel, 2010, p. 32

The rigour for the mentor-coach in this type of feedback is not to interpret or add in our own observations. This is about the mentee stepping up and taking a close look at themselves, expanding their awareness and their possibilities for moving forward. It is the mentee's work.

In working with drama education pioneer Dorothy Heathcote in the 1970s, I learned that role-playing is a strategy that we can use to help ourselves "switch on the watcher" within ourselves. When we agree to take on a role, to imagine ourselves in another's shoes, we agree to the convention that we are watching ourselves, somewhat outside ourselves, as we inhabit the role. Within improvisation and script, we pretend together, while at the same time observing ourselves and each other interacting. Because the roles are not who we really are, we have a heightened capacity to watch ourselves in the moment.

From Jeanie

The idea of being an observer of ourselves is central to mentor-coaching and building capacity. However, being in the experience as we watch ourselves in the experience is not easy. By holding up the mirror, the mentor-coach supports the mentee in enhancing her or his skill at doing just that, sometimes in the moment, other times in reflecting back past interactions and behaviours. If we want to change our actions and reactions, we need to be aware of what we are truly up to, and this requires the cultivation of our observer self. Usually, if we do not like our results, we try to change our action…and we get more of the same. We need to work at the level of the observer to be able to create new possibilities.

"It is only through becoming a new observer that new opportunities for action arise. We build our futures through the actions made possible by the observer who is constituted by the distinctions and discourses we are immersed in. Part of the possibility of transformation thus lies in becoming astute and wise observers of the observer we are…"
—Olalla, 2004, pp. 114–115

Drawing on a metaphor used in *Leadership on the Line* (Heifetz & Linsky, 2002), another way to think of this feedback approach is that the mentor-coach is holding up the mirror so that the mentee can learn to be on the balcony and on the dance floor at the same time, able to be in the experience and be an observer of self and others in the experience at the same time.

> "The observational challenge is to see the subtleties that normally go right by us. Seeing the whole picture requires standing back and watching even as you take part in the action being observed… The goal is to come as close as you can to being in both places simultaneously, as if you had one eye looking from the dance floor and one eye looking down from the balcony, watching all the action, including your own."
>
> —*Heifetz & Linsky, 2002, pp. 52, 54*

Mentor-Coaching in Action

Holding Up the Mirror: Opportunities and Examples

Opportunity: To invite the mentee to notice the impact of their behaviour within a specific remembered context

Mentor-coach: What is your best guess regarding the impact of the way in which you gave your feedback to the teacher?

Opportunity: To support the mentee in noticing the presence of a particular strength or value

Mentor-coach: What strength is present in you right now as you step into this challenge?

Opportunity: To invite the mentee "to the balcony" as an observer, as they recall a challenging interaction that they wish had turned out differently

Mentor-coach: From the metaphorical balcony, what do you now notice about your own behaviour in your interactions with the student?

continued…

Opportunity: To reflect back a visible bodily response or energy shift so that the mentee can notice and make his or her own meaning

Mentor-coach: I am noticing a shift in your energy... What is happening now for you?

Reflection: Holding Up the Mirror

In a discussion or journal, consider and respond to the questions below.

1. When is it easiest to observe yourself? When is it most challenging?

2. How do you support yourself in noticing your own thoughts, feelings, and behaviours in the moment?

3. Who holds up the mirror for you in your leadership? in your teaching? What is the impact for you?

4. How will you support yourself in holding up the mirror for the mentee without interpreting or sharing your observations?

5. How will you continue to cultivate the capacity to be on the dance floor and on the balcony at the same time as a leader? as a teacher? as a mentor-coach?

Exercises: Practice in Holding Up the Mirror

1. Practise setting the intention of observing yourself up close, as you are participating or interacting as a leader in different situations and contexts. Use a journal to capture your observations, reflections, and surprises.

2. Using the premise that it is "only through becoming a new observer that new opportunities for action arise" (Olalla, 2004, p. 114), choose a current challenge that you are facing as a leader or teacher and invite your observer self to see anew. Generate possibilities for new behaviours for yourself within the context. Then experiment with some of the new possibilities, noticing the results and the impact.

3. Try holding up the mirror for others in your life, inviting them to notice and remembering not to add your own observations or interpretations.

3. Sharing Observations: INCITE

In this feedback approach, we share observations with the mentee to raise awareness and provoke further reflection in the mentee.

As a learning partnership and reflective process, mentor-coaching invites input from the mentor-coach, in service of the mentee, based on gathering wisdom, observations over time, a sense of what the mentee wants, their learning journey, and so on. The observations shared might include

- observed behaviours,

- assumptions, and

- the presence of a core value or belief.

As mentor-coach, it is important to offer observations without judgment and without becoming attached to the mentee's responses or choices that grow out of the sharing. Be clear that it is the mentee's work, so it is the mentee who will receive the offerings and make meaning from them. Sometimes, the observations we share can be very impactful. At other times, the mentee may not feel our observations are relevant. What is important is not to be invested in our performance as mentor-coach and thus be attached to whether the mentee is excited about what we are offering.

One of the subtleties of providing this form of feedback is to cultivate a sense of when sharing will be useful to the mentee and when it will get in the way of her or his own exploring, gathering clarity, and momentum. Asking permission is helpful as it gives the mentee the option to hear what is on offer or not. Similarly, accessing intuition supports knowing what and when to share. We may feel in our gut that the mentee is ready to be challenged. Conversely, we may sense that the mentee is too vulnerable to receive a challenging observation.

By sharing observations, we provide "outside" feedback for the mentee. In *Thinking, Fast and Slow*, Kahneman (2011) discusses the important role that an "outside view" (p. 245) plays, when one is looking to move ahead with the attention and intention that capacity building requires. Kahneman reminds us that the outside perspective, like that provided by our feedback, can help to extend the learner's thinking beyond the automatic impressions and desires of "fast thinking" (p. 13) to deliberate and "slow thinking" that is more conducive to detailed, specific processing.

Mentor-Coaching in Action

Sharing Observations: Opportunities and Examples

Opportunity: Noticing when and where the mentee is operating at his or her best

Mentor-coach: Based on your description, I can see your full self standing at the front of the room at the meeting and really speaking the truth as you see it now.

Opportunity: Noticing when and where the mentee is challenged or does not seem to be accessing their fully resourced self

Mentor-coach: What is the story you are telling yourself around this…?

Opportunity: Noticing the mentee's assumptions as they navigate their leadership

Mentor-coach: It sounds like you are making an assumption about how this meeting with the parents will go…

Opportunity: Helping the mentee name something that is getting in the way

Mentor-coach: I've noticed you seem to have a lot of rules around how you are supposed to behave within this relationship…

Reflection: Sharing Observations

In a discussion or journal, consider and respond to the questions below.

1. What supports you in being fully present and highly observant as a leader? as a teacher? as a mentor-coach?

2. How does your intuition serve you in offering observations to others?

3. What helps you stay quiet after offering an observation?

4. How do you know when to share an observation with the mentee?

5. How do you stay away from judgment and remain "unattached" as you offer an observation to the mentee?

Exercises: Practice in Sharing Observations

1. Practise being highly observant of others when you are in conversations. Notice what strategies help you heighten your awareness. With permission, experiment with sharing some of your observations to further the others' awareness. Ask for feedback regarding how the observations landed and their usefulness.

2. Set the intention to notice assumptions others are making. Practise sharing what you are noticing in the form of an observation. Offer your observation without judgment and without being attached to others' responses.

3. Watch for energy shifts in your conversations with the mentee or others. When one happens, share your noticing of it within the conversation and notice how the mentee or others respond. What is the impact of sharing energy shifts with others?

Challenging the Mentee

Feedback includes asking permission to offer challenges to the mentee's thinking, noticing, assumptions, perspectives, and so on. As mentor-coach, we may give these challenges in the form of an acknowledgement, holding up the mirror, or sharing an observation, thereby inviting new perspectives and possibilities.

Offering challenges may invite the mentee to move out beyond her or his comfort zone or beyond a constrained perspective. This type of stretching is an essential part of mentor-coaching, as it supports the mentee in stepping into new challenges, behaviours, and learning.

Clearly, challenging the mentee requires a healthy level of trust between the mentor-coach and the mentee. If challenging happens too soon in the relationship, it can be uncomfortable or even counter-productive. As with providing other feedback, when offering a challenge, it is important for us not to be attached: the mentee responds in the moment, making their own meaning and taking the challenge where they need or want to.

Mentor-Coaching in Action

Challenging the Mentee: Opportunities and Examples

Opportunity: Noticing a possible limiting perspective and challenging the mentee to take a broader view

Mentor-coach: It sounds like you have lots of ideas for how you want it done. I'm curious, how will you continue to invite the other stakeholders to co-create this initiative with you?

Opportunity: Challenging the mentee to find a way to apply one of their learning intentions to the task at hand

Mentor-coach: I have a challenge for you, if you are interested... Given your wish to expand your creativity, what is a creative way to explore this new possibility?

continued...

Opportunity: Challenging the mentee to stretch the new learning by taking it on

Mentor-coach: My sense is that you are ready to dial it up. What are you willing to take on that will really stretch your learning around this?

Reflection: On Challenges

In a discussion or journal, consider and respond to the questions below.

1. What challenges have you received from others that really supported your learning and growth?

2. What was the impact on you?

3. What helped you hear, or live into, the challenges?

4. How does offering challenges to the mentee and others support risk taking, new perspectives, learning, and stretching?

5. What are your challenges in framing and offering challenges as a mentor-coach? as a leader? as a teacher?

Exercises: Practice in Challenging

1. When mentor-coaching, listen for the opportunity for the mentee to "stretch" in areas where it feels like he or she is interested in taking further risk for learning and growth. Practise asking permission and then offering a challenge for the mentee to grow into.

2. Experiment with offering a variety of challenges to the mentee and others, based on where they are and what they want, moving forward. Challenges can grow out of many areas: concrete actions and intentions, reflective activities, creative expression, new perspectives, and so on.

3. Try inviting the mentee and others to be intentional about challenging themselves as they step into desired change. Encouraging the mentee to identify and experiment with challenges supports capacity building.

Role-Playing Scenarios: Practising Giving Feedback in a Safe Place

Along with helping us heighten our observer selves, role-playing allows us to practise new skills within a safe space for experimenting and taking risks. In the spirit of learning and growth, here are a few scenarios and a role-playing frame for both mentor-coach and mentee to practise the complex skill of giving and receiving feedback.

Frame for Role-Playing

- An invitation to try on the feedback skills in a safe place

- Being authentic in role: thinking and feeling as if you were this imagined person interacting

- Keeping it spontaneous and "real"

Scenario 1: Processing Challenging Feedback

Mentee (Person A)

As a mentee, you have just received challenging feedback from a staff member or a parent, and you want to process the feedback with your mentor-coach so that you can take it in and be thoughtful about what to do with it.

Mentor-Coach (Person B)

Your mentee has sent you an email ahead of today's conversation, telling you that they have just received challenging feedback from a staff member or a parent, and they want to process the feedback with you, their mentor-coach.

Scenario 2: Offering Challenging Feedback

a) Seeking Support: How to Offer Feedback

Mentee (Person B)

As a mentee, you need to give a teacher or colleague some challenging feedback and you want support from your mentor-coach, so that you can offer feedback that the person will really "hear" and that will be impactful.

Mentor-Coach (Person A)

Your mentee has sent you an email ahead of today's conversation. The message says that they need to give a teacher or colleague some feedback and they want support from you, so that they can be prepared to offer feedback that the person will really "hear" and that will be impactful.

b) "Trying It On": Rehearsing the Feedback

Mentee (Person B)

The mentee now rehearses offering the feedback to the teacher or colleague.

Teacher/Colleague (Person A, formerly mentor-coach)

The mentor-coach now assumes the role of the teacher or colleague receiving the feedback, so that the mentee can practise offering feedback.

As you role-play together, feel free to call "time outs" along the way. This technique serves to heighten the observation and understanding of the mentee, inviting them to unpack what has happened, make changes, rewind the scene, and so on. During the "time out," the mentor-coach steps out of role and becomes the mentor-coach again, asking questions to further the mentee's understanding of what is unfolding in the scenario for the mentee and their teacher or colleague. The questions highlight challenges that the mentee needs to address in order for the feedback to be heard, to land, and so on.

References

Adams, M. (2011, September 28). Guidelines for great question askers. *Inquiry Institute Newsletter.*

Andreas, S. (2012). *Transforming negative self-talk: Practical, effective exercises.* New York, NY: W.W. Norton.

Baldwin, C. (2005). *Storycatcher: Making sense of our lives through the power of story.* Novato, CA: New World Library.

Batt, E. G. (2010). Cognitive coaching: A critical phase in professional development to implement sheltered instruction. *Teaching and Teaching Education, 26*(4), 997–1005.

Benard, B., & Slade, S. (2009). Listening to students: Moving from resilience research to youth development practice and school connectedness. In R. Gilman, E. S. Heubner, & M. J. Furlong (Eds.), *Handbook of positive psychology in schools.* New York, NY: Routledge.

Biswas-Diener, R., & Dean, B. (2007). *Positive psychology coaching: Putting the science of happiness to work for your clients.* Hoboken, NJ: Wiley.

Boyatzis, R., & McKee, A. (2005). *Resonant leadership.* Boston, MA: Harvard Business.

Bronson, H. (2007). *Investigating teacher leadership as a means of building school capacity.* (Unpublished doctoral dissertation). Ontario Institute for Studies in Education of the University of Toronto.

Brown, B. (2010). *The gifts of imperfection: Let go of who you think you are supposed to be and embrace who you are.* Center City, MN: Hazelden.

Brown, B. (2012). *Daring greatly: How the courage to be vulnerable transforms the way we live, love, parent and lead.* New York, NY: Gotham.

Buckingham, M., & Clifton, D. O. (2001). *Now, discover your strengths.* New York, NY: Free Press.

Bush, R. N. (1984). *Effective staff development in making schools more effective: Proceedings of three state conferences.* San Francisco, CA: Far West Laboratory.

Carroll, M. (2010, March). Beyond the elevator speech. *Shambhala Sun.*

Carson, R. (1983). *Taming your gremlin.* New York, NY: HarperCollins.

Cashman, K. (1999). *Leadership from the inside out.* Provo, UT: Executive Excellence.

Cashman, K. (2008). *Leadership from the inside out* (2nd ed). Oakland, CA: Berrett-Koehler.

Cholle, F. P. (2012). *The intuitive compass: Why the best decisions balance reason and instinct.* San Francisco, CA: Jossey Bass.

Cooperrider, D., & Whitney, D. (2005*). Appreciative inquiry: A positive revolution in change.* Oakland, CA: Berrett-Koehler.

Cordingley, P., & Bell, M. (2012). *Understanding what enables high quality professional learning: A report on the research evidence.* Coventry, UK: Centre for the Use of Research and Evidence in Education (CUREE).

Covey, S. R. (1989). *The 7 habits of highly effective people.* New York, NY: Free Press.

Covey, S. R., & Merrill, R. (2006). *The speed of trust: The one thing that changes everything.* New York, NY: Free Press.

Creelman, D. (Interviewer), & Cooperrider, D. (Interviewee). (2001). [Interview transcript]. Retrieved from https://appreciativeinquiry.case.edu/practice/quotesDetail.cfm?coid=875.

Csikszentmihalyi, M. (1996). *Creativity: Flow and the psychology of discovery and invention.* New York, NY: Harper Perennial.

Daloz, L. A. (2000). Foreword. In L. J. Zachary, *The mentor's guide: Facilitating effective learning relationships.* San Francisco, CA: Jossey Bass.

Deci, E. L., & Ryan, R. M. (2008). Self-determination theory: A macro theory of human motivation, development and health. *Canadian Psychology, 49*(3), 182–185.

Duckworth, A. L., Peterson, C., Matthews, M. D., & Kelly, D. R. (2007). Grit: Perseverance and passion for long-term goals. *Journal of Personality and Social Psychology, 92*(6), 1087–1101.

DuFour, R., & Marzano, R. J. (2011). *Leaders learning: How district, school and classroom leaders improve student achievement*. Bloomington, IN: Solution Tree.

Dweck, C. (2006). *Mindset: The new psychology of success*. New York, NY: Random House.

Dweck, C. (2010). Mind-sets and equitable education. *Principal Leadership, 10*(5), 26–29.

Edmondson, A. C. (2003). Managing the risk of learning: Psychological safety in work teams. In M. West, D. Tjosvold, & K. Smith (Eds.), *International handbook of organizational teamwork and cooperative working*. Chichester, UK: Wiley.

Edmondson, A. C. (2008, July–August). The competitive imperative of learning. *Harvard Business Review*.

Edmondson, A. C. (2012). *Teaming: How organizations learn, innovate, and compete in the knowledge economy*. San Francisco, CA: Jossey-Bass.

Epston, D. (1996). *Catching up with David Epston: A collection of narrative practice-based papers, published between 1991 and 1996*. Adelaide, AU: Dulwich Centre.

Fowler, C. J. H., & Mayes, T. J. (2000). Learning relationships from theory to design. In D. Squires, G. Conole, & G. Jacobs (Eds.), *The changing face of learning technology*. Cardiff, UK: University of Wales Press.

Freire, P. (2000). *Pedagogy of the oppressed*. New York, NY: Continuum.

Fritz, R. (1991). *Creating*. New York, NY: Fawcett.

Fullan, M. (2001). *Leading in a culture of change*. San Francisco, CA: Jossey-Bass.

Fullan, M. (2011). Motion leadership: The skinny on becoming change savvy. Preconference workshop. International Conference of Principals. *Leading Student Achievement: An International Odyssey*. Retrieved from http://www.michaelfullan.ca/images/handouts/ 11_TheSkinny_A4.pdf.

Fullan, M. (2013). *Great to excellent: Launching the next stage of Ontario's education agenda*. Toronto, ON: Queen's Printer for Ontario.

Fullan, M., & Langworthy, M. (2013). *Towards a new end: New pedagogies for deep learning*. Seattle, WA: Collaborative Impact.

Gallagher, W. (2009). *Rapt: Attention and the focused life*. New York, NY: Penguin.

Gallwey, T. W. (2000). *The inner game of work*. New York, NY: Bantam.

Goleman, D. (2006). *Social intelligence: The new science of human relationships*. New York, NY: Bantam.

Gregory, J. B., & Levy, P. E. (2013). Humanistic/person-centred approaches. In J. Passmore, D. B. Peterson, & T. Freire (Eds.), *The Wiley-Blackwell handbook of the psychology of coaching and mentoring*. Chichester, UK: Wiley.

Gulamhussein, A. (2013). *Teaching the teachers: Effective professional development in an era of high stakes accountability*. Alexandria, VA: Center for Public Education.

Haidt, J. (2001). The emotional dog and its rational tail: A social intuitionist approach to moral judgment. *Psychological Review, 108*(4), 814–834.

Hall, L. M., & Duval, M. (2003). *Coaching conversations: Robust conversations that coach*. Clifton, CO: Neuro-Semantic Publications.

Hanson, R. (2011). *Just one thing*. Oakland, CA: New Harbinger.

Hanson, R. (2013). *Hardwiring happiness: The new brain science of contentment, calm and confidence*. New York, NY: Crown.

Hargreaves, A., & Shirley, D. (2009). *The fourth way: The inspiring future for educational change*. Thousand Oaks, CA: Corwin.

Hargrove, R. (1995). *Masterful coaching*. San Francisco, CA: Jossey-Bass.

Hargrove, R. (2007). *Masterful coaching* (2nd ed). San Francisco, CA: Jossey-Bass.

Hattie, J. (2012). Know thy impact. *Educational leadership, 70*(1), 18–23.

Hattie, J., & Timperley, H. (2007). The power of feedback. *Review of Educational Research, 77*(1), 81–112.

Hayashi, S. K. (2011). *Conversations for change: 12 ways to say it right when it matters most.* New York, NY: McGraw-Hill.

Hayes, S. (2007). Hello, darkness: Discovering our values by confronting our fears. *Psychotherapy Networker, 31*(5).

Heathcote, D. (1984). *Dorothy Heathcote: Collected writings on education and drama.* London, UK: Hutchinson.

Heifetz, R. A. (1998). *Leadership without easy answers.* Boston, MA: Harvard Business.

Heifetz, R., & Linsky, M. (2002). *Leadership on the line: Staying alive through the dangers of leading.* Boston, MA: Harvard Business.

Hicks, D. (2011). *Dignity: The essential role it plays in resolving conflict.* New Haven, CT: Yale University Press.

Holmes, C. (Interviewer), & Senge, P. (Interviewee). (2009). A conversation with Peter Senge and Charles Holmes [Interview transcript]. Retrieved from http://www.connectingforchange.ca/petersenge_charlesholmes.

Hopmann, S. T. (2008). No child, no school, no state left behind: Schooling in the age of accountability. *Journal of Curriculum Studies, 40*(4), 417–456.

Institute for Education Leadership. (2013). *The Ontario leadership framework: A school and system leader's guide to putting Ontario's leadership framework into action.* Retrieved from https://iel.immix.ca/storage/6/1380680840/OLF_User_Guide_FINAL.pdf.

International Coach Federation. "Core competencies?" (n.d-a) Retrieved from http://coachfederation.org/credential/landing.cfm?ItemNumber=2206.

International Coach Federation. "What is professional coaching?" (n.d-b) Retrieved from http://coachfederation.org/need/landing.cfm?ItemNumber=978.

Interstate School Leaders Licensure Consortium (ISLLC). (2008). *Standards.*

Jayaram, K., Moffit, A., & Scott, D. (2012, January). Breaking the habit of ineffective professional development for teachers. *McKinsey on society*, 2012. Retrieved from http://mckinseyonsociety.com/downloads/reports/Education/MoSociety_Teacher_PD-v4.pdf.

Joyce, B., & Showers, B. (1980). Improving inservice training: The message of research. *Educational Leadership, 37*(5), 379–385.

Joyce, B., & Showers, B. (1982, October). The coaching of teaching. *Educational Leadership, 40*(1), 4–10.

Joyce, B., & Showers, B. (1996). The evolution of peer coaching. *Educational Leadership, 53*(6), 12–16.

Joyce, B., & Showers, B. (2002). *Student achievement through staff development* (3rd ed.). Alexandria, VA: Association for Supervision and Curriculum Development.

Kahneman, D. (2011). *Thinking, fast and slow.* Toronto, ON: Doubleday.

Katz, S., & Dack, L. A. (2013). *Intentional interruption: Breaking down learning barriers to transform professional practice.* Thousand Oaks, CA: Corwin.

Katzenmeyer, M., & Moller, G. (2001). *Awakening the sleeping giant: Helping teachers develop as leaders* (2nd ed.). Thousand Oaks, CA: Corwin.

Kaufman, S. B. (2013). *Ungifted: Intelligence redefined: The truth about talent, practice, creativity, and the many paths to greatness.* New York, NY: Basic.

Kegan, R., & Lahey, L. L. (2009). *Immunity to change: How to overcome it and unlock potential in yourself and your organization.* Boston, MA: Harvard Business.

Kimsey-House, H., Kimsey-House, K., Sandahl, P., & Whitworth, L. (2011). *Co-active coaching: Changing business, transforming lives* (3rd ed.). Boston, MA: Nicholas Brealey.

Kirschenbaum, H., & Henderson, V. L. (1989). *The Carl Rogers reader.* New York, NY: Houghton Mifflin.

Kluger, A. N., & DeNisi, A. (1996). The effects of feedback interventions on performance: A historical review, a meta-analysis, and a preliminary feedback intervention theory. *Psychological Bulletin, 119*(2), 254–284.

Knight, J. (1998). *The effectiveness of partnership learning: A dialogical methodology for staff development.* Lawrence, KS: University of Kansas Center for Research on Learning.

Knight, J. (2007). *Instructional coaching: A partnership approach to improving instruction.* Thousand Oaks, CA: Corwin Press.

Knowles, M. (1984). *The adult learner: A neglected species* (3rd ed.). Houston, TX: Gulf.

Kretlow, A., & Bartholomew, C. (2010). Using coaching to improve the fidelity of evidence-based practices: A review of studies. *Teacher Education and Special Education, 33*(4), 279–299.

Kretlow, A., Cooke, N., & Wood, C. (2012). Using in-service and coaching to increase teachers' accurate use of research-based strategies. *Remedial and Special Education, 33*(6), 348–361.

Langer, E. J. (2005). *On becoming an artist: Reinventing yourself through mindful creativity.* New York, NY: Random House.

Leithwood, K. (2013). *Strong districts and their leadership.* Institute for Education Leadership. Retrieved from http://www.ontariodirectors.ca/downloads/Strong%20 Districts-2.pdf.

Leithwood, K., Louis, K. S., Anderson, S., & Wahlstrom, K. (2004). *How leadership influences student learning.* The Wallace Foundation. Retrieved from http://www.wallacefoundation. org/knowledge-center/school-leadership/key-research/documents/how-leadership-influences-student-learning.pdf.

Leithwood, K., & Riehl, C. (2003). *What we know about successful school leadership.* National College for School Leadership. Retrieved from http://dcbsimpson.com/randd-leithwood-successful-leadership.pdf.

Lerner, H. (1985). *The dance of anger.* New York, NY: HarperCollins.

Lerner, H. (2001). *The dance of connection.* New York, NY: HarperCollins.

Lieberman, A., & Miller, L. (2004). *Teacher leadership.* San Francisco, CA: Jossey-Bass.

Lieberman, M. (2013). *Social: Why our brains are wired to connect.* New York, NY: Crown.

Markova, D. (2000). *I will not die an unlived life: Reclaiming purpose and passion.* Berkeley, CA: Conari.

Martel, Y. (2009). *What is Stephen Harper reading? Yann Martel's recommended reading for a prime minister and book lovers of all stripes.* Toronto, ON: Vintage.

McCashen, W. (2005). *The strengths approach: A strengths-based resource for sharing power and creating change.* Victoria, AU: Innovative.

Meister, J., & Willyerd, K. (2010). *The 2020 workplace: How innovative companies attract, develop, and keep tomorrow's employees today.* New York, NY: HarperCollins.

Mourshed, M., Chijioke, C., & Barber, M. (2010). *How the world's most improved school systems keep getting better: Executive summary.* McKinsey & Company. Retrieved from http:// mckinseyonsociety.com/how-the-worlds-most-improved-school-systems-keep-getting-better/.

Nagata, A. (n.d.). *Transformative learning in intercultural education.* Human Dignity and Humiliation Studies. Retrieved from http://www.humiliationstudies.org/documents/ NagataTransformativeLearning.pdf.

Nishimura, J. (1989). *Change in teaching practice: Collegial partnership.* (Unpublished master's paper). Ontario Institute for Studies in Education of the University of Toronto.

Nye, Joseph S. (2011). *The future of power.* New York, NY: Public Affairs.

O'Donohue, J. (2006, March 17). *The subversive spirit of creativity.* Speech presented at Psychotherapy Networker Symposium. Washington, DC.

Olalla, J. (2004). *From knowledge to wisdom: Essays on the crisis in contemporary learning.* Boulder, CO: Newfield.

Oliver, M. (2008). Instructions for living a life. In *Red bird: Poems*. Boston, MA: Beacon.

Palmer, P. (1998). *The courage to teach: Exploring the inner landscape of a teacher's life*. San Francisco, CA: Jossey-Bass.

Palmer, P. (2000). *Let your life speak: Listening for the voice of vocation*. San Francisco, CA: Jossey-Bass.

Paul Hamlyn Foundation (2012, March). *Learning futures: A vision for engaging schools*. Retrieved from http://www.innovationunit.org/sites/default/files/Learning%20_Futures_Engaging_Schools.pdf.

Penenberg, A. (Interviewer), & Ries, E. (Interviewee). (2012). How Eric Ries coined "the pivot" and what your business can learn from it. [Interview video]. Retrieved from http://www.fastcompany.com/1836238/how-eric-ries-coined-pivot-and-what-your-business-can-learn-it.

Pink, D. (2010). *Drive: The surprising truth about what motivates us*. New York, NY: Riverhead.

Raney, P., & Robbins, P. (1989). Professional growth and support through peer coaching. *Educational Leadership, 46*(8), 35–38.

Remen, N. (1996). *Kitchen table wisdom: Stories that heal*. New York, NY: Riverhead.

Reynolds, M. (2014). *The discomfort zone: How leaders turn difficult conversations into breakthroughs*. Oakland, CA: Berrett-Koehler.

Robinson, J. (2010). *Mentoring and coaching school leaders: A phenomenological study of adaptive expertise for school administrators*. (Unpublished doctoral dissertation). University of Phoenix.

Robinson, J. (2011). Mentoring and coaching school leaders: A qualitative study of adaptive expertise for school administrators. *The Register, 13*(2), 22–25.

Robinson, K., & Aronica, L. (2009). *The element: How finding your passion changes everything*. New York, NY: Viking.

Robinson, V. M. J., & Timperley, H. S. (2007). The leadership of the improvement of teaching and learning: Lessons from initiatives that have positive outcomes for students. *Australian Journal of Education, 51*(3), 247–262.

Rock, D. (2006). *Quiet leadership: Six steps to transforming performance at work*. New York, NY: HarperCollins.

Rock, D. (2009). *Your brain at work: Strategies for overcoming distraction, regaining focus, and working smarter all day long*. New York, NY: HarperCollins.

Rushkoff, D. (2013). *Present shock: When everything happens now*. New York, NY: Penguin.

Scott, S. (2002). *Fierce conversations: Achieving success at work and in life one conversation at a time*. New York, NY: Berkley.

Scott, S. (2009). *Fierce leadership: A bold alternative to the worst "best" practices of business today*. New York, NY: Crown.

Seale, A. (2008). *The manifestation wheel*. Newburyport, MA: Weiser Books.

Seligman, M. E. (2002). *Authentic happiness: Using the new psychology to realize your potential for lasting fulfillment*. New York, NY: Simon and Shuster.

Senge, P., Scharmer, O., Jaworski, J., & Flowers, B. S. (2004). *Presence: An exploration of profound change in people, organizations and society*. New York, NY: Random House.

Showers, B. (1982). *Transfer of training: The contribution of coaching*. Eugene, OR: Center for Educational Policy and Management.

Showers, B. (1984). *Peer coaching: A strategy for facilitating transfer of training*. Eugene, OR: Center for Educational Policy and Management.

Siegel, D. J. (2007). *The mindful brain: Reflection and attunement in the cultivation of well-being*. New York, NY: Norton.

Siegel, D. J. (2010). *Mindsight: The new science of personal transformation*. New York, NY: Bantam.

Siegel, D. J., & Hartzell, M. (2003). *Parenting from the inside out: How a deeper understanding can help you raise children who thrive*. New York, NY: Tarcher.

Silsbee, D. (2008). *Presence-based coaching: Cultivating self-generative leaders through mind, body and heart*. San Francisco, CA: Jossey Bass.

Sinetar, M. (1998). *The mentor's spirit: Life lessons on leadership and the art of encouragement*. New York, NY: St. Martin's.

Slinger, J. L. (2004). Cognitive coaching: Impact on student and influence on teachers. *Dissertation Abstracts International, 65*(7), 2567. (University Microfilms No. 3138974).

Speck, M., & Knipe, C. (2001). *Why can't we get it right? Professional development in our schools*. Thousand Oaks, CA: Corwin.

Spoth, J., Toman, S., Leichtman, R., & Allen, J. (2013). Gestalt approach. In J. Passmore, D. B. Peterson, & T. Freire (Eds.), *The Wiley-Blackwell handbook of the psychology of coaching and mentoring*. Chichester, UK: Wiley.

Stober, D. R. (2006). Coaching from the humanistic perspective. In D. Stober, & A. Grant (Eds.), *Evidence based coaching handbook: Putting best practices to work for your clients*. Hoboken, NJ: Wiley.

Stone, D., & Heen, S. (2014). *Thanks for the feedback: The science and art of receiving feedback well*. New York, NY: Penguin.

Suggett, N. (2006). *Time for coaching*. Nottingham, UK: National College for School Leadership.

Timperley, H., & Earl, L. (2011). *State of the art: Teacher effectiveness and professional learning*. Session presented at 24th International Congress for School Effectiveness and Improvement. Limassol, Cypress.

Tippett, K. (Interviewer), & Hamilton, A. (Interviewee). (2014). [Interview transcript]. Retrieved from http://www.onbeing.org/program/ann-hamilton-making-and-the-spaces-we-share/transcript/6148.

Tippett, K. (Interviewer), & Langer, E. (Interviewee). (2015). [Interview transcript]. Retrieved from http://www.onbeing.org/program/ellen-langer-science-of-mindlessness-and-mindfulness/transcript/7906#main_content.

Tolle, E. (1999). *The power of now: A guide to spiritual enlightenment*. Novato, CA: New World Library.

Tryon, B. L. (2012). *Assessing collaborative conversations between mentor coaches and school administrators: A qualitative study*. (Unpublished doctoral dissertation). Abraham S. Fischler College of Education, Nova Southeastern University.

Vogt, E. E., Brown, J., & Isaacs, D. (2003). *The art of powerful questions: Catalyzing insight, innovation, and action*. Mill Valley, CA: Whole Systems.

Wallace Foundation. (2007, March). *A Wallace perspective: Getting principal mentoring right: Lessons from the field*. New York, NY: The Wallace Foundation.

Wheatley, M. J. (2002). *Turning to one another: Simple conversations to restore hope to the future*. Oakland, CA: Berrett-Koehler.

Wheatley, M. J. (2005). *Finding our way: Leadership for an uncertain time*. Oakland, CA: Berrett-Koehler.

Whitmore, J. (2009). *Coaching for performance: GROWing human potential and purpose* (4th ed.). London, UK: Nicholas Brealey.

Whitworth, L., Kimsey-House, H., Kimsey-House, K., & Sandahl, P. (2007). *Co-active coaching: New skills for coaching people towards success in work and life* (2nd ed.). Boston, MA: Nicholas Brealey.

Whyte, D. (2001). *Crossing the unknown sea: Work as a pilgrimage of identity*. New York, NY: Riverhead.

Wiliam, D. (2012). Feedback: Part of a system. *Educational Leadership, 70*(1), 30–34.

Zander, R. S., & Zander, B. (2002). *The art of possibility: Transforming professional and personal life*. Boston, MA: Harvard Business.

Index

A

Accountability
  in conversations, 202–203
  creation of culture of, 54–55
  mentor-coaching relationship/
    process and, 18
  in results domain of mentor-
    coaching model, 90
Acknowledgements/acknowledging,
  238–241
Action
  confirming in conversations,
    202, 203
  designing in conversations, 198,
    199–200, 201
  as focus in coaching relationship,
    10–11
  mentor-coaching relationship/
    process and, 17
  in professional learning/
    development session, 38
  propelling into, 196
  scope of term, 201
  stepping up to, in conversations,
    198, 199, 206
Advice/advising
  inquiring vs., 20
  mentee asking for, 177–178
  pull to give, 172
  questions intended for, 161
  resisting tug to give, 174–175
Agenda
  awareness of, 191–192
  changes, in conversations, 206
  clarification of, 207
  client's choice, 10
  in conversations, 10, 168–170,
    189–190, 194, 205, 206–207
  and focus, 148, 168–170, 189
  holding the space for, 170
  importance, 189
  lack of, 206–207
  in professional learning/
    development session, 37
  questions focusing on, 168–169
  questions supporting, 152
  setting, 169

Alignment
  in conversations, 196, 198
  within mentor-coaching model,
    88, 94
  parental, 95
  and values, 215
Allen, J., 101
Anderson, S., 6, 33, 40
Aronica, L., *The Element,* 70
Articulating of responsibility in
  conversations, 202, 203
"The Art of Powerful Questions"
  (Vogt; Brown; Isaacs), 145
Assumptions
  in "listening for" questions, 163
  in mentees' conversations, 139
  questions challenging mentee's
    beliefs and, 154
Attunement(s)
  in conversations, 207
  defined/about, 122
  in professional learning/
    development session, 37
Authenticity
  defined, 64
  of leaders, 41
  in mentor-coaching relationship,
    10–11, 64–65
Autonomy, 51–52
Awareness. *See also* Self-awareness
  of agenda focus, 148
  and being in the moment, 102
  co-creation of, 210–223
  in conversations, 191–192, 193,
    208, 210–223
  of current reality relative to goal/
    desired change, 211
  deepening of, 191, 192
  feedback and, 228
  internal dialogue and, 184
  of internal/external resources,
    212–215
  mentor-coaching relationship/
    process and, 17–18
  mentor-coach's mindset and, 113
  of mindset, 221–223
  of obstacles, 217–218

and possibilities, 193
and presence in mentee, 110–111
in professional learning/
  development session, 37
of purpose, 220–221
questions expanding, 150–151,
  153–154, 162, 208, 211, 212,
  214–216, 218, 220–223
seven dimensions of, 210–223
of strengths/gifts, 212
stuckness and expansion of, 208
of values, 215–216
of vision, 218–220

B

Baldwin, C., 71
Bartholomew, C., 31–32
Bearing witness, 182
Being
  about, 99–100
  and action, in conversations, 198
  as central to mentor-coaching, 99
  coach-like, 118
  conversations and, 10
  and destination of conversations,
    194
  doing vs., 99
  feedback and, 233
  inside-out approach and, 94
  in mentor-coaching relationship, 93
Being in the moment, fully present.
    See also Presence
  about, 102–103, 120–122
  awareness and, 102
  and being with, 102
  centring and, 104–105
  defined, 65
  in feedback, 238
  listening deeply and, 162
  in mentor-coaching relationship, 65
  and mindfulness, 103
  presence and, 100
Bell, M., 33–34, 35
  "Understanding What Enables
    High Quality Professional
    Learning," 35

brainstorming in, 194
and capacity building, 10, 185
centrality to learning, 185–186
challenges of navigating, 205–210
and change, 194
choices in, 196
in coaching, 10
common language in, 181
completion of, 203
confirming action in, 202, 203
and connection, 180–181
definitions of, 180, 185–186
designing of action in, 198,
    199–200, 201
destination, 189, 190, 194
distractions in, 207
engagement in, 196, 198
feedback in, 194
focus in, 189–190
and forward journey, 10
GO (Green Zone), 188, 198–205
holding the space in, 194
importance in, 190
inquiry propelling, 144
inside-out approach, 193
intentionality in, 10, 191, 192,
    194, 206
internal, 183–185
lack of agenda for, 206–207
LIST (learning, intentionality,
    support, and trust) in, 204–205
mindset in, 221–223
not getting through all layers of,
    209–210
not unfolding sequentially, 207
obstacles in, 200, 217–218
one at a time, 181
options in, 195, 196
possibilities in, 192–196
PROCEED WITH CAUTION
    (Yellow Zone), 188, 192–198
questions in, 10
range of strategies in, 185–186
and relationships, 181
securing accountability in,
    202–203
and self-observation, 182
spontaneity in, 188
stepping into action phase, 198,
    199, 200, 206
STOP (Red Zone), 188, 189–192
structured, 15

stuckness in, 208–209
superficiality in, 205–206
values in, 215–216
vision/purpose in, 218–221
when mentoring meets
    coaching, 15
Cooperrider, D., 43, 55
Cordingley, P., 33–34
    "Understanding What Enables
        High Quality Professional
        Learning," 35
Creativity
    accessing, 70, 112
    mentor-coaching relationship/
        process and, 17
    and presence, 112
    questions accessing, 157
Creelman, D., 43
Curiosity
    and development of presence, 112
    mentee's agenda vs., 160
    mentor-coaching relationship/
        process and, 17–18
    questions from, 165–166

D

Dack, L. A., 25
Daring Greatly (Brown), 67
Deci, E. L., 51–52
DeNisi, A., 235
Dignity, 63
Directionality, 41
Distractions. *See also* Interference;
        Obstacles
    in conversations, 207
    in listening through, 131
Doing
    being vs., 99
    and destination of conversations,
        194
    feedback and, 233
    in mentor-coaching relationship, 93
    working from inside out and, 94
Duckworth, A. L., 213
DuFour, R., 32
Duval, M., 44
Dweck, C., 69, 112, 230

E

Edmondson, A. C., 54–55, 61
Educational leadership. *See* Leadership
The Element (Robinson; Aronica), 70

Energy
    in "listening for" questions, 164
    in mentees' conversations, 140
Engagement
    about, 107–108
    in conversations, 196, 198
    deep, 111
Experience/expertise/wisdom
    sharing, 18, 176–178

F

Feedback
    acknowledging: INSPIRE, 237,
        238–241
    and being in the moment, 238
    and brain's negativity bias, 228–229
    and capacity building, 225, 229,
        233–234
    challenges/challenging in,
        227–231, 248–249
    and connection, 225
    and constructive criticism, 227
    in conversations, 194
    defined, 225
    fear and, 229
    as gift, 232–233
    and growth, 227–228, 229
    and growth vs. fixed mindset,
        230–231
    holding up mirror: INSIGHT,
        237, 241–245
    impactful, 234–235, 237–247
    "landing" of, 236
    for leaders, 227
    and learning, 225, 227–228
    linking to desired results, 233–237
    mentee response to, 235–237
    in mentor-coaching relationship,
        226
    and metacognition, 233
    mindfulness in providing, 226
    and observation, 241–245
    past experience with, 226–227
    "positive," 227
    practising giving in safe place,
        250–251
    and reflection/self-reflection,
        241–245
    self-generated, 232–233
    sharing observations: INCITE,
        237, 245–247
    shifting frame of, 231–237

mentor as "thinking partner" in mentor-coaching relationship, 60–61

mentor-coaches as, 20

mentors as, 20

and strengths vs. weaknesses, 27

synergy in, 50–51

Paul Hamlyn Foundation, *Learning Futures*, 86

Peer coaching, 29, 32

Peterson, C., 213

Possibilities

    in conversations, 192–196, 194, 195–196

    mentor-coaching relationship/ process and, 18

    for moving forward, 194

    questions generating, 156

Presence. *See also* Being in the moment, fully present

    and accessing intuition, 110

    and being in the moment, 100, 102–103

    and centring, 104–105

    cultivating heightened awareness around, 110–111

    defined, 7, 100

    and engagement, 107–108

    essential aspects, 101–110

    of leaders, 42

    of mentor-coach, 100–110

    and mindfulness, 103–104

    and openness, 109

    practices to develop, 111–112

    as quality of coach, 11

    and rapt attention, 108–109

    and stillness, 105–107

Professional learning/development

    capacity building and, 25, 35–39

    coaching and, 29–30

    integrating learning/skills/ behaviours, 30–32

    lifelong, 33

    in mentor-coaching model, 82

    mentor-coach's stance and, 29

    outside-in approach and, 80–81

    and school culture, 35–39

    and student achievement, 33–34

    three reports regarding, 34–39

Psychological safety, 54–55

Purpose, in conversation(s), 220–221

Q

Questions

    accessing creativity, 157

    and actualization of resources, 201–202

    and advising/fixing, 161

    and alignment in conversations, 198

    and articulating of responsibility, 203

    asking "Why?" 161

    and awareness expansion, 150–151, 153–154, 162, 208, 211, 212, 214–216, 218, 220–223

    best, 145–147

    and capacity building, 156–157, 161

    challenging mentee's beliefs/ assumptions, 154

    choice extending, 150

    choosing options in conversations, 196

    closed, 160

    confirming action, 203

    in conversations, 10

    curiosity and, 160, 165–166

    current conditions and, 154

    and current reality vs. goal/desired change, 211

    and designing in conversations, 201

    and destination of conversations, 190

    for each zone in mentor-coaching model, 96

    and engagement in conversations, 198

    and focus on agenda, 168–169, 190

    and forward movement/change, 155, 209–210

    impactful, 144–167

    in inside-out approach, 85

    and internal/external resources, 214–215

    leading/suggestive, 160

    and learning edge, 157

    linking to matters of importance, 190

    "listening for" and, 163–168

    and mentee's agenda, 152

    and mentee's generation of own questions, 158

    mentee's language generating, 162–163

    mentee's planning style and, 199–200

    in mentor-coaching model, 85, 89–90

    and mindset awareness expansion, 222–223

    and obstacles, 218

    open-ended, 154, 197

    opening range of possibilities in conversations, 195–196

    open vs. closed, 167

    and possibilities generation, 156

    problem focused, 161–162

    and purpose, 221

    and reflection, 155

    replay/feedback on, 165–166

    securing LIST in conversations, 204–205

    separating person from problem, 157–158

    serving mentee's vision and larger purpose, 155–156

    stacked, 161

    and strengths/gifts, 212

    and trust, 152, 197

    types of, 152–160

    types to avoid, 160–162

    and values, 216

    and vision, 220

R

Rapt attention, 108–109, 111

Reflection

    feedback and, 237, 241–245

    mentor-coaching relationship/ process and, 17–18

    mentor-coach's mindset and, 113

    questions inviting, 155

Relationship(s). *See also* Mentor-coaching relationship; Partners/partnership

    about, 50–51

    centrality in mentor-coaching relationship, 57–58

    in coaching, 10–11

    connection through conversations and, 181

    conversations and, 181

    importance of being in, 50–56

Credits

Adult Learner: A Neglected Species (3rd edition) by M. Knowles, © 1984 Gulf; **41:** Excerpt from *Leadership from the Inside Out* (2nd Edition) by K. Cashman, © 2008 Berrett-Koehler Publishers, Inc.; **41:** Excerpt from *The Gifts of Imperfection: Let Go of Who You Think You're Supposed to Be and Embrace Who You Are* by B. Brown, © 2010 Hazleden; **42:** Excerpt from *Mindsight: The New Science Of Personal Transformation* by D. Siegel © 2010 Bantam Books; **42:** Excerpt from "Beyond the Elevator Speech" by M. Carroll, *Shambhala Sun*, March 2010; **42–43:** Excerpt from *Fierce Leadership* by S. Scott, © 2009 Crown Business; **43:** Excerpt from *The Future of Power* by J. Nye, © 2011 Public Affairs; **43:** Excerpt from Interview: David Cooperrider and Appreciative Inquiry by D. Creelman. Found at http://www4.hr.com, © 2001; **43–44:** Excerpt from *Immunity to Change: How To Overcome It And Unlock Potential In Yourself And Your Organization* by R. Kegan & L. L. Lahey, © 2009 by Harvard Business Publishing; **44:** Excerpt from *Coaching Conversations: Robust Conversations that Coach* by L. M. Hall and M. Duval, © 2003 Neuro-Semantic Publications; **44:** Excerpt from *Resonant Leadership* by R. Boyatzis and A. McKee, © 2005 Harvard Business Publishing; **44–45:** Reprinted by permission of B. Tucker; **45:** Excerpt from *Leadership in a Culture of Change* by M. Fullan, © 2001 Jossey-Bass; **45, 46:** Excerpts from *What We Know About Successful School Leadership* by K. Leithwood and C. Riehl in Division A of AERA, Autumn 2003, NCSL; **47:** Reprinted by permission of Jane Morton; **47:** Reprinted by permission of Liana Lafranier; **47:** Reprinted by permission of Karin Schmidlechner; **48:** Reprinted by permission of Carol Rolheiser. **CHAPTER 3: 50:** Excerpt from *Dignity: The Essential Role it Plays in Resolving Conflict* by D. Hicks, © 2011, published by Yale University Press; **51:** Excerpts from "Mentoring and Coaching School Leaders: A qualitative study of adaptive expertise for school administrators" by Dr. Joanne Robinson in OPC Register: Summer 2011. Vol. 13, No. 2, Published by Ontario Principals' Council. © 2011. Reprinted by permission of Dr. Joanne Robinson; **51:** Excerpt from "Social and Sociological Factors in Development of Expertise" by H. A. Mieg in *The Cambridge Handbook of Expertise and Expert Performance*, K. A. Ericsson et al. (editors), © 2006 Cambridge University Press; **51:** Excerpt from *Ungifted: Intelligence Redefined: The Truth About Talent, Practice, Creativity, and the Many Paths to Greatness* by Scott Barry Kaufman. Published by Basic Books, © 2012; **52:** Excerpt from "The Interpersonal Relationship in the Facilitation of Learning" in *Humanizing Education* by Carl Rogers, © 1967, in *The Carl Rogers Reader* by H. Kirschenbaum and V. L. Henderson, © 1989 Houghton Mifflin Company; **52–53:** Excerpt from *Towards a New End: New Pedagogies for Deep Learning* by M. Fullan and M. Langworthy, © 2013 Collaborative Impact; **54:** Excerpt from "Managing the Risk of Learning: Psychological Safety in Work Teams" by A. Edmonson, in *International Handbook of Organizational Teamwork and Cooperative Working*, M. West et al. (editors), © 2003 Wiley & Sons Ltd.; **55:** Adapted and reprinted with permission from "The Competitive Imperative of Learning" by Amy C. Edmonson. *Harvard Business Review*, July/August 2008; **56:** Excerpt from "Learning Relationships from Theory to Design," in. D. Squires, G. Console, and G. Jacobs (eds), *The Changing Face of Learning Technology*, © 2000 University of Wales Press; **57:** Excerpt from "Gestalt Approach" by J. Spoth et al., in *The Wiley-Blackwell Handbook of the Psychology of Coaching and Mentoring*, J. Passmore et al. (editors), © 2013 John Wiley & Son; **58:** Reprinted by permission of Sally Peterson; **61:** Reprinted by permission of Dufferin R. Worden; **61:** Excerpt from *Teaming: How Organizations: Learn, Innovate, and Compete in the Knowledge Economy* by A. Edmondson, © 2012 Jossey-Bass; **63:** Excerpt from *Dignity: The Essential Role It Plays in Resolving Conflict* by D. Hicks, © 2011 Published in Yale University Press; **64:** Excerpt from "Counseling and Psychotherapy" by C. Rogers, © 1942 in *The Carl Rogers Reader* by H. Kirschenbaum and V. L. Henderson, © 1989 Houghton Mifflin Company; **64:** Excerpt from *The Gifts of Imperfection: Let Go of Who You Think You're Supposed to Be and Embrace Who You Are* by B. Brown, © 2010 Hazleden; **65:** Excerpt from *Rapt: Attention and the Focused Life* by W. Gallagher, © 2009 The Penguin Press; **65:** Excerpt from *The Speed of Trust: The One Thing That Changes Everything* by S. R. Covey and R. Merrill, © 2006 Free Press; **67:** Excerpt from *Daring Greatly: How the Courage to Be Vulnerable Transforms the Way We Live, Love, Parent and Lead* by B. Brown, © 2012 Gotham; **67:** Excerpt from *Walking on Water: Reflections on Faith and Art* by M. L'Engle, © 1980 Harold Shaw Publishers; **68:** Excerpt from *The Mindful Brain: Reflection and Attunement in the Cultivation of Well-Being* by D. Siegel, © 2007 W.W. Norton & Company; **68:** Excerpt from *The Courage to Teach: Exploring the Inner Landscape of a Teacher's Life* by P. Palmer © 1998 Jossey-Bass; **68:** Excerpt from *On Love and Other Difficulties* by R. M. Rilke, © W.W. Norton and Company; **69:** Reprinted by permission of Brian Jones; **69:** Excerpt of Kaufman el al. (2009) quoted in "Humanistic/Person-centered Approaches" by J. B. Gregory and P. E. Levy in *The Wiley-Blackwell Handbook of the Psychology of Coaching and Mentoring*, J. Passmore et al. (editors), © 2013 John Wiley & Sons; **70:** Excerpt from *The Subversive Spirit of Creativity* by J. O'Donohue. Speech presented at Psychotherapy Networker Symposium, March 17, 2006; **70:** Excerpt from *Creativity: Flow and the Psychology of Discovery and Invention* by M. Csikszentmihalyi, © 1996 Harper Perennial; **71:** Excerpt from *The Intuitive Compass: Why the Best Decisions Balance Reason and Instinct* by F. Cholle © 2012 Jossey-Bass; **71:** Excerpt from *The Manifestation Wheel* by A. Seale, © 2008 Weiser Books; **71:** Excerpt from *Storycatcher: Making Sense of Our Lives Through the Power of Story* by C. Baldwin, © 2005 New World Library; **72:** Excerpt from *Kitchen Table Wisdom: Stories That Heal* by

Naomi Remen, © 1996 Riverhead Books. **CHAPTER 4 77:** Excerpt from *Leadership in a Culture of Change* by M. Fullan, © 2001 Jossey-Bass; **77:** Excerpt from *The Courage to Teach: Exploring the Inner Landscape of a Teacher's Life* by P. Palmer © 1998 Jossey-Bass; **78, 79:** Excerpts from *Immunity to Change: How To Overcome It And Unlock Potential In Yourself And Your Organization* by R. Kegan & L. L. Lahey, © 2009 by Harvard Business Publishing; **80:** Excerpt from "Draft: Strong Districts and their Leadership" by K. Leithwood, © 2013 The Council of Ontario Directors of Education and the Institute for Education Leadership; **81:** Excerpt from "Breaking the Habit of Ineffective Professional Development for Teachers" by K. Jayaram, A. Moffit, and D. Scott, © 2012 McKinsey Report; **82:** Excerpt from *Mindsight: The New Science Of Personal Transformation* by D. Siegel © 2010 Bantam Books; **82:** Excerpt from *Teacher Leadership* by A. Liebermann and L. Miller, © 2004 Jossey-Bass; **83:** Reprinted by permission of Carol Ann Fisher; **86:** Excerpt from *Learning Futures: A Vision for Engaging Schools*, March 2012, Paul Hamlyn Foundation, www.innovationunit.org; **86:** Reprinted by permission of Steph Cook; **89:** Reprinted by permission of Laurie Dodson; **95:** Excerpt from *Presence: An Exploration of Profound Change in People, Organizations and Society* by Peter Senge et al., © 2004 Random House. **CHAPTER 5: 98:** Excerpt from *Presence-Based Coaching: Cultivating Self-Generative Leaders Through Mind, Body and Heart* by D. Silsbee, © 2008 Jossey-Bass; **100:** Excerpt from *The Gifts of Imperfection: Let Go of Who You Think You're Supposed to Be and Embrace Who You Are* by B. Brown, © 2010 Hazleden; **100:** Excerpt from Transformative Learning in Intercultural education by A. Nagata, Human Dignity and Humiliation Studies, www.humiliationstudies.org; **101:** Excerpt from "Gestalt Approach" by J. Spoth et al., in *The Wiley-Blackwell Handbook of the Psychology of Coaching and Mentoring*, J. Passmore et al. (editors), © 2013 John Wiley & Sons; **101:** Reprinted by permission of the International Coach Federation; **101:** Reprinted by permission of Patty Lowry; **102:** Excerpt from *Mindsight: The New Science Of Personal Transformation* by D. Siegel © 2010 Bantam Books; **102:** Excerpt from *The Power of Now: A Guide to Spiritual Enlightenment* by E. Tolle, © 1999 New World Library; **103:** Excerpt from a radio interview with Dr. Ellen Langer: On Being with Krista Tippett: "Science of Mindlessness and Mindfulness," www.OnBeing.org; **105:** Excerpt from *Presence-Based Coaching: Cultivating Self-Generative Leaders Through Mind, Body and Heart* by D. Silsbee, © 2008 Jossey-Bass; **106:** Excerpt from *The Mentor's Spirit: Life Lessons on Leadership and the Art of Encouragement*, by M. Sinetar, © 1998 St. Martin's Press; **106:** Excerpt from *What is Stephen Harper Reading?* by Y. Martel, © 2009 Vintage Canada Edition; **107:** Excerpt from *On Becoming an Artist: Reinventing Yourself Through Mindful Creativity* by E. Langer, © 2005 Random House; **108:** Excerpt from *Your Brain at Work: Strategies for Overcoming Distraction, Regaining Focus, and Working Smarter All Day Long* by D. Rock, © 2009 HarperCollins; **112:** Excerpt from *Mindset: The New Psychology of Success* by C. Dweck, © 2006 Random House. **CHAPTER 6: 119:** Excerpt from *Storycatcher: Making Sense of Our Lives Through the Power of Story* by C. Baldwin, © 2005 New World Library; **120:** Excerpt from *Presence-Based Coaching: Cultivating Self-Generative Leaders Through Mind, Body and Heart* by D. Silsbee, © 2008 Jossey-Bass; **120–121:** Reprinted by permission of Mary Ann Tucker; **121:** Excerpt from *Present Shock: When Everything Happens Now* by D. Rushkoff, © 2013 Current, Penguin Group; **123:** Excerpt from *Parenting from the Inside Out: How a Deeper Understanding Can Help You Raise Children Who Thrive* by D. Siegel and M. Hartzell, © 2003 Penguin Putnam; **123:** Excerpt from "Listening to Students: Moving from Resilience Research to Youth Development Practice and School Connectedness" by B. Benard and S. Slade in *Handbook of Positive Psychology in Schools*, R. Gilman et al. (editors), © 2009 Routledge; **128:** Excerpt from *Masterful Coaching*, 3rd Edition, by R. Hargrove, © 2008 Jossey-Bass; **129:** Reprinted by permission of Linda Beale; **129:** Reprinted by permission of Val Fox; **132:** Reprinted by permission of Teresa Hadley and Tracy Vanslyke; **133:** Excerpt from *The 7 Habits of Highly Effective People: Powerful Lessons in Personal Change* by S. M. R. Covey, © 2013 Simon & Shuster; **141:** Reprinted by permission of Barbara Bower. **CHAPTER 7: 143:** Excerpt from *Appreciative Inquiry: A Positive Revolution in Change* by D. Cooperrider and D. Whitney, © 2005 by Berrett-Koehler Publishers, Inc.; **144:** Excerpt from *I Will Not Die an Unlived Life: Reclaiming Purpose and Passion* by D. Markova © 2000 Conari Press; **145:** Reprinted by permission of Dr. Heike Bronson; **145:** Random House Dictionary of English Language, © 1966 Random House; **148–149:** "Awareness: The Light of Focused Attention [figure]" from THE INNER GAME OF WORK by W. Timothy Gallwey, copyright © 1999 by W. Timothy Gallwey. Used by permission of Random House, an imprint and division of Penguin Random House LLC. All rights reserved; **157:** Excerpt from *The Strengths Approach: A strengths-based resource for sharing power and creating change* by W. McCashen, © 2005 St Luke's Innovative Resources; **159:** Excerpt from *The Art of Powerful Questions* by E. E. Vogt, J. Brown, and D. Isaacs, © 2003 Whole Systems Associates; **159:** Reprinted by permission of Teresa Hadley and Tracy Vanslyke; **163:** Excerpt from *Your Brain at Work: Strategies for Overcoming Distraction, Regaining Focus, and Working Smarter All Day Long* by D. Rock, © 2009 HarperCollins; **163:** Excerpt from *Become an Outstanding Question Asker* by M. G. Adams, © 2007 International Ask a Question Day; **166:** Excerpt from *Co-Active Coaching: Changing Business, Transforming Lives*, 3rd Edition, by H. Kimsey-House et al., © 2011 Nicholas Brealey Publishing; **167:** Excerpt from *Letters to a Young Poet* by R. M. Rilke, © 1934 W.W. Norton & Company;

The Ontario Principals' Council (OPC) is committed to supporting school leaders throughout the education system. Education Leadership Canada® (ELC), our professional development unit, seeks input from a multitude of sources to identify, design, develop and deliver the learning and support needs of our Members and colleagues. ELC offers multiple professional development opportunities for current and aspiring school leaders. These include skills assessments, needs identification, mentoring support from experienced peers, workshop sessions, and online learning opportunities. The OPC recognizes the value of job-embedded learning, sharing promising practices and the distributed leadership model of principals sharing with principals.